America's 50 Fastest Growing Jobs

J. Michael Farr
With data and other contributions from various
U.S. Department of Labor publications.
Second Edition

This newly revised edition includes:

- The newest growth projections for jobs
- Completely updated and revised job descriptions
- All new information, based on latest government data
- 100 additional job projections (totaling 500)

- A new appendix on projections for the self-employed
- Expanded tables on occupations by training required
- A new section on growth projections by industries

80282

Other Titles of Interest Published by JIST and Available from Bookstores

Also Available From Distributors and Libraries

- *The Occupational Outlook Handbook*—Current descriptions for more than 250 jobs, based on the U.S. Department of Labor book with the same title.
- *The Resume Solution—How to Write (and Use) a Resume That Gets Results* by David Swanson—Provides step-by-step directions, worksheets, and many examples for creating a superior resume.
- *The Very Quick Job Search—Get a Good Job in Less Time* by Mike Farr—Thorough career planning and proven techniques to cut your job search time in half.
- *The Enhanced Guide for Occupational Exploration*—Provides descriptions of 2,500 jobs, organized by interest areas.
- *The Complete Guide for Occupational Exploration*—A 1993 revision of the older *Guide for Occupational Exploration*, cross-references over 12,000 job titles by interest area.
- *The Job Doctor* by Philip Norris, Ed.D.—Full of easy-to-follow tips on finding a job, completing a resume, and conducting interviews.
- *Job Savvy—How to Be a Success at Work* by LaVerne Ludden, Ed.D.—Practical advice on how to survive the first days on a new job and position yourself for raises and promotions.
- *Mind Your Own Business!—Getting Started as an Entrepreneur* by LaVerne Ludden, Ed.D. and Bonnie Maitlen, Ed.D.—A how-to guide for considering or starting self-employment or a small business.

Other books in the "Top Jobs" series include:

- *America's 50 Fastest Growing Jobs*
- *America's Top Federal Jobs*
- *America's Top Medical Jobs*
- *America's Top Office, Management, and Sales Jobs*
- *America's Top 300 Jobs, revised edition (based on The Occupational Outlook Handbook)*
- *Career Guide to America's Top Industries*

Compiler/Author: J. Michael Farr
Project Director: Spring Dawn Reader
Editor: Sara Adams
Composition: Carolyn J. Newland
Cover Design: Robert Steven Pawlak

Errors and omissions: We have been careful to provide accurate information throughout this book. But it is possible that errors have been inadvertently introduced. Please consider this in making any career plans or other important decisions. Trust your own judgment above all else and in all things.

©1994, **JIST Works, Inc.** Reorder #AFF4
Printed in U.S.A.

99 98 97 96 95 94 93 9 8 7 6 5 4 3 2 1

JIST Works, Inc.
720 North Park Avenue
Indianapolis, IN 46202-3431
Phone: **(317) 264-3720** Fax: **(317) 264-3709**

ISBN: 1-56370-091-3

About This Book

The U.S. government lists over 20,000 job titles. That's far too many to consider if you are making career plans. But many of these occupations are very specialized and have few people working in them. In fact, over 90 percent of the people in the United States work in just a few hundred major occupations. These jobs are the ones we cover in this book.

Some jobs are projected to grow much faster than average over the next 10 years. While we have provided data on the growth projections and other details of all major occupations in this book, we have given particular attention to the fastest growing ones. The 50 fastest growing jobs are listed in the Table of Contents within major clusters. Each of these jobs is cross-referenced to a thorough job description in chapter 3 which provides details on:

- Nature of Work & Working Conditions
- Skills & Abilities Required
- Future Employment Outlook
- Average Earnings

- Related Occupations
- Education & Training Requirements
- Employment Opportunities
- Sources of Additional Information

But this book is much more than a simple listing and description of the fastest growing jobs. Here are some of the reasons:

Some Reasons You Should Read This Book

1. **It provides you with information about trends in the economy and the workplace:** Several articles in this book will provide you with well-researched and written information about important trends that are affecting virtually everyone who will work over the next decade.

2. **The career information is the most accurate and timely information available:** Most of the information in this book is based on original source documents from the U.S. Department of Labor, Bureau of Labor Statistics. There is no more reliable source of this information anywhere.

3. **All important careers are covered:** While we emphasize those jobs that are growing most rapidly, there is information on over 300 major occupations. Separate tables and appendices provide important information on several hundred major occupations, including those that are not growing rapidly.

Who Should Use This Book

Many people will find this a useful book. The groups it will especially help include:

1. **Those Exploring Career Options:** If you are planning your career, jobs that are growing quickly are obviously good ones to consider since they often offer superior opportunities. You can find out a great variety of information on the fastest growing jobs in this book, as well as valuable information on a variety of jobs that are not listed among the fastest growing.

2. **Students and Those Considering Additional Education or Training:** Knowing which jobs are growing will help you identify those with the best prospects. A new appendix arranged by various levels of education also gives you occupations to consider.

3. **Job Seekers**: If you hope to interview for one of the fastest growing jobs listed in this book, the information provided will be invaluable in preparing you for interviews and salary negotiations. There is also an entire chapter covering career planning and effective job-seeking skills.

4. **Employers:** An important source of information for writing job descriptions, establishing salary ranges, and knowing what to require of a new employee (and what to ask in an interview).

5. **Counselors, Instructors and Others:** An important source of information for all career professionals including those providing career counseling to individuals, and those planning future education and training programs.

How Best to Use This Book

Each section of this book has been designed to be read by itself. This allows you to go directly to a chapter or appendix to get the information you want without having to read the entire book.

To give you the background necessary to interpret each section by itself, there is some repetition of information essential to the understanding of that section. This repetition should not cause a problem since these narrative sections are often quite brief and each provides different details not found elsewhere.

There are many ways you might use the information in this book. We suggest that you begin by reading the Table of Contents carefully to determine which sections would provide you with the most useful information. Then turn to those sections and follow up by browsing the other sections for supportive information as needed.

For example, you could look up the data on the job you are interested in as well as similar jobs requiring similar training or experience. This would help you determine which jobs pay well, have higher growth projections, and other important details. If one or more of these jobs were among the fastest growing ones, you could then read the description of those jobs to get considerable additional information. The job search section could then help you define what skills you have to support that job and teach you the basics of an effective job search and interview process.

There are many other ways to use this book. We hope you find it both interesting and useful!

P.S. The terms "job" and "occupation" are used interchangeably throughout this book. While some argue technical differences between the terms, for our purposes they mean the same thing.

TABLE OF CONTENTS

CHAPTER FOUR: Information on the 250 Most Popular Jobs — Where About 85 Percent of All People Work

This chapter provides information on the approximately 250 most popular jobs in the country—including projected growth and the major reasons for this growth. While all of the fastest growing jobs will be listed among them, a chart provides information on many jobs that are not listed in the earlier chapters of this book. Many of these previously unlisted jobs are also growing, though not as quickly. But even for those with slow or no growth projections, all of these occupations employ many people and will have many openings to replace those who have left their jobs.

CHAPTER FIVE: Making Career Decisions and Getting a Good Job—in Less Time

If you are making career plans or looking for a job, this chapter will provide you with specific techniques for doing both. This chapter was written by Mike Farr, whose job search books have sold more than 600,000 copies. Though short, this chapter emphasizes results-oriented, career-planning and job-search techniques. Topics include: • Changing Jobs and Careers Is Often Healthy • But Not Just Any Job Should Do—Or Any Job Search • Six Steps for a Successful Job Search • Know Your Skills • Have a Clear Job Objective • Know Where and How to Look • Traditional Job Search Methods • Contact Employers Directly • Where the Jobs Are • JIST Cards • Telephone Contacts • Spend at Least Twenty-Five Hours a Week • Get Two Interviews a Day • Answering Interview Questions • Follow Up on All Contacts • Thank-You Notes • Essential Job Search Data Writing Your Resume • Skills and Combination Resumes • The Quick Job Search Review.

APPENDIX A: Employment Projections Through the Year 2005 for the 500 Largest Occupations

This appendix provides information on the projected growth or decline of approximately 500 occupations. These jobs account for over 90 percent of the jobs people hold in this country. It includes an introduction that reviews major growth trends plus a a listing of the 500 major occupations that provides details on total employment, projected growth, annual openings, and worker characteristics.

APPENDIX B: Employment and Trends by Major Industry.

A new section provides details and comments on trends in all major industries. It contains helpful information to determine trends in an industry where you are currently employed or are considering for the future.

APPENDIX C: Earnings, Education Required, Employment Rates, and Other Details for Over 200 Jobs.

One series of tables arrange major occupations based on the level of education or training they typically require. This is useful for determining those occupations typically held by a high school or college graduate, for example, and selecting those that seem most interesting, are projected to grow quickly are better paying or other criteria. Another table lists jobs in alphabetical order and notes the education typically required by those employed in that job. A separate narrative section also provides information on the major sources of training and education available.

APPENDIX D: Projections for Self-Employed Workers

A new appendix that provides growth projections and other information on jobs held by significant numbers of self-employed workers.

CHAPTER ONE:
Labor Market and Career Planning Trends Through the Year 2005

The labor market is changing rapidly. Over 20 million new jobs are projected to be added to our work force over the next 10 years. That would increase our labor force to about 150 million people by the year 2005—a 20 percent increase. While many new jobs will be created, many more existing jobs will also be affected by changing technologies, new products and techniques, foreign trade, and other factors.

This means that most people will be affected by these changes and it is clear that some occupations will do better than others. Few jobs will remain the same and many people will need to upgrade their skills, change jobs or even change careers.

No one can be sure of what will happen in the future, but some trends in the labor market do give clues on what is likely to happen. In making decisions about your education or career, it is important to understand these trends and to make good choices based on this information. This chapter provides an overview of some of the major trends, while other sections of the book will provide additional details.

Most People Will Change Jobs and Careers

Young people tend to change jobs more frequently, but even workers over age 25 will change jobs an average of eight or more times during their working lives. Most people will also change their career—going from a truck driver to a teacher, for example—three or more times during their working lives. And the trend for changing jobs and careers more often is increasing. Sometimes, these changes will not be anticipated or will occur in unpredictable ways. For these reasons, preparing now for your next job or career change makes more sense than ever.

Some Jobs Will Grow More Rapidly Than Others

While there will be growth in most occupations, some will grow much more rapidly than others—and some will even decline. Obviously, occupations that are expected to grow will offer many good opportunities and these jobs are the focus of this book. The jobs that are growing the fastest tend to require education and training beyond the high school level. This "upgrading" of skills is an important trend in our labor force since even entry-level jobs now typically require good academic skills as well as training beyond high school.

The Service Economy Is Becoming Increasingly Important

Only about 25 percent of the work force have jobs manufacturing products, most of the rest of us are employed in the "service" sector. These jobs are in government, business services, health care, retail trade, and other fields that do not produce goods. While manufacturing remains an important part of our economy, most people work in other areas now and this trend is likely to increase. In fact, almost all of the new jobs are projected to be in the service-producing rather than the manufacturing sector of our economy.

Jobs Will Increase in Health Care

As the large numbers of "baby boomers" (born from 1946 through 1964) age, the average age of our population will also increase. This and the many new and improved medical services becoming available will result in increased life-spans and an increase in demand for medical services of all kinds. That is the primary reason why so many of the most rapidly growing jobs are in the health care field.

Demand for Business Services Will Grow

Job demand for those who provide services to business are expected to increase rapidly. These jobs include many requiring advanced training such as computer technicians and systems analysts, as well as those requiring less training such as janitors. Jobs in accounting, marketing, office workers, engineering, finance, truck driving, and many others providing services to businesses are expected to grow.

The Increasing Importance of Small Businesses

Two out of three workers employed by businesses now work for small employers—those employing fewer than 500 workers. The largest employers now employ fewer workers than they did 10 years ago and most of the new jobs are being created by small employers. This means that you are far more likely now to work for a small employer than a large one. Jobs with small employers tend to require more flexibility and more rapid adaptation to change. While large employers remain an important part of our economy, small employers have become increasingly important.

Education and Government Jobs

Increases are projected for jobs at all levels of the educational system. The enrollments at elementary schools and high schools should continue to increase as the children of the baby boomers —and their grandchildren—pass through school. More people going to college and post high school training will increase jobs in the post-secondary system as well. Government jobs will also increase, but not as rapidly as in the past, and most new jobs will be at the state and local rather than the federal level.

Retail Trade

Jobs in restaurants, auto repair, grocery stores, hotels, department stores, and other retail businesses are expected to grow quickly. Many of these jobs do not require advanced training but those jobs also tend to be lower-paying.

Should I Consider Only the Fastest Growing Jobs?

With all the change that is projected in the coming years, it would seem wise to consider those jobs that are growing most rapidly. These jobs are projected to increase the numbers of people they employ and offer better than average opportunities for employment and security. But there will be many opportunities in jobs that are growing at average or even below-average rates. Some of these occupations are very large and there will be many new openings due to retirement, people leaving the field, and other reasons. Information on many of these jobs is provided in the appendices of this book and you should consider them, if that is what you want to do, even if they are not listed among the most rapidly growing of jobs.

Most Good Jobs Require More Education

Back when factory jobs were plentiful, many people could get a good-paying factory job right out of high school. Today, there is intense competition for the relatively few of these jobs that come open. If you look at the occupations that are shrinking, many are those primarily held by people with lower levels of education.

Most of the new jobs now require training or education beyond high school. Even entry-level jobs typically held by high school graduates often now require some experience with using computers. This upgrading of the skills required to obtain the better jobs will continue. This will mean that those now employed will need to continue their education to keep up with the changing technology that affects their jobs and entry-level workers will need more education in order to be considered for many of the better jobs.

The projected demand for college graduates will remain strong, though some fields will do better than others. College graduates, on the average, earn much more than those with a high school degree and this earnings gap has widened over the past 10 years. But a four-year college degree is not essential in order to do well in the labor market. Many of the rapidly growing jobs, for example, will require technical training that can be obtained in one or two years at a private vocational school or community college.

Recent studies have shown that the additional cost of education or training is often quickly paid back in higher earnings. And the increased earnings often last a lifetime, making a major difference in lifestyle. So consider investing in yourself and don't eliminate jobs that interest you if they require additional education. Instead, consider getting it.

Career Planning and Job Seeking Skills Are More Important Than Ever

One thing is clear: in order to succeed in today's labor market, you will need to spend more time on career planning and preparation. People who do will more likely do better in the labor market—and they are more likely to find a career that is satisfying to them. Good career planning includes more than just picking a job. It includes knowing what you want to accomplish, using the skills that you enjoy, seeking a work environment that is satisfying to you, and (among other things) finding work that is meaningful to you.

Because you are also more likely now to change jobs than in the past, it is also wise to learn more about how to conduct a more effective job search. The average length of unemployment ranges from 12 to 16 weeks and can be much higher for some people. For example, older workers and those with higher earnings are two groups who take longer than average to find new jobs. With the major changes in the labor market, many people find that they are forced to look for work and don't know how to go about doing it effectively. The traditional job seeking techniques simply don't work very well and this can lead to a frustrating and negative life experience.

Certain job search techniques have been found to reduce the time it takes to find a job and to increase your chances of getting the more desirable ones. Over time, this can make a big difference in your earnings and long-term career satisfaction. A chapter in this book provides a brief review of effective career planning and job seeking techniques, though we encourage you to learn more if this is important to you.

It makes sense to learn as much as you can about career planning and job seeking. In today's economy, knowing these techniques are becoming essential economic survival skills. Those who do a thorough job in planning their careers will clearly do better than those who do not.

CHAPTER TWO:
The Fastest Growing Jobs[1]

This chapter will provide you with a listing of the fastest growing jobs in our economy, arranged in order of the percentage of growth projected for each. It also provides brief reviews of the trends in each major occupational cluster of jobs.

A List of the 50 Fastest Growing Jobs[2]

The Top 50 Fastest Growing Jobs

Occupation	% Growth Projected	Numerical Growth	Estimated Total Employment 1990
1. Homemaker-home health aides	88	343,000	391,000
2. Paralegals	85	77,000	90,000
3. Computer systems analysts	79	366,000	463,000
4. Physical therapists	76	67,000	88,000
5. Medical assistants	74	122,000	165,000
6. Operations research analysts	73	42,000	57,000
7. Human services workers	71	103,000	145,000
8. Radiologic technologists	70	103,000	149,000
9. Medical secretaries *	68	158,000	232,000
10. Psychologists	64	79,000	125,000
11. Travel agents	62	82,000	132,000
12. Correction officers	61	142,000	230,000
13. Flight attendants	59	59,000	101,000
14. EEG Technologists	57	3,800	6,700
15. Computer programmers	56	317,000	565,000
16. Services sales representatives	55	325,000	588,000
17. Surgical technologists	55	21,000	38,000
18. Occupational therapists	55	20,000	36,000
19. Medical records technicians	54	28,000	52,000
20. Nuclear medicine technologists	53	5,500	10,000
21. Management analysts and consultants	52	79,000	151,000
22. Respiratory therapists	52	31,000	60,000
23. Preschool workers	49	490,000	990,000
24. Marketing, advertising, and public relations managers	47	203,000	427,000
25. Legal secretaries*	47	133,000	281,000
26. Podiatrists	46	7,300	16,000
27. Registered nurses	44	767,000	1,727,000
28. Hotel managers and assistants	44	45,000	102,000

The Top 50 Fastest Growing Jobs

Occupation	% Growth Projected	Numerical Growth	Estimated Total Employment 1990
29. Nursing aides and psychiatric aides	43	587,000	1,374,000
30. Licensed Practical Nurses	42	269,000	644,000
31. Health services managers	42	108,000	257,000
32. Information clerks	41	584,000	1,418,000
33. Dental hygienists	41	40,000	97,000
34. Actors, directors, and producers	41	39,000	95,000
35. Gardeners and groundskeepers	40	348,000	874,000
36. Securities and financial services sales representatives	40	76,000	191,000
37. Recreational therapists	39	13,000	32,000
38. Computer and office machine repairers	38	60,000	156,000
39. Animal caretakers except farm	38	40,000	106,000
40. Dancers and choreographers	38	3,300	8,600
41. Dispensing opticians	37	24,000	64,000
42. Chefs, cooks, and other kitchen workers	34	1,035,000	3,069,000
43. Secondary school teachers	34	437,000	1,280,000
44. Accountants and auditors	34	340,000	985,000
45. Guards	34	298,000	883,000
46. Teacher aides	34	278,000	808,000
47. Lawyers and judges	34	217,000	633,000
48. Physicians	34	196,000	580,000
49. Social workers	34	150,000	438,000
50. Electrical and, electronic engineers	34	145,000	426,000

*The descriptions for Medical secretaries and Legal secretaries are listed under the general "Secretaries" heading in the section titled Administrative Support Occupations Including Clerical.

Other Rapidly Growing Jobs

We have included additional jobs in this category, most of which employ larger numbers of workers. The list does not include some smaller occupations that are also growing quickly. Descriptions for each of these jobs—and many others—can be found in another book titled *America's Top 300 Jobs*, published

---

1 Much of the information in this chapter is based on several U.S. Department of Labor publications including a chapter titled "Tomorrow's Jobs" from the 1992-93 *Occupational Outlook Handbook*, "Outlook 1990-2005" (Bureau of Labor Statistics Bulletin 2402), and *America's Top 300 Jobs*, Revised Edition, published by JIST Works, Inc.

2 The information in this list is based on data obtained from the U.S. Department of Labor. The list is arranged in order of the projected growth anticipated for each job, from higher to lower. Note that these are projections and the actual growth may be more or less than projected. A description of each of these jobs is included in the next chapter.

by JIST Works, Inc., or the *Occupational Outlook Handbook*, published by the U.S. Department of Labor.

Occupation	% Growth Projected	Numerical Growth	Estimated Total Employment 1988
51. Engineering science and data processing managers	34	108,000	315,000
52. Property and real estate managers	34	76,000	225,000
53. Counter and rental clerks	34	74,000	215,000
54. Dental assistants	34	60,000	176,000
55. Reservation and transportation ticket agents and travel clerks	34	52,000	150,000
56. Counselors	34	49,000	144,000
57. Hotel and motel desk clerks	34	40,000	118,000
58. Aircraft pilots	34	31,000	90,000
59. Speech-language pathologists and audiologists	34	23,000	68,000
60. Biological scientists	34	21,000	62,000
61. Physician assistants	34	18,000	53,000
62. Actuaries	34	4,400	13,000
63. Construction contractors and managers	33	60,000	183,000
64. Bus drivers	32	177,000	561,000
65. Restaurant and food service managers	32	177,000	556,000
66. Personnel, training, and labor relations specialists and managers	32	144,000	456,000
67. Visual artists	32	73,000	230,000
68. Veterinarians	31	14,000	47,000
69. Landscape architects	31	6,200	20,000
70. Civil engineers	30	59,000	198,000
71. Inspectors and compliance officers except construction	30	46,000	156,000
72. Emergency medical technicians	30	26,000	89,000
73. Meteorologists	30	1,600	5,500
74. Retail sales workers	29	1,381,000	4,754,000
75. Electricians	29	158,000	548,000
76. Adult education teachers	29	152,000	517,000
77. Dispatchers	29	60,000	209,000
78. Water and waste treatment plant operators	29	23,000	78,000
79. Ophthalmic laboratory technicians	29	5,600	19,000

Additional Details About the Fastest Growing Jobs

An estimated 25 million jobs will be added to the U.S. economy by 2005. Those jobs will not be evenly distributed across major industry and occupational groups. While the fastest growing jobs will be an important part of the overall growth of the labor market, it is important to understand the effects of major trends within the society and within major occupational groups

as well. The information in this section will give you a better idea of these issues.

Many Jobs Require More Education

Occupations that require more education will generally grow faster than occupations with the lowest educational requirements. Look over the lists of the fastest growing jobs found earlier in this chapter and you will notice that almost all of the fastest growing jobs will require special training beyond high school. Only two occupational groups, health services and personal services, for example, had less than one-half of their workers with an educational attainment of high school or less in 1990.

Three of the fastest growing occupational groups are the executive, administrative, and managerial; professional specialty; and technicians and related support occupations. Not surprisingly, these occupations usually require the highest levels of education and skill. These three major occupational groups, which represented just over one-fourth of total employment in 1990, are expected to account for 41 percent of the increase in employment between 1990 and 2005.

In recent years, the educational attainment of the labor force has risen dramatically. Between 1975 and 1990, the proportion of the labor force aged 25 to 64 with at least one year of college increased from 33 to 47 percent, while the proportion with four years of college or more increased from 18 to 26 percent. Even when workers with varying levels of education are employed within an occupation, those with a higher level of education often earn considerably more than their less educated counterparts. (See the table below.)

Median Annual Earnings by Occupation and Level of Education, 1987

Occupation	Total, all levels	Less than High School	High School	1-3 Years college	4 years college or more
Total, all occupations	$21,543	$15,249	$18,902	$21,975	$31,029
Executive, administrative, and managerial	30,264	22,306	23,286	27,255	37,252
Professional speciality	30,116	19,177	23,233	27,458	31,311
Technicians and related support	24,489	16,207	21,358	23,830	28,004
Marketing and sales	22,220	13,746	17,654	22,546	32,747
Administrative support occupations including clerical	17,120	15,535	16,554	17,491	20,823
Service occupations	13,443	10,764	13,093	16,937	21,381
Precision production, craft, and repair	24,856	20,465	25,140	27,042	30,938
Operators, fabricators, and laborers	18,132	15,365	19,303	21,627	22,114
Agriculture, forestry, fishing, and related workers	11,781	10,571	12,730	16,331	17,130

Jobs That Are Rapidly Declining

While the focus of this book is on jobs that are growing, some jobs will not grow in the numbers of people they employ and some will decline. Office and factory automation, changes in consumer demand, and increased use of imports are some of the reasons that will cause employment to stagnate or decline in many occupations that require little formal education. Laborers, assemblers, typists, and word processors are examples of occupations that will decline in number. Opportunities for high school dropouts will become increasingly limited. Illiterate workers will find it difficult, if not impossible, to find jobs.

Consider the table that follows. It includes the occupations that have the largest reductions in the numbers of people they employ. In most cases, these are jobs that do not require training beyond the high school level.

Occupations with the largest job declines, 1990-2005, moderate alternative projection (numbers in thousands)			
	Employment		Number	Percent
Occupation	1990	2005	change	change
Farmers	1,074	850	-224	-20.9
Bookkeeping, accounting, and auditing clerks	2,276	2,143	-133	-5.8
Child care workers, private households	314	190	-124	-39.5
Sewing machine operators, garmet	585	469	-116	-19.8
Electric and electronic assemblers	232	128	-105	-45.1
Typists and word processors	972	869	-103	-10.6
Cleaners and servants, private household	411	310	-101	-24/5
Farm workers	837	745	-92	-11.0
Electrical and electronic equipment assemblers, precision	171	90	-81	-47.5
Textile draw-out and winding machine operators and tenders	199	138	-61	-30.6
Switchboard operators	246	189	-57	-23.2
Machine forming operators and tenders, metal and plastic	174	131	-43	-24.5
Machine tool cutting operators and tenders, metal and plastic	145	104	-42	-28.6
Telephone and cable TV line installers and repairers	133	92	-40	-30.4
Ce ntral office and PBX installers and repairers	80	46	-34	-42.5
Central office operators	53	22	-31	-59.2
Statistical clerks	85	54	-31	-36.1
Packaging and filling machine operators and tenders	324	297	-27	-8.3
Station installers and repairers, telephone	47	21	-26	-55.0
Bank tellers	517	492	-25	-4.8
Lathe and turning machine tool setters and set-up operators, metal and plastic	80	61	-20	-24.4
Grinders and polishers, hand	84	65	-19	-22.5
Electromechanical equipment assemblers, precision	49	31	-18	-36.5
Grinding machine setters and set-up operators, metal and plastic	72	54	-18	-25.1
Service station attendants	246	229	-17	-7.1
Directory assistance operators	26	11	-16	-59.4

Occupations with the largest job declines, 1990-2005, moderate alternative projection (numbers in thousands)			
	Employment		Number	Percent
Occupation	1990	2005	change	change
Butchers and meatcutters	234	220	-14	-5.9
Chemical equipment controllers, operators, and tenders	75	61	-14	-19.1
Drilling and boring machine tool setters and set-up operators, metal and plastic	52	39	-13	-25.6
Meter readers, utilities	50	37	-12	-24.8

Important Trends in Major Sectors of the Labor Market

Growth of Service Jobs: By the year 2005, projections indicate that nearly four out of five jobs will be in industries that provide services. Expansion of service sector employment is linked to a number of different factors, including changes in consumer tastes and preferences, legal and regulatory changes, advances in science and technology, and changes in the organization and management of businesses. Contrary to popular beliefs, many of these jobs pay well.

Many people think of a service economy as one in which the work force is dominated by retail sales workers, restaurant workers and cashiers. In reality, the fastest growing occupations will be those that require the most educational preparation. Some of the most rapidly growing occupations require above-average math, language and reasoning skills. More than half of the 50 fastest growing occupations had a majority of workers with education or training beyond high school in 1990.

The two largest industries in the services division are health services and business services. Together, they account for 6.1 million of the projected increase in jobs, or about one-fourth of the total.

Health Care: Health care will continue to be one of the most important industry groups in terms of job creation. Employment in health industries is projected to grow from 8.9 to 12.8 million. New technology and a growing and aging population will increase the demand for health services. Because of the rapid expansion, six of the 10 fastest growing occupations between 1990 and 2005 will be health related. Improvements in medical technology and a growing and aging population will increase the demand for health services. Employment in home health care services—the fastest growing industry in the economy—nursing homes, and offices and clinics of physicians and other health practitioners is projected to increase the most rapidly throughout this period. Hospitals will, however, continue to employ the most health care workers.

Business Services: Another important industry group that is expected to generate many jobs is business services. These industries employed 5.2 million workers in 1990 and are projected to employ 7.6 million in the year 2005. Personnel supply services, which includes temporary help agencies, is the largest industry in this group and will add many new jobs. Business services also includes one of the fastest growing industries in the economy—

computer and data processing services. This industry's rapid growth stems from advances in technology, worldwide trends toward office and factory automation, and increases in demand from business firms, government agencies, and individuals.

Education and Social Services: Jobs in all levels of education will grow, based on population growth at the elementary, high school and post-secondary age groups. In addition to traditional- aged students, more adults, foreign and part-time students will also increase enrollments. Increased need for child care and the needs of an aging population are also expected to increase demand for social services.

A Look at the Rapidly Growing Occupational Groups

While certain industries such as health care and business services are expected to grow rapidly, there are certain types of jobs within these and other industries that will also grow rapidly. Following are overviews of those expected to grow the fastest as well as those that are not growing as rapidly or even declining. Please note that particular jobs within each cluster may grow or decline faster or more slowly than the group as a whole.

Technicians and Related Support Occupations: Workers in this group provide technical assistance to engineers, scientists, and other professional workers, as well as operate and program technical equipment. Employment in this cluster is expected to increase 37 percent, from 4.2 to 5.8 million, making it the fastest growing occupational group in the economy. It also contains the second-fastest growing occupation—paralegals. Employment of paralegals is expected to skyrocket due to their increased use in the rapidly expanding legal services industry. Most of the jobs for technicians, however, will be in the large and rapidly growing health services and data processing industries.

Professional Specialty Occupations: Employment in this cluster of jobs is expected to grow 32 percent, from 15.8 to 20.9 million jobs. Much of this growth is a result of rising demand for engineers; computer specialists; lawyers; health diagnosing and treating occupations, and secondary school teachers.

Service Occupations: Note that "service occupations" refers to a cluster of similar jobs rather than to the much broader "service industry" mentioned previously. Jobs in the service occupations group include a wide range of workers in protective services, food and beverage preparation, and cleaning and personal services. These occupations are expected to grow 29 percent, from 19.2 to 24.8 million, because the growing population and economy, combined with higher incomes and increased leisure time, will spur demand for all types of services.

Executive, Administrative, and Managerial Occupations: Employment in this cluster is expected to increase 27 percent, from 12.5 to 15.9 million. Growth will be spurred by the increasing number and complexity of business operations and result in large employment gains in the services industry division. However, many businesses will streamline operations, reducing administrative costs and employing fewer managers, thus offsetting increases in employment.

Employment in these occupations tends to be driven by industry growth. For example, opportunities for health services managers will increase much faster than average, while only average growth is expected for wholesale and retail buyers and merchandise managers.

Hiring requirements in many managerial and administrative jobs are rising. Work experience, specialized training, or graduate study will be increasingly necessary. Familiarity with computers is required in a growing number of firms, due to the widespread use of computerized management information systems.

Marketing and Sales Occupations: Employment in this large cluster is projected to increase 24 percent, from 14.1 to 17.5 million jobs. Demand for services sales representatives, travel agents and securities and financial services sales representatives is expected to grow much faster than the average due to strong growth in the industries that employ them. Many part- and full-time job openings are expected for retail sales workers and cashiers due to the large size, high turnover, and faster-than-average employment growth in these occupations. The outlook for higher paying sales jobs will be more competitive.

Additional details on these and other occupational clusters that are growing more slowly are provided in the next chapter.

Many Job Openings Occur Due to Simple Turnover and Replacement Needs

Replacement openings occur as people leave occupations. Some change careers, while others are promoted to other occupations. Still others stop working in order to return to school, to assume household responsibilities, or to retire.

Most jobs through the year 2005 will become available as a result of replacement needs. Thus, even occupations with little, no, or slower-than-average employment growth may still offer many job openings.

Occupations with the most replacement openings tend to be large, with low pay and status, low training requirements, and a high proportion of young and part-time workers. Jobs for cashiers, waiters and waitresses and child care workers are examples of jobs that have high turnover.

Those occupations with relatively few replacement openings usually have lengthy training requirements, a high proportion of prime working age, full-time workers, and provide high pay and status. Physical therapists, lawyers, and aircraft pilots are examples of workers who have generally spent several years acquiring training that may not be applicable to other occupations.

A Few Words on Selecting a Career

A job is something you may take simply because it is available when you need one. A career is a longer-term decision to work within a certain area of expertise that may require special training or experience. When considering a longer-term career choice, it is important to understand that it is often better to prepare for or to select a job that you will really enjoy—AND that will help you enter or prepare to enter a career that interests you. This increases your chances for long-term career satisfaction.

Most people will change their jobs many times and their careers several times during their work lives. When you are doing this, consider factors other than simply how fast that occupational group is growing. Even in careers that are projected to have slow or no growth, opportunities will remain. But if you ARE interested in a career within an occupation that is growing quickly, that can certainly work to your long-term advantage.

a bachelor's degree regardless of the amount of experience he or she possesses. These managers establish and implement policies, goals, objectives, and procedures for their departments; evaluate personnel and work; develop reports and budgets; and coordinate activities with other department heads, the top administrator, and professional colleagues.

Although there are many common elements involved in running a health facility, there are significant differences among settings that affect job duties. For example, hospital and nursing home management differ in important aspects. The chief hospital administrator works with the governing board in establishing general policies and an operating philosophy and provides direction to assistant administrators and department heads who carry out those policies. Nursing home administrators need many of the same management skills but are much more involved in detailed management decisions than hospital administrators. Administrative staffs in nursing homes are typically much smaller than those in hospitals—nursing home administrators often have only one or two assistants, sometimes none. Nursing home administrators directly manage personnel, finance, operations, and admissions. They analyze data and make daily management decisions in all of these areas. Because many nursing home residents are long term—staying for months or even years—administrators must try to create an environment that nourishes residents' psychological, social, and spiritual well-being, as well as tending to their health care needs. This long-term residency allows the nursing home administrator to have direct contact with the patients, something that few hospital administrators are able to do unless a problem arises.

In the growing field of group practice management, managers need to be able to work effectively with the physicians who own the practice. Specific job duties vary according to the size of the group. While an office manager handles business affairs in very small medical groups, leaving policy decisions to the physicians themselves, larger groups generally employ a full-time administrator to advise on business strategies and coordinate the day-to-day management of the practice.

A small group of 10 or 15 physicians might employ a single administrator to oversee personnel matters, billing and collection, budgeting, planning, equipment outlays, advertising, and patient flow, whereas a large practice of 40 or 50 physicians requires a chief administrator and several business assistants, each responsible for a different functional area of management. In addition to providing overall management direction, the chief administrator is responsible for assuring that the practice maintains or strengthens its competitive position. Assuring competitiveness might entail market research to analyze the services the practice currently offers and those it might offer; negotiating contracts with hospitals or other health care providers to gain access to specialized facilities and equipment; or entering joint ventures for the purchase of an expensive piece of medical equipment such as a magnetic resonance imager. Health services managers in health maintenance organizations (HMO's) perform all of the functions of those in large medical group practices.

Some health services managers oversee the activities of several or many facilities in multi-facility health organizations.

Working Conditions

Health services managers often work long hours. Facilities such as nursing homes and hospitals operate around the clock, and administrators and managers may be called at all hours to deal with emergencies. The job also may include travel to attend meetings or to inspect satellite health care facilities.

Employment

Health services managers held about 257,000 jobs in 1990. Nearly three-fifths of all jobs were in hospitals. About a quarter of health services managers worked in nursing and personal care facilities and in offices of physicians. The remainder worked in other health and allied services, home health agencies, medical and dental laboratories, and offices of dentists and other practitioners.

Training, Qualifications, and Advancement

Knowledge of management principles and practices is the essential requirement for a position in this field, and such knowledge often is gained through work experience. Nonetheless, formal educational preparation is important, especially for those who wish to advance in the profession. For many chief administrative positions, a graduate degree in health services administration, nursing administration, or business administration is a decided asset. For all health specialist positions and some generalist positions, employers seek applicants who have had clinical experience (as nurses or therapists, for example) as well as academic preparation in business or health services administration.

Many hospitals are setting up separate ventures such as outpatient surgical centers, alcoholism treatment centers, and home health care services. To operate and manage these subsidiary companies, hospitals look for managers with well-established skills in marketing and finance. Nonetheless, graduate education in health services administration remains a prerequisite for many upper level administrative positions within hospitals and their subsidiaries.

Academic programs in health administration, leading to a bachelor's, master's, or doctoral degree, are offered by colleges, universities, and schools of public health, medicine, allied health, public administration, and business administration. The various degree programs provide different levels of career preparation. The master's degree—in hospital administration, health administration, health sciences, public health, public administration, or business administration—is regarded as the standard credential for many positions in this field. Educational requirements vary with the size of the organization and the amount of responsibility involved. Generally, larger organizations require more specialized academic preparation than smaller ones do.

In 1991, 29 colleges and universities offered bachelor's degree programs in health services administration. Sixty schools had accredited programs leading to the master's degree in health services administration, according to the Accrediting Commission on Education for Health Services Administration.

To enter graduate programs, applicants must have a bachelor's degree. Some schools seek students with undergraduate degrees in business or health administration; however, many programs prefer those students with a liberal arts or social science background. Competition for entry to these programs is keen, and applicants need above-average grades to gain admission. The programs generally last between 2 and 3 years. They include up to 1 year of supervised administrative experience, undertaken after completion of course work in such areas as hospital organization and management, accounting and budget control, personnel administration, strategic planning, and management of health information systems.

New graduates with master's degrees in health or hospital administration may be hired by hospitals as assistant administrators. Others may start as managers of nonhealth departments, like finance, and work up to top administrative positions. Postgraduate residencies and fellowships are offered by hospitals and other health facilities; these are normally staff jobs.

Growing numbers of graduates from master's degree programs are also taking jobs in HMO's, large group medical practices, clinics, and multifacility nursing home corporations. Students should be aware, however, that mid-level job transfers from one setting to another may be difficult. Employers place a high value on experience in similar settings because some of the management skills are unique to each setting.

New recipients of bachelor's degrees in health administration usually begin as administrative assistants or assistant department heads in larger hospitals, or as department heads or assistant administrators in small hospitals or in nursing homes.

The Ph.D. degree usually is required for positions in teaching, consulting, or research. Nursing service administrators are usually chosen from among supervisory registered nurses with administrative abilities and advanced education.

Licensure is not required in most areas of health services management, except for nursing home or long-term care administration. All States and the District of Columbia require nursing home administrators to pass a licensing examination, complete a State-approved training program, and pursue continuing education. Most States have additional specific requirements, so persons interested in nursing home administration should contact the individual agencies of the State in which they wish to work for information.

Health services managers are often responsible for millions of dollars of facilities and equipment and hundreds of employees. To make effective decisions, they need to be open to different opinions and good at sifting through contradictory information. To motivate subordinates to implement their decisions, they need strong leadership qualities. Interpersonal skills are important in all settings, but nowhere more so than in medical groups, where success depends on developing a good working relationship with the physician-owners. Tact, diplomacy, and communication skills are essential.

Like their counterparts in other kinds of organizations, health services managers need to be self-starters. In order to create an atmosphere favorable to good patient care, they must like people, enjoy working with them, and be able to deal effectively with them. They also should be good at public speaking.

Health services managers may advance by moving into more responsible and higher paying positions within their own institution; advancement occurs with promotion to successively more responsible jobs such as assistant or associate administrator and, finally, CEO. Health services managers sometimes begin their careers in small hospitals in positions with broad responsibilities, such as assistant administrator. Managers also advance by shifting to another health care facility or organization.

Job Outlook

Employment of health services managers is expected to grow much faster than the average for all occupations through the year 2005 as health services continue to expand and diversify. Hospitals will continue to employ the greatest number of health services managers, although the number of jobs will not be growing as fast as in other areas. Opportunities for managers in hospitals should be best in large hospitals with subsidiaries that provide such services as ambulatory surgery, alcohol and drug abuse rehabilitation, hospice facilities, or home health care.

Employment in home health agency and nursing and long-term care facilities will be growing the fastest. this is due to an increased number of elderly who will need care. demand in medical group practices will grow, too. as medical group practices become larger and more complex, more job opportunities for clinical department heads like director of nursing services should emerge. moreover, the increased complexity of group practices should also increase the number of associate administrators.

Health services managers in hospitals will face very keen competition for upper level management jobs, a reflection of the pyramidal management structure characteristic of most large and complex organizations.

In nursing homes and other long-term care facilities, where a graduate degree in health administration is not ordinarily a requirement, job opportunities for individuals with strong business or management skills will continue to be good.

Earnings

The type and size of the facility greatly affects the earnings of administrators. For example, the Medical Group Management Association reported that the median salary for administrators in group practices was $58,000 in 1990. The median salary for those in small group practices—with net revenues of $2 million or less—was $40,200; for those in very large group practices—with net revenues over $10 million—$96,000.

According to the American Hospital Association, half of all hospital CEO's earned $121,500 or more in 1991. The lowest 10 percent earned less than $71,000; the top 10 percent earned $203,400 or more.

Clinical department heads' salaries varied too. According to a survey by *Modern Healthcare* magazine, average salaries in 1991 for heads of the following clinical departments were: Medical records, $41,700; imaging/radiology, $46,600; physical therapy, $47,100; rehabilitation services, $51,000; and nursing services, $59,700.

Management incentive bonuses based on job performance are increasingly commonplace in executive compensation packages.

Related Occupations

Health services managers have training or experience in health and in management. Other occupations that require knowledge of both fields are public health directors, social welfare administrators, directors of voluntary health agencies and health professional associations, and underwriters in health insurance companies and HMO's.

Sources of Additional Information

Information about health administration and academic programs in this field is available from:

- American College of Healthcare Executives, 840 North Lake Shore Dr., Chicago, IL 60611.
- Association of University Programs in Health Administration, 1911 North Fort Myer Dr., Suite 503, Arlington, VA 22209.

For a list of accredited graduate programs in health services administration, contact:

- Accrediting Commission on Education for Health Services Administration, 1911 North Fort Myer Dr., Suite 503,

Arlington, VA 22209.

Information about health administration and job opportunities in group medical practices is available from:

- Medical Group Management Association, 104 Inverness Terrace East, Englewood, CO 80112-5306.

For information about career opportunities in long-term care, contact:

- American College of Health Care Administrators, 325 S. Patrick St., Alexandria, VA 22314.

Hotel Managers and Assistants

(D.O.T. 187.117-038, .167-046, -078, -106, -110, -122; and 320)

Nature of the Work

Across the Nation, hotels and motels are a welcome haven for weary travelers. For vacationing families and persons whose jobs take them out of town, a comfortable room, good food, and a helpful hotel staff can make being away from home an enjoyable experience. They may be guests overnight at a roadside motel, spend several days at a towering downtown convention hotel, or a week at a large resort complex with tennis courts, a golf course, and a variety of other recreational facilities. At each, hotel managers and assistant managers work to insure that guests' visits are pleasant.

Hotel managers are responsible for the efficient and profitable operation of their establishments. In a small hotel, motel, or inn with a limited staff, a single manager may direct all aspects of operations. However, large hotels may employ hundreds of workers, and the manager may be aided by a number of assistant managers assigned among departments responsible for various aspects of operations. The *general manager* has overall responsibility for the operation of the hotel. Within guidelines established by the owners of the hotel or executives of the hotel chain, the general manager sets room rates, allocates funds to departments, approves expenditures, and establishes standards for service to guests, decor, housekeeping, food quality, and banquet operations. Assistant managers must ensure that the day-to-day operations of their departments meet the general manager's standards.

Resident managers live in hotels and are on call 24 hours a day to resolve any problems or emergencies, although they normally work an 8-hour day. As the most senior assistant manager, they oversee the day-to-day operations of the hotel. In many hotels, the general manager also serves as the resident manager.

Executive housekeepers are responsible for ensuring that guest rooms, meeting and banquet rooms, and public areas are clean, orderly, and well maintained. They train, schedule, and supervise the work of housekeepers, inspect rooms, and order cleaning supplies.

Front office managers coordinate reservations and room assignments and train and direct the hotel's front desk staff that deals with the public. They ensure that guests are handled courteously and efficiently, complaints and problems are resolved, and requests for special services are carried out.

Food and beverage managers direct the food services of hotels. They oversee the operation of hotels' restaurants, cocktail lounges, and banquet facilities. They supervise and schedule food and beverage preparation and service workers, plan menus, estimate costs, and deal with food suppliers.

Convention services managers coordinate the activities of large hotels' various departments for meetings, conventions, and other special events. They meet with representatives of groups or organizations to plan the number of rooms to reserve, the desired configuration of hotel meeting space, and any banquet services needed. During the meeting or event, they resolve unexpected problems and monitor activities to check that hotel operations conform to the expectations of the group.

Other assistant managers may be specialists responsible for activities such as personnel, accounting and office administration, marketing and sales, security, maintenance, and recreational facilities. (For more information, see the related statements on marketing, advertising, and public relations managers elsewhere in this book.) Managers who work for chains may be assigned to organize and staff a newly built hotel, refurbish an older hotel, or reorganize a hotel or motel that is not operating successfully.

Working Conditions

Since hotels are open around the clock, night and weekend work is common. Many hotel managers work considerably more than 40 hours per week. Managers who live in the hotel usually have regular work schedules, but they may be called for work at any time. Some employees of resort hotels are managers during the busy season and have other duties the rest of the year.

Hotel managers sometimes experience the pressures of coordinating a wide range of functions. Conventions and large groups of tourists may present unusual problems. Dealing with irate patrons can also be stressful. The job can be particularly hectic for front office managers around checkin and checkout time.

Employment

Hotel managers and assistant managers held about 102,000 wage and salary jobs in 1990. An additional number—primarily owners of small hotels and motels—were self-employed. Others were employed by companies that manage hotels and motels under contract.

Training, Qualifications, and Advancement

Postsecondary training in hotel or restaurant management is preferred for most hotel management positions, although a college liberal arts degree may be sufficient when coupled with related hotel experience. In the past, most managers were promoted from the ranks of front desk clerks, housekeepers, waiters and chefs, and hotel sales workers. While some persons still advance to hotel management positions without the benefit of education or training beyond high school, increasingly, postsecondary education is preferred. Nevertheless, experience working in a hotel—even part time while in school—is an asset to all persons seeking to enter hotel management careers. Restaurant management training or experience is also a good background for entering hotel management because the success of a hotel's food service and beverage operations is often of great importance to the profitability of the entire establishment.

A bachelor's degree in hotel and restaurant administration provides particularly strong preparation for a career in hotel management. In 1991, over 160 colleges and universities offered bachelor's and graduate programs in this field. Over 800 community and junior colleges, technical institutes, vocational and trade schools, and other academic institutions also have programs leading to an associate degree or other formal recognition in hotel or restaurant management. Graduates of hotel or restaurant management programs usually start as trainee assistant managers, or at least advance to such positions more quickly.

Hotel management programs usually include instruction in hotel administration, accounting, economics, marketing, housekeeping, food service management and catering, hotel maintenance engineering, and data processing—reflecting the widespread use of computers in hotel operations such as reservations, accounting, and housekeeping management. Programs encourage part-time or summer work in hotels and restaurants because the experience gained and the contacts made with employers may benefit students when they seek full-time employment after graduation.

Hotel managers must be able to get along with all kinds of people, even in stressful situations. They need initiative, self-discipline, and the ability to organize and direct the work of others. They must be able to solve problems and concentrate on details.

Sometimes large hotels sponsor specialized on-the-job management training programs which enable trainees to rotate among various departments and gain a thorough knowledge of the hotel's operation. Other hotels may help finance the necessary training in hotel management for outstanding employees.

Most hotels promote employees who have proven their ability. Newly built hotels, particularly those without well-established on-the-job training programs, often prefer experienced personnel for managerial positions. Large hotel and motel chains may offer better opportunities for advancement than small, independently owned establishments, but relocation every several years often is necessary for advancement. They have more extensive career ladder programs and offer managers the opportunity to transfer to another hotel or motel in the chain or to the central office if an opening occurs. Career advancement can be accelerated by completion of certification programs offered by the associations listed below. These programs generally require a combination of course work, examinations, and experience.

Job Outlook

Employment of salaried hotel managers is expected to grow much faster than the average for all occupations through the year 2005 as more hotels and motels are built. Business travel will continue to grow, and increased domestic and foreign tourism will also create demand for additional hotels and motels. Most openings are expected to occur as experienced managers transfer to other occupations, retire, or stop working for other reasons.

Opportunities to enter hotel management are expected to be very good for persons who have college degrees in hotel or restaurant management.

Earnings

Salaries of hotel managers varied greatly according to their responsibilities and the size of the hotel in which they worked. In early 1991, annual salaries of assistant hotel managers averaged nearly $31,000, based on a survey conducted for the American Hotel and Motel Association. Assistants employed in large hotels with

over 350 rooms averaged over $36,000 in 1991, while those in small hotels with no more than 150 rooms averaged less than $25,000. Salaries of assistant managers also varied because of differences in duties and responsibilities. For example, food and beverage managers averaged $38,900, according to the same survey, whereas front office managers averaged $25,000. The manager's level of experience is also an important factor.

In 1991, salaries of general managers averaged nearly $56,000, ranging from an average of about $42,300 in hotels and motels with no more than 150 rooms to an average of about $81,800 in large hotels with over 350 rooms. Managers may earn bonuses ranging up to 15 percent of their basic salary in some hotels. In addition, they and their families may be furnished with lodging, meals, parking, laundry, and other services.

Most managers and assistants receive 3 to 11 paid holidays a year, paid vacation, sick leave, life insurance, medical benefits, and pension plans. Some hotels offer profit-sharing plans, educational assistance, and other benefits to their employees.

Related Occupations

Hotel managers and assistants are not the only workers concerned with organizing and directing a business in which pleasing people is very important. Others with similar responsibilities include restaurant managers, apartment building managers, department store managers, and office managers.

Sources of Additional Information

For information on careers and scholarships in hotel management, contact:

- The American Hotel and Motel Association (AH&MA), Information Center, 1201 New York Ave. NW., Washington, DC 20005- 3931.

For information on educational programs, including correspondence courses, in hotel and restaurant management, write to:

- The Educational Institute of AH&MA, P.O. Box 1240, East Lansing, MI 48826.

Information on careers in housekeeping management may be obtained from:

- National Executive Housekeepers Association, Inc., 1001 Eastwind Dr., Suite 301, Westerville, OH 43081.

For information on hospitality careers, as well as how to purchase a directory of colleges and other schools offering programs and courses in hotel and restaurant administration, write to:

- Council on Hotel, Restaurant, and Institutional Education, 1200 17th St. NW., Washington, DC 20036-3097.

General career information and a directory of accredited private trade and technical schools offering programs in hotel-motel management may be obtained from:

- National Association of Trade and Technical Schools, P.O. Box 10429, Department BL, Rockville, MD 20850.

Management Analysts and Consultants

(D.O.T. 100.117-014; 161.117-014, .167-010, .267 except -014 and -030; 169.167-074; and 375.267-026)

Nature of the Work

A rapidly growing small company needs a better system of

control over inventories and expenses. An established manufacturing company decides to relocate to another State and needs assistance planning the move. After acquiring a new division, a large company realizes that its corporate structure must be reorganized. A division chief of a government agency wants to know why the division's contracts are always going over budget. These are just a few of the many organizational problems that management analysts, as they are called in government agencies, and management consultants, as business firms refer to them, help solve. Although their job titles may differ, their job duties are essentially the same.

The work of management analysts and consultants varies from employer to employer and from project to project. For example, some projects require several consultants to work together, each specializing in one area; at other times, they will work independently. In general, analysts and consultants collect, review, and analyze information; make recommendations; and often assist in the implementation of their proposal.

Both public and private organizations use consultants for a variety of reasons. Some don't have the internal resources needed to handle a project; others need a consultant's expertise to determine what resources will be required—or problems encountered—if they pursue a particular course of action; while others want to get outside advice on how to resolve organizational problems that have already been identified or to avoid troublesome problems that could arise.

Firms providing consulting services range in size from solo practitioners to large international organizations employing thousands of consultants. These services usually are provided on a contract basis—a company solicits proposals from consulting firms specializing in the area in which it needs assistance. These proposals include the estimated cost and scope of the project, staffing requirements, and the deadline. The company then selects the proposal which best meets its needs.

Upon getting an assignment or contract, consultants define the nature and extent of the problem. During this phase of the job, they may analyze data such as annual revenues, employment, or expenditures; interview employees; or observe the operations of the organizational unit.

Next, they use their knowledge of management systems and their expertise in a particular area to develop solutions. In the course of preparing their recommendations, they must take into account the general nature of the business, the relationship the firm has with others in that industry, and the firm's internal organization, as well as information gained through data collection and analysis.

Once they have decided on a course of action, consultants usually report their findings and recommendations to the client, often in writing. In addition, they often make oral presentations regarding their findings. For some projects, this is all that is required; for others, consultants may assist in the implementation of their suggestions.

Management analysts in government agencies use the same skills as their private-sector colleagues to advise managers in government on many types of issues—most of which are similar to the problems faced by private firms. For example, if an agency is planning to purchase several personal computers, it first must determine which type to buy, given its budget and data processing needs. Management analysts would assess the various types of machines available and determine which best meets their department's needs.

Working Conditions

Management analysts and consultants usually divide their time between their offices and their Client's operation. Although much of their time is spent indoors in clean, well-lighted offices, they may have to visit a Client's production facility where conditions may not be so favorable. They must follow established safety procedures when making field visits to sites where they may encounter potentially hazardous conditions.

Typically, analysts and consultants work at least 40 hours a week. Overtime is common, especially when deadlines must be met. In addition, because they must spend a significant portion of their time with clients, they may travel frequently.

Self-employed consultants can set their workload and hours and work at home. On the other hand, their livelihood depends on their ability to maintain and expand their client base, which can be difficult at times.

Employment

Management analysts and consultants held about 151,000 jobs in 1990. Almost half of these workers were self-employed. Most of the rest worked in management consulting firms and for Federal, State, and local governments. The majority of those working for the Federal Government were found in the Department of Defense.

Management analysts and consultants are found throughout the country, but employment is concentrated in metropolitan areas.

Training, Qualifications, and Advancement

There are no universal educational requirements for entry level jobs in this field. However, employers in private industry prefer to hire those with a master's degree in business administration or a discipline related to the firms' area of specialization. Those individuals hired straight out of school with only a bachelor's degree are likely to work as research associates or junior consultants, rather than full-fledged management consultants. It is possible for research associates to advance up the career ladder if they demonstrate a strong aptitude for consulting, but, more often, they need to get an advanced degree to do so.

Many entrants to this occupation have, in addition to the appropriate formal education, several years of experience in management or in another occupation.

Most government agencies hire those with a bachelor's degree and no work experience as entry level management analysts, and often provide formal classroom training in management analysis.

Many fields of study provide a suitable formal educational background for this occupation because of the diversity of problem areas addressed by management analysts and consultants. These include most areas of business and management, as well as computer and information sciences and engineering.

Management analysts and consultants who are hired directly from school sometimes participate in formal company training programs. These programs may include instruction on policies and procedures, computer systems and software, and management practices and principles. Because of their previous industry experience, most who enter at middle levels do not participate in formal company training programs. However, regardless of background, analysts and consultants routinely attend conferences to keep abreast of current developments in their field. Additionally, some large firms offer in-house formal training programs for all levels of staff.

Management analysts and consultants often work under little or no supervision, so they should be independent and self-motivated. Analytical skills, strong oral communication and written skills, good judgment, the ability to manage time well, and creativity in developing solutions to problems are other desirable qualities for prospective management analysts and consultants.

In large consulting firms, beginners usually start as a member of a consulting team. The team is responsible for the entire project and each consultant is assigned to a particular area. As consultants gain experience, they may be assigned to work on one specific project full-time, taking on more responsibility and managing their own hours. At the senior level, consultants may supervise entry level workers and become increasingly involved in seeking out new business. Those with exceptional skills may eventually become a partner or principal in the firm. Others with entrepreneurial ambition may open their own firm.

The Institute of Management Consultants (a division of the Council of Consulting Organizations) offers the Certified Management Consultant (CMC) designation to those who pass an examination and meet minimum levels of education and experience. Certification is not mandatory for management consultants to practice, but it may give a jobseeker a competitive advantage.

Job Outlook

Employment of management analysts and consultants is expected to grow much faster than the average for all occupations through the year 2005 as industry and government increasingly rely on outside expertise to improve the performance of their organizations. Growth is expected in large consulting firms, but also in small consulting firms whose consultants will fill specialized niches. Most job openings, however, will result from the need to replace personnel who transfer to other fields or leave the labor force.

Increased foreign competition has caused American industry to take a closer look at its operations. In a more competitive international market, firms cannot afford inefficiency and wasted resources or else they risk losing their share of the market. Management consultants are being increasingly relied upon to help reduce costs, streamline operations, and develop marketing strategies. As businesses downsize and eliminate needed functions, consultants will be used to perform those functions on a contractual basis. On the other hand, businesses undergoing expansion will also need the skills of management consultants to help with organizational, administrative, and other issues. Continuing changes in the business environment also are expected to lead to demand for management consultants: Firms will use consultants' expertise to incorporate new technologies, to cope with more numerous and complex government regulations, and to adapt to a changing labor force. As businesses rely more on technology, there are increasing roles for consultants with a technical background, such as engineering or biotechnology, particularly when combined with an MBA.

Federal, State, and local agencies also are expected to expand their use of management analysts. In the era of budget deficits, analysts' skills at identifying problems and implementing cost reduction measures are expected to become increasingly important.

In the private sector, job opportunities are expected to be best for those with a graduate degree and some industry expertise, while opportunities for those with only a bachelor's degree will be best in the Federal Government. Consultants with special knowledge or skills in the environmental field, in human resources administration, and in the health care field are expected to have better job prospects than others.

Because many small conconsulting firms fail each year for lack of managerial expertise and clients, those interested in opening their own firm should have good organizational and marketing skills, plus several years of consulting experience.

Despite projected rapid employment growth and higher than average turnover, competition for jobs as management consultants is expected to be keen in the private sector. Because management consultants can come from such diverse educational backgrounds, the pool of applicants from which employers hire is quite large. Additionally, the independent and challenging nature of the work combined with high earnings potential make this occupation attractive to many.

Earnings

Salaries for management analysts and consultants vary widely by experience, education, and employer. In 1990, those who were wage and salary workers had median annual earnings of about $39,900. The middle 50 percent earned between $28,000 and $53,100.

In 1989, according to the Association of Management Consulting Firms (ACME), earnings—including bonuses and/or profit sharing—for research associates in ACME member firms averaged $31,800; for entry level consultants, $40,900; for management consultants, $58,900; for senior consultants, $79,300; for junior partners, $110,600; and for senior partners, $183,800.

In the Federal Government, the average salary for management analysts in 1991 was $41,353.

Typical benefits for salaried analysts and consultants include health and life insurance, a retirement plan, vacation and sick leave, profit sharing, and bonuses for outstanding work. In addition, all travel expenses usually are reimbursed by their employer. Self-employed consultants usually have to maintain an office and do not receive employer-provided benefits.

Related Occupations

Management analysts and consultants collect, review, and analyze data; make recommendations; and assist in the implementation of their ideas. Others who use similar skills are managers, computer systems analysts, operations research analysts, economists, and financial analysts.

Sources of Additional Information

Information about career opportunities in management consulting is available from:

- The Council of Consulting Organizations, Inc., 251 Fifth Ave., New York, NY 10175.

For information about a career as a State or local government management analyst, contact your State or local employment service.

Persons interested in a management analyst position in the Federal Government can obtain information from:

- U.S. Office of Personnel Management, 1900 E St. NW., Washington, DC 20415.

Marketing, Advertising, and Public Relations Managers

(D.O.T. 141.137-010; 159.167-022; 163.117-014, -018, -022, -026, .167-010, -018, -022, .267-010; 164.117-010, -014, -018, .167-010; 185.117-014, .157-010, -014; 187.167-162; 189.117-018)

Nature of the Work

The fundamental objective of any firm is to market its products or services profitably. In very small firms, all marketing responsibilities may be assumed by the owner or chief executive officer. In large firms, which may offer numerous products and services nationally or even worldwide, experienced marketing, advertising, and public relations managers coordinate these and related activities.

In large firms, the executive vice president for marketing directs the overall marketing policy—including market research, marketing strategy, sales, advertising, promotion, pricing, product development, and public relations activities. These activities are supervised by middle and supervisory managers who oversee staffs of professionals and technicians.

Marketing managers develop the firm's detailed marketing strategy. With the help of subordinates, including product development managers and market research managers, they determine the demand for products and services offered by the firm and its competitors and identify potential consumers—for example, business firms, wholesalers, retailers, government, or the general public. Mass markets are further categorized according to various factors such as region, age, income, and lifestyle. Marketing managers develop pricing strategy with an eye towards maximizing the firm's share of the market and ultimately its profits. In collaboration with sales, product development, and other managers, they monitor trends that indicate the need for new products and services and oversee product development. Marketing managers work with advertising and promotion managers to best promote the firm's products and services and to attract potential users.

Sales managers direct the firm's sales program. They assign sales territories and goals and establish training programs for their sales representatives. Managers advise their sales representatives on ways to improve their sales performance. In large, multiproduct firms, they oversee regional and local sales managers and their staffs. Sales managers maintain contact with dealers and distributors. They analyze sales statistics gathered by their staffs to determine sales potential and inventory requirements and monitor the preferences of customers. Such information is vital to develop products and maximize profits.

Except in the largest firms, advertising and promotion staffs are generally small and serve as a liaison between the firm and the advertising or promotion agency to which many advertising or promotional functions are contracted out. Advertising managers oversee the account services, creative services, and media services departments. The account services department is managed by account executives, who assess the need for advertising and, in advertising agencies, maintain the accounts of clients. The crea-tive services department—which develops the subject matter and presentation of advertising—is supervised by a creative director, who oversees the copy chief and art director and their staffs. The media services department is supervised by the media director, who oversees planning groups which select the communication media—for example, radio, television, newspapers, magazines, or outdoor signs—to disseminate the advertising.

Promotion managers—who supervise staffs of promotion specialists—direct promotion programs, which combine advertising with purchase incentives to increase sales of products or services. In an effort to establish closer contact with purchasers—dealers, distributors, or consumers—promotion programs may involve direct mail, telemarketing, television or radio advertising, catalogs, exhibits, inserts in newspapers, in-store displays and product endorsements, and special events. Purchase incentives may include discounts, samples, gifts, rebates, coupons, sweepstakes, and contests.

Public relations managers supervise public relations specialists. Public relations managers direct publicity programs to a targeted public, using any necessary communication media, designed to maintain the support of the specific group upon whom their organization's success depends, such as consumers, stockholders, or the general public. For example, public relations managers may clarify or justify the firm's point of view on health or environmental issues to community or special interest groups. They may evaluate advertising and promotion programs for compatibility with public relations efforts. Public relations managers in effect serve as the eyes and ears of top management—observing social, economic, and political trends that might ultimately have an impact upon the firm, and making recommendations to enhance the firm's public image in view of those trends. Public relations managers may confer with labor relations managers to produce internal company communications—such as news about employee-management relations—and with financial managers to produce company reports. They may assist company executives in drafting speeches, arranging interviews, and other forms of public contact; oversee company archives; and respond to information requests. In addition, public relations managers may handle special events such as sponsorship of races, parties introducing new products, or other activities by which the firm seeks public attention through the press without advertising directly.

Working Conditions

Marketing, advertising, and public relations managers are provided with offices close to top managers. Long hours, including evenings and weekends, are not uncommon. Working under pressure is unavoidable as schedules change, problems arise, and deadlines and goals must be met. Marketing, advertising, and public relations managers meet frequently with other managers; some meet with the public and government officials.

Substantial travel may be involved. For example, attendance at meetings sponsored by associations or industries is often mandatory. Sales managers travel to national, regional, and local offices and to various dealers and distributors. Advertising and promotion managers may travel to meet with clients or representatives of communications media. Public relations managers may travel to meet with special interest groups or government officials. Job transfers between headquarters and regional offices are common—particularly among sales managers—and may disrupt family life.

Employment

Marketing, advertising, and public relations managers held about 427,000 jobs in 1990. These managers are found in virtually every industry. Industries employing them in significant numbers include motor vehicle dealers; printing and publishing firms; advertising agencies; department stores; computer and data processing services firms; and management and public relations firms.

Training, Advancement, and Other Qualifications

A wide range of educational backgrounds are suitable for entry into marketing, advertising, and public relations managerial jobs, but many employers prefer a broad liberal arts background. A bachelor's degree in sociology, psychology, literature, or philosophy, among other subjects, is acceptable. However, requirements vary depending upon the particular job.

For marketing, sales, and promotion management positions, some employers prefer a bachelor's or master's degree in business administration with an emphasis on marketing. Courses in business law, economics, accounting, finance, mathematics, and statistics are also highly recommended. In highly technical industries, such as computer and electronics manufacturing, a bachelor's degree in engineering or science combined with a master's degree in business administration may be preferred. For advertising management positions, some employers prefer a bachelor's degree in advertising or journalism. The curriculum should include courses in marketing, consumer behavior, market research, sales, communications methods and technology, and visual arts—for example, art history and photography. For public relations management positions, some employers prefer a bachelor's or master's degree in public relations or journalism. The curriculum should include courses in advertising, business administration, public affairs, political science, and creative and technical writing. For all specialties, courses in management and completion of an internship while in school are highly recommended. Familiarity with computerized word processing and data base applications also is important for many marketing, advertising, and public relations management positions.

Most marketing, advertising, and public relations management positions are filled by promoting experienced staff or related professional or technical personnel—for example, sales representatives, purchasing agents, buyers, product or brand specialists, advertising specialists, promotion specialists, and public relations specialists. In small firms, where the number of positions is limited, advancement to a management position may come slowly. In large firms, promotion may occur more quickly.

Although experience, ability, and leadership are emphasized for promotion, advancement may be accelerated by participation in management training programs conducted by many large firms. Many firms also provide their employees with continuing education opportunities, either in-house or at local colleges and universities, and encourage employee participation in seminars and conferences, often provided by professional societies. In addition, numerous marketing and related associations, often in collaboration with colleges and universities, sponsor national or local management training programs. Courses in these schools include brand and product management, international marketing, sales management evaluation, telemarketing and direct sales, promotion, marketing communication, market research, organizational communication, and data processing systems procedures and management. Many firms pay all or part of the cost for those who successfully complete courses.

Persons interested in becoming marketing, advertising, and public relations managers should be mature, creative, highly motivated, resistant to stress, and flexible, yet decisive. The ability to communicate persuasively, both orally and in writing, with other managers, staff, and the public is vital. Marketing, advertising, and public relations managers also need tact, good judgment, and exceptional ability to establish and maintain effective personal relationships with supervisory and professional staff members and client firms.

Because of the importance and high visibility of their jobs, marketing, advertising, and public relations managers are often prime candidates for advancement. Well-trained, experienced, successful managers may be promoted to higher positions in their own or other firms. Some become top executives. Managers with extensive experience and sufficient capital may open their own businesses.

Job Outlook

Employment of marketing, advertising, and public relations managers is expected to increase much faster than the average for all occupations through the year 2005. Increasingly intense domestic and foreign competition in products and services offered consumers should require greater marketing, promotional, and public relations efforts. In addition to much faster than average growth, many job openings will occur each year to replace managers who move into top management positions, transfer to other jobs, or leave the labor force. However, many of these highly coveted jobs will be sought by other managers or highly experienced professional and technical personnel, resulting in substantial job competition. College graduates with extensive experience, a high level of creativity, and strong communication skills should have the best job opportunities.

Projected employment growth varies by industry. For example, employment of marketing, advertising, and public relations managers is expected to grow very rapidly in most services industries—such as computer and data processing firms, and management, public relations, and advertising firms—and in motor vehicle dealerships. More moderate growth is projected in manufacturing industries overall.

Earnings

The median annual salary of marketing, advertising, and public relations managers was $41,400 in 1990. The lowest 10 percent earned $20,300 or less, while the top 10 percent earned $78,500 or more. Many earn bonuses equal to 10 percent or more of their salaries. Surveys show that salary levels vary substantially depending upon the level of managerial responsibility, length of service, education, and the employer's size, location, and industry. For example, manufacturing firms generally pay marketing, advertising, and public relations managers higher salaries than nonmanufacturing firms. For sales managers, the extent of their sales territory is another important factor.

According to a 1990 survey by Abbot, Langer and Associates, of Crete, Illinois, median annual incomes ranged from $30,500 for a top sales promotion manager to $63,700 for a regional sales manager. The median annual income for a top advertising manager was $45,000; for a product/brand manager, $53,400.

Like other managers, marketing, advertising, and public relations managers typically receive a range of fringe benefits that includes health and life insurance, vacation and sick leave, and a pension, among others.

Related Occupations

Marketing, advertising, and public relations managers direct the sale of products and services offered by their firms and the communication of information about their firms' activities. Other personnel involved with marketing, advertising, and public relations include art directors, commercial and graphic artists, copy chiefs, copywriters, editors, lobbyists, market research analysts, public relations specialists, promotion specialists, sales representatives, and technical writers.

Sources of Additional Information

For information about careers in sales and marketing management, contact:

- American Marketing Association, 250 S. Wacker Dr., Chicago, IL 60606.
- Sales and Marketing Executives, International, 458 Statler Office Tower, Cleveland, OH 44115.

For information about careers in advertising management, contact:

- American Association of Advertising Agencies, 666 Third Ave., 13th Floor, New York, NY 10017.
- American Advertising Federation, Education Services Department, 1400 K St. NW., Suite 1000, Washington, DC 20005.

Information about careers in promotion management is available from:

- Council of Sales Promotion Agencies, 750 Summer St., Stamford, CT 06901.
- Promotion Marketing Association of America, Inc., 322 Eighth Ave., Suite 1201, New York, NY 10001.

Information about careers in public relations management is available from:

- Public Relations Society of America, 33 Irving Place, New York, NY 10003-2376.

Property and Real Estate Managers

(D.O.T. 186.117-042, -046, -058, and -062, .167-018, -030, -038, -042, -046, -062, and -066; 187.167-190; 189.157; 191.117-030 and -042 through -050).

Nature of the Work

Many people own real estate in the form of a home, but, to businesses and investors, real estate is more than simply the roof over their heads and the ground under their feet. For them, real estate is a valuable asset—land and structures, such as office buildings, shopping centers, and apartment complexes—that can produce income and appreciate in value over time if well managed. Real estate can be a source of income when it is leased to others, and a substantial business expense when it is leased from others. Property managers administer income-producing commercial and residential properties and manage the communal property and services of condominium and community associations. Real estate managers plan and direct the purchase, development, and disposal of real estate for businesses.

The majority of property and real estate managers work in the field of property management. When owners of apartments, office buildings, retail and industrial properties, or condominiums lack the time or expertise to assume the day-to-day management of their real estate investments, they often hire a property manager, or contract for one's services with a real estate management company. Most property managers handle several properties simultaneously. Property managers act as the owners' agent and adviser for the property. They market vacant space to prospective tenants, through the use of a leasing agent, advertising, or by other means, and establish rental rates in accordance with prevailing local conditions. They negotiate and prepare lease or rental agreements with tenants and collect their rent payments and other fees. Property managers also handle the bookkeeping for the property. They see to it that rents are received and make sure that mortgages, taxes, insurance premiums, payroll, and upkeep and maintenance bills are paid on time. They also supervise the preparation of financial statements and periodically report to the owners on the status of the property, occupancy rates, dates of lease expirations, and other matters.

Property managers negotiate contracts for janitorial, security, groundskeeping, trash removal, and other services. When contracts are awarded competitively, managers must solicit bids from several contractors and recommend to the owners which bid to accept. They monitor the performance of the contractors, and investigate and resolve complaints from tenants. Managers also purchase all supplies and equipment needed for the property, and make arrangements with specialists for any repairs that cannot be handled by the regular property maintenance staff.

Property managers hire the maintenance, stationary engineering, and on-site management personnel. At smaller properties, the property manager might employ only a building engineer who maintains the building's heating, ventilation, and air-conditioning systems and performs other routine maintenance and repair. Larger properties require a sizable maintenance staff supervised by a full-time on-site or resident manager, who works under the direction of the property manager.

Although some on-site managers oversee large office buildings or shopping centers, most manage apartments. They train, supervise, and assign duties to the maintenance staff and routinely inspect the grounds, facilities, and equipment, determine what repairs and maintenance are needed, and assign workers to do them. Occasionally, outside contractors are required, and the on-site manager may obtain bids for the work and submit them to the property manager. On-site managers schedule routine servicing of the heating, ventilation, and air-conditioning systems and insure that the work of the maintenance staff and contract workers is up to standards or contract specifications. They keep records of expenditures incurred for operating the property and submit regular expense reports to the property manager or owners. They may recruit maintenance staff, interview the job applicants, and recommend to the property manager qualified candidates for employment.

Tenant relations is an important part of the work of on-site managers, particularly apartment managers. Apartment managers handle tenants' requests for service or repairs and try to resolve complaints. They show vacant apartments to prospective

training, and job placement. Rehabilitation counselors interview individuals with disabilities and their families, evaluate school and medical reports, and confer and plan with physicians, psychologists, occupational therapists, employers, and others. Conferring with the client, they develop and implement a rehabilitation program, which may include training to help the person become more independent and employable. They also work toward increasing the client's capacity to adjust and live independently.

Employment counselors help individuals make wise career decisions. They help clients explore and evaluate their education, training, work history, interests, skills, personal traits, and physical capacities, and may arrange for aptitude and achievement tests. They also work with individuals in developing jobseeking skills and assist clients in locating and applying for jobs.

Mental health counselors work with individuals and groups to promote optimum mental health. They help individuals deal with such concerns as addictions and substance abuse, family, parenting, and marital problems, suicide, stress management, problems with self-esteem, issues associated with aging, job and career concerns, educational decisions, and issues of mental and emotional health. Mental health counselors work closely with other mental health specialists, including psychiatrists, psychologists, clinical social workers, psychiatric nurses, and school counselors.

Counselors specialize in many other areas, including marriage and family, multicultural, and gerontological counseling.

Working Conditions

Most school counselors work the traditional 9- to 10-month school year with a 2- to 3-month vacation, although an increasing number are employed on 10 1/2- or 11-month contracts. They generally have the same hours as teachers.

Rehabilitation and employment counselors generally work a standard 40-hour week. Self-employed counselors and those working in mental health and community agencies often work evenings to counsel clients who work during the day. College career planning and placement counselors may work long and irregular hours during recruiting periods.

Since privacy is essential for confidential and frank discussions with clients, counselors usually have private offices.

Employment

Counselors held about 144,000 jobs in 1990. School counseling was the largest specialty.

In addition to elementary and secondary schools and colleges and universities, counselors worked in a wide variety of public and private establishments. These include health care facilities; job training and vocational rehabilitation centers; social agencies; correctional institutions; and residential care facilities, such as halfway houses for criminal offenders and group homes for children, the aged, and the disabled. Counselors also worked in organizations engaged in community improvement and social change, as well as drug and alcohol rehabilitation programs and State and local government agencies. A growing number of counselors are in private practice, health maintenance organizations, and group practice.

Training, Other Qualifications, and Advancement

Generally, counselors have a master's degree in college student affairs, elementary or secondary school counseling, gerontological counseling, marriage and family counseling, substance abuse counseling, rehabilitation counseling, agency or community counseling, mental health counseling, counseling psychology, career counseling, or a related field.

Graduate level counselor education programs in colleges and universities are usually in departments of education or psychology. Courses are grouped into eight core areas: Human growth and development; social and cultural foundations; helping relationships; groups; lifestyle and career development; appraisal; research and evaluation; and professional orientation. In an accredited program, 48 to 60 semester hours of graduate study, including a period of supervised clinical experience in counseling, are usually required for a master's degree. The Council for Accreditation of Counseling and Related Educational Programs (CACREP) accredits graduate counseling programs.

In 1991, 34 States had some form of counselor credentialing legislation—licensure, certification, or registry—for practice outside schools. Requirements vary from State to State. In some States, credentialing is mandatory; in others, voluntary.

Many counselors elect to be Nationally certified by the National Board for Certified Counselors (NBCC), which grants the credential "National Certified Counselor." In order to be certified, a counselor must hold a master's degree in counseling, have at least 2 years of professional counseling experience, and pass NBCC's National Counselor Examination. This national certification is distinct from State certification.

All States require school counselors to hold State school counseling certification. Some States require public school counselors to have both counseling and teaching certificates. Depending on the State, a master's degree in counseling and 2 to 5 years of teaching experience may be required for a counseling certificate.

Vocational and related rehabilitation agencies generally require a master's degree in rehabilitation counseling, counseling and guidance, or counseling psychology for rehabilitation counselor jobs. Some, however, may accept applicants with a bachelor's degree in rehabilitation services, counseling, psychology, or related fields. Experience in employment counseling, job development, psychology, education, or social work may be helpful.

The Council on Rehabilitation Education (CORE) accredits graduate programs in rehabilitation counseling. A minimum of 2 years of study—including a period of supervised clinical experience—are required for the master's degree. Some colleges and universities offer a bachelor's degree in rehabilitation services education.

In most State vocational rehabilitation agencies, applicants must pass a written examination and be evaluated by a board of examiners. Many employers require rehabilitation counselors to be certified. To become certified, counselors must meet educational and experience standards established by the Commission on Rehabilitation Counselor Certification, and pass a written examination. They are then designated as "Certified Rehabilitation Counselors."

Some States require counselors in public employment offices to have a master's degree; others accept a bachelor's degree with appropriate counseling courses.

Mental health counselors generally have a master's degree in mental health counseling, another area of counseling, or in psychology or social work. They are voluntarily certified by the National Academy of Certified Clinical Mental Health Counselors. Generally, to receive this certification, a counselor must have a master's degree in counseling, 2 years of post-master's experience, a period of supervised clinical experience, a taped sample of clinical work, and a passing grade on a written examination.

Some employers provide training for newly hired counselors. Many have work-study programs so that employed counselors can earn graduate degrees. Counselors must participate in graduate studies, workshops, institutes, and personal studies to maintain their certificates and licenses.

Persons interested in counseling should have a strong interest in helping others and the ability to inspire respect, trust, and confidence. They should be able to work independently or as part of a team.

Prospects for advancement vary by counseling field. School counselors may move to a larger school; become directors or supervisors of counseling or pupil personnel services; or, usually with further graduate education, become counselor educators, counseling psychologists, or school administrators.

Rehabilitation, mental health, and employment counselors may become supervisors or administrators in their agencies. Some counselors move into research, consulting, or college teaching, or go into private practice.

Job Outlook

Overall employment of counselors is expected to grow faster than the average for all occupations through the year 2005. In addition, replacement needs should increase significantly by the end of the decade as the large number of counselors now in their 40's and 50's reach retirement age.

Employment of school counselors is expected to grow faster than average because of increasing secondary school enrollments, State legislation requiring counselors in elementary schools, and the expanded responsibilities of counselors. Counselors are increasingly becoming involved in crisis and preventive counseling, helping students deal with issues ranging from drug and alcohol abuse to death and suicide.

Faster than average growth is also expected for rehabilitation and mental health counselors. Insurance companies are increasingly allowing for reimbursement of counselors, enabling many counselors to move from schools and government agencies to private practice. The number of people who need rehabilitation services will rise as advances in medical technology continue to save lives that only a few years ago would have been lost. In addition, more rehabilitation and mental health counselors will be needed as society focuses on ways of developing mental well-being, such as controlling job and family-related stress, with the help of counselors.

The number of employment counselors, who work primarily for State and local governments, could be limited by budgetary constraints.

Earnings

Median earnings for full-time educational and vocational counselors were about $31,000 a year in 1990. The middle 50 percent earned between $24,200 and $40,000 a year. The bottom 10 percent earned less than $17,700 a year, while the top 10 percent earned over $49,300 a year.

The average salary of school counselors in the 1990-91 academic year was about $38,000, according to the Educational Research Service. Some school counselors earn additional income working summers in the school system or in other jobs.

Self-employed counselors who have well-established practices generally have the highest earnings, as do some counselors working for private companies, such as insurance companies and private rehabilitation companies.

Related Occupations

Counselors help people evaluate their interests, abilities, and disabilities, and deal with personal, social, academic, and career problems. Others who help people in similar ways include college and student personnel workers, teachers, personnel workers and managers, social workers, psychologists, psychiatrists, members of the clergy, occupational therapists, training and employee development specialists, and equal employment opportunity/affirmative action specialists.

Sources of Additional Information

For general information about counseling, as well as information on school, college, mental health, rehabilitation, multicultural, career, marriage and family, and gerontological counselors, contact:

- American Association for Counseling and Development, 5999 Stevenson Ave., Alexandria, VA 22304.

For information on accredited counseling and related training programs, contact:

- Council for Accreditation of Counseling and Related Educational Programs, American Association for Counseling and Development, 5999 Stevenson Ave., Alexandria, VA 22304.

For information on national certification requirements and procedures for counselors, contact:

- National Board for Certified Counselors, P.O. Box 5406, Greensboro, NC 27435.

For information about rehabilitation counseling, contact:

- National Rehabilitation Counseling Association, 633 So. Washington St., Alexandria, VA 22314.
- National Council on Rehabilitation Education, 1213 29th St. NW., Washington, DC 20007.

For information on certification requirements for rehabilitation counselors, contact:

- Commission on Rehabilitation Counselor Certification, 1835 Rohlwing Rd., Suite E, Rolling Meadows, IL 60008.

For general information about school counselors, contact:

- American School Counselor Association, 5999 Stevenson Ave., Alexandria, VA 22304.

State departments of education can supply information on colleges and universities that offer approved guidance and counseling training for State certification and licensure requirements.

State employment service offices have information about job opportunities and entrance requirements for counselors.

Dancers and Choreographers

(D.O.T. 151.027-010, and .047-010)

Nature of the Work

From ancient times to the present, dancers have expressed

ideas, stories, rhythm, and sound with their bodies. They may perform in classical ballet, which includes the stylized, traditional repertory, or modern dance, which allows more free movement and self-expression. Others perform in dance adaptations for musical shows, in folk, ethnic, and jazz dances, and in other popular kinds of dancing. In addition to being an art form for its own sake, dance also complements opera, musical comedy, and television performances. Therefore, many dancers sing and act, as well as dance.

Dancers most often perform as a group, although a few top artists dance solo. Many dancers combine stage work with teaching.

Choreographers create original dances. They may also create new interpretations to traditional dances like the "Nutcracker" since few dances are "written down." Choreographers instruct performers at rehearsals to achieve the desired effect. They also audition performers.

Working Conditions

Dancing is strenuous. Rehearsals require very long hours and usually take place daily, including weekends and holidays. For shows on the road, weekend travel often is required. Most performances take place in the evening, and dancers must become accustomed to working late hours.

Due to the physical demands, most dancers stop performing by their late thirties, but they sometimes continue to work in the dance field as a choreographer, a dance teacher/coach, or an artistic director. Some celebrated dancers, however, continue performing beyond the age of 50.

Employment

Professional dancers held an average of about 8,600 jobs at any one time in 1990. Many others were between engagements so that the total number of people employed as dancers over the course of the year was greater. In addition, there were many dance instructors in secondary schools, colleges and universities, dance schools, and private studios. Many teachers also performed from time to time.

New York City is the home of most of the major dance companies. Other cities with full-time professional dance companies are Atlanta, Boston, Chicago, Cincinnati, Cleveland, Dallas, Houston, Milwaukee, Philadelphia, Pittsburgh, Salt Lake City, San Francisco, and Seattle.

Training and Other Qualifications

Training depends upon the type of dance. Early ballet training begins at 5 to 8 years of age and is usually given by private teachers and independent ballet schools. Serious training traditionally begins between the ages of 10 and 12. Students who demonstrate potential in the early teens receive more intensive and advanced professional training at regional ballet schools or schools conducted under the auspices of the major ballet companies. Leading dance school companies often have summer training programs from which they select candidates for admission to their regular full-time training program. Most dancers have their professional auditions by age 17 or 18; however, training and practice never end. For example, professional ballet dancers have 1 to 1 1/2 hours of lessons every day, and spend many additional hours practicing and rehearsing.

Early and intensive training also is important for the modern dancer, but modern dance generally does not require as many years of training as ballet.

Because of the strenuous and time-consuming training required, a dancer's formal academic instruction may be minimal. However, a broad, general education including music, literature, history, and the visual arts is helpful in the interpretation of dramatic episodes, ideas, and feelings.

Many colleges and universities confer bachelor's or higher degrees in dance, generally through the departments of physical education, music, theater, or fine arts. Most programs concentrate on modern dance but also offer courses in ballet/classical techniques.

A college education is not essential to obtaining employment as a professional dancer. In fact, ballet dancers who postpone their first audition until graduation may compete at a disadvantage with younger dancers. On the other hand, a college degree can be helpful for the dancer who retires at an early age, as often happens, and wishes to enter another field of work.

A college education is also an advantage for college or university teaching. However, it is not necessary for teaching dance or choreography in a studio. Studio schools usually require teachers to have experience as performers; colleges and conservatories generally require graduate degrees, but performance experience often may be substituted.

The dancer's life is one of rigorous practice and self-discipline; therefore, patience, perseverance, and a devotion to dance are essential. Good health and physical stamina are necessary in order to practice and perform and to follow the rugged schedule often required. Good feet and normal arches also are required. Above all, one must have flexibility, agility, coordination, grace, a sense of rhythm, and a feeling for music, as well as a creative ability to express oneself through movement.

Seldom does a dancer perform unaccompanied. Therefore, ability to function as part of a team is important. Dancers also should be prepared to face the anxiety of intermittent employment and rejections when auditioning for work.

For dancers, advancement takes the form of a growing reputation, bigger and better roles, and higher pay.

Job Outlook

Dancers face keen competition. The number of applicants will continue to exceed the number of job openings. Only the most talented will find regular employment.

Employment of dancers is expected to grow much faster than the average for all occupations through the year 2005 due to the public's continued interest in this form of artistic expression. In addition to jobs arising from increased demand, some job openings will occur as dancers leave the occupation and as dance companies search for and find outstanding talent.

The best job opportunities are expected to be with national dance companies because of the demand for performances outside of New York City. Opera companies will also provide some employment opportunities. Dance groups affiliated with colleges and universities and television and motion pictures will also offer some opportunities. In addition, the growing popularity of dance in recent years has resulted in increased employment opportunities in teaching dance.

Earnings

Earnings of most professional dancers are governed by union

contracts. Dancers in the major opera ballet, classical ballet, and modern dance corps belong to the American Guild of Musical Artists, Inc., AFL-CIO; those on live or videotaped television belong to the American Federation of Television and Radio Artists; those who perform in films and on TV belong to the Screen Actors Guild or the Screen Extras Guild; and those in musical comedies are members of Actors' Equity Association. The unions and producers sign basic agreements specifying minimum salary rates, hours of work, and other conditions of employment. However, the separate contract signed by each dancer with the producer of the show may be more favorable than the basic agreement.

For 1991-92, the minimum weekly salary for dancers in ballet and modern productions was $555. For new first year dancers being paid for single performances, the basic rate was $230 per performance and $60 per rehearsal hour. Dancers on tour received an additional allowance for room and board. The minimum performance rates for dancers on television was $569 for a 1-hour show. The normal workweek is 30 hours including rehearsals and matinee and evening performances. Extra compensation is paid for additional hours worked.

Some new choreographers receive a minimum fee of $400 for a ballet and $30 per performance in royalties.

Earnings from dancing are generally low because dancers' employment is irregular. They often must supplement their income by taking temporary jobs unrelated to dancing.

Dancers covered by union contracts are entitled to some paid sick leave, paid vacations, and various health and pension benefits—extended sick pay, child birth provisions—provided by their unions. Employers contribute toward these benefits. Most other dancers do not receive any fringe benefits.

Related Occupations

Other occupations require the dancer's knowledge of conveying ideas through physical motion including ice skater, dance critic, dance instructor, dance notator, and dance therapist. Athletes in most sports also need the same strength, flexibility, agility, and body control.

Sources of Additional Information

For information about colleges and universities that teach dance, including details on the types of courses offered, send a stamped, self-addressed envelope to:

- National Association of Schools of Dance, 11250 Roger Bacon Dr., Reston, VA 22090.

For information on all aspects of dance, including job listings, send a self-addressed stamped envelope to:

- American Dance Guild, 33 West 21st St., Third Floor, New York, NY 10010.

For information on which associations to contact and references for reading materials, send a self-addressed stamped envelope to:

- Associated Actors and Artistes of America, 165 West 46th St., New York, NY 10036.

Electrical and Electronics Engineers

(D.O.T. 003.061, .167 except -034, -062, and -070, and .187)

Nature of the Work

Electrical and electronics engineers design, develop, test, and supervise the manufacture of electrical and electronic equipment. Electrical equipment includes power generating and transmission equipment used by electric utilities, and electric motors, machinery controls, and lighting and wiring in buildings, automobiles, and aircraft. Electronic equipment includes radar, computer hardware, and communications and video equipment.

The specialties of electrical and electronics engineers include several major areas—such as power generation, transmission, and distribution; communications; computer electronics; and electrical equipment manufacturing—or a subdivision of these areas—industrial robot control systems or aviation electronics, for example. Electrical and electronics engineers design new products, write performance requirements, and develop maintenance schedules. They also test equipment, solve operating problems, and estimate the time and cost of engineering projects.

Working Conditions

Many engineers work in laboratories industrial plants or construction sites where they inspect supervise or solve onsite problems. Others work in an office almost all of the time. Engineers in branches such as civil engineering may work outdoors part of the time. A few engineers travel extensively to plants or construction sites.

Many engineers work a standard 40-hour week. At times deadlines or design standards may bring extra pressure to a job. When this happens engineers may work long hours and experience considerable stress.

Employment

Electrical and electronics engineers held about 426,000 jobs in 1990, making it the largest branch of engineering. Most jobs were in firms that manufacture electrical and electronic equipment, business machines, professional and scientific equipment, and aircraft and parts. Computer and data processing services firms, engineering and business consulting firms, public utilities, and government agencies accounted for most of the remaining jobs.

Training Other Qualifications and Advancement

A bachelor's degree in engineering from an accredited engineering program is usually required for beginning engineering jobs. College graduates with a degree in a physical science or mathematics may occasionally qualify for some engineering jobs especially in engineering specialties in high demand. Most engineering degrees are granted in branches such as electrical mechanical or civil engineering. However engineers trained in one branch may work in another. This flexibility allows employers to meet staffing needs in new technologies and specialties in short supply. It also allows engineers to shift to fields with better employment prospects or ones that match their interests more closely.

In addition to the standard engineering degree many colleges offer degrees in engineering technology which are offered as either 2- or 4-year programs. These programs prepare students for practical design and production work rather than for jobs that require more theoretical scientific and mathematical knowledge. Graduates of 4-year technology programs may get jobs similar to those obtained by graduates with a bachelors degree in engineering. However some employers regard them as having skills between those of a technician and an engineer.

Graduate training is essential for engineering faculty positions but is not required for the majority of entry level engineering jobs. Many engineers obtain a master's degree to learn new technology to broaden their education and to enhance promotion opportunities.

Nearly 260 colleges and universities offer a bachelor's degree in engineering and nearly 100 colleges offer a bachelor's degree in engineering technology. Although most institutions offer programs in the larger branches of engineering only a few offer some of the smaller specialties. Also programs of the same title may vary in content. For example some emphasize industrial practices preparing students for a job in industry while others are more theoretical and are better for students preparing to take graduate work. Therefore students should investigate curriculums carefully before selecting a college. Admissions requirements for undergraduate engineering schools include courses in advanced high school mathematics and the physical sciences.

In a typical 4-year college curriculum the first 2 years are spent studying basic sciences (mathematics physics and chemistry) introductory engineering and the humanities social sciences and English. In the last 2 years most courses are in engineering usually with a concentration in one branch. For example the last 2 years of an aerospace program might include courses such as fluid mechanics heat transfer applied aerodynamics analytical mechanics flight vehicle design trajectory dynamics and aerospace propulsion systems. Some programs offer a general engineering curriculum; students then specialize in graduate school or on the job.

A few engineering schools and 2-year colleges have agreements whereby the 2-year college provides the initial engineering education and the engineering school automatically admits students for their last 2 years. In addition a few engineering schools have arrangements whereby a student spends 3 years in a liberal arts college studying preengineering subjects and 2 years in the engineering school and receives a bachelor's degree from each. Some colleges and universities offer 5-year master's degree programs.

Some 5- or even 6-year cooperative plans combine classroom study and practical work permitting students to gain valuable experience and finance part of their education.

All 50 States and the District of Columbia require registration for engineers whose work may affect life health or property or who offer their services to the public. In 1990 nearly 500000 engineers were registered. Registration generally requires a degree from an engineering program accredited by the Accreditation Board for Engineering and Technology 4 years of relevant work experience and passing a State examination. Some States will not register people with degrees in engineering technology.

Beginning engineering graduates usually do routine work under the supervision of experienced engineers and in larger companies may also receive formal classroom or seminar-type training. As they gain knowledge and experience they are assigned more difficult tasks with greater independence to develop designs solve problems and make decisions. Engineers may become technical specialists or may supervise a staff or team of engineers and technicians. Some eventually become engineering managers or enter other managerial management support or sales jobs. Some engineers obtain graduate degrees in business administration to improve advancement opportunities; others obtain law degrees and become patent attorneys. Many high level executives in government and industry began their careers as engineers.

Engineers should be able to work as part of a team and should have creativity an analytical mind and a capacity for detail. In addition engineers should be able to express themselves well—both orally and in writing.

Job Outlook

Employment opportunities for electrical and electronics engineers are expected to be good through the year 2005 because employment is expected to increase faster than the average for all occupations. The majority of job openings will result from the need to replace electrical and electronics engineers who transfer to other occupations or leave the labor force.

Increased demand by businesses and government for computers and communications equipment is expected to account for much of the projected employment growth. Consumer demand for electrical and electronic goods and increased research and development on computers, robots, and other types of automation should create additional jobs.

Since many electrical engineering jobs are defense related, expected cutbacks in defense spending could result in layoffs of electrical engineers, especially if a defense-related project or contract is unexpectedly canceled. Furthermore, engineers who fail to keep up with the rapid changes in technology in some specialties risk technological obsolescence, which makes them more susceptible to layoffs or, at a minimum, likely to be passed over for advancement.

Earnings

Starting salaries for engineers with the bachelors degree are significantly higher than starting salaries of bachelors degree graduates in other fields. According to the College Placement Council engineering graduates with a bachelors degree averaged about $31,900 a year in private industry in 1990; those with a master's degree and no experience $36,200 a year; and those with a Ph.D. $50,400. Starting salaries for those with the bachelor's degree vary by branch as shown in the following tabulation.

	Starting salary
Petroleum	$35,202
Chemical	35,122
Metallurgical	32,235
Mechanical	32,064
Electrical	31,778
Nuclear	31,750
Industrial	30,525
Aerospace	30,509
Mining	29,383
Civil	28,136

As shown in the following tabulation, the average salary for engineers in private industry in 1990 was $31,412 at the most junior level, and $93,514 at senior managerial levels. Experienced midlevel engineers with no supervisory responsibilities averaged $49,195.

	Average salary
Engineers I	$31,412
Engineers II	35,389

kept on hand, for example, operations research analysts might talk with engineers about production levels; discuss purchasing arrangements with industrial buyers; and examine data on storage costs provided by the accounting department.

With this information in hand, the operations research analyst is ready to select the most appropriate analytical technique. There may be several techniques that could be used, or there may be one standard model or technique that is used in all instances. In a few cases, the analyst must construct an original model to examine and explain the system. In almost all cases, the selected model must be modified to reflect the specific circumstances of the situation.

A model for airline flight scheduling, for example, might take into account the amount of fuel required to fly the routes, several projected levels of passenger demand, varying ticket prices, pilot scheduling, and maintenance costs. The analyst chooses the values for these variables, enters them into a computer, which has already been programmed to make the calculations required, and runs the program to produce the best flight schedule consistent with several sets of assumptions. The analyst would probably design a model that would take into account wide variations in the different variables.

At this point, the operations research analyst presents the final work to management along with recommendations based on the results of the analysis. Additional runs based on different assumptions may be needed to help in making the final decision. Once a decision has been reached, the analyst works with the staff to ensure its successful implementation.

Working Conditions

Operations research analysts generally work regular hours in an office environment. Because they work on projects that are of immediate interest to management, analysts often are under pressure to meet deadlines and may work more than a 40-hour week. The work is sedentary in nature, and very little physical strength or stamina is required.

Employment

Operations research analysts held about 57,000 jobs in 1990. They are employed in most industries. Major employers include manufacturers of chemicals, machinery, and transportation equipment; firms providing transportation and telecommunications services; public utilities; banks; insurance agencies; and government agencies at all levels. Some analysts work for management consulting agencies that develop operations research applications for firms that do not have an in-house operations research staff.

Most analysts in the Federal Government work for the Armed Forces. In addition, many operations research analysts who work in private industry do work directly or indirectly related to National defense.

Training, Other Qualifications, and Advancement

Employers strongly prefer applicants with at least a master's degree in operations research or management science, mathematics, statistics, business administration, computer science, industrial engineering, or other quantitative disciplines. A high level of computer skills is also required.

The organizations often sponsor skill-improvement training for experienced workers, helping them keep up with new developments in operations research techniques as well as advances in computer science. Some analysts attend advanced university classes on these subjects.

Operations research analysts must be able to think logically and work well with people. Thus, employers prefer workers with good oral and written communication skills. The computer is the most important tool for quantitative analysis, and training or experience in programming is a must.

Beginning analysts usually do routine work under the supervision of experienced analysts. As they gain knowledge and experience, they are assigned more complex tasks, with greater autonomy to design models and solve problems. Operations research analysts advance by assuming positions as technical specialists or supervisors. The skills acquired by operations research analysts are useful for upper level jobs in an organization, and experienced analysts with leadership potential often leave the field altogether to assume nontechnical managerial or administrative positions.

Job Outlook

Employment of operations research analysts is expected to grow much faster than the average for all occupations through the year 2005 due to the increasing importance of quantitative analysis in decisionmaking and the increasing availability of computing resources. In addition to jobs arising from the increased demand for these workers, many openings will occur each year as workers transfer to other occupations or leave the labor force altogether.

More and more organizations are using operations research techniques to improve productivity and reduce costs. This reflects growing acceptance of a systematic approach to decisionmaking as well as more affordable computers, which give even small firms access to operations research applications. The interplay of these two trends should greatly stimulate demand for these workers in the years ahead.

Much of the job growth is expected to occur in the transportation, manufacturing, finance, and services sectors. Firms in these sectors recognize that quantitative analysis can achieve dramatic improvements in operating efficiency and profitability. More airlines, for example, are using operations research to determine the best flight and maintenance schedules, select the best routes to service, analyze customer characteristics, and control fuel consumption, among other things. Motel chains are beginning to utilize operations research analysis to improve their efficiency. For example, they analyze automobile traffic patterns and customer attitudes to determine location, size, and style of new motels. Like other management support functions, operations research is spread by its own success. When one firm in an industry increases productivity by adopting a new procedure, its competitors usually follow. This competitive pressure will contribute to demand for operations research analysts.

Demand also should be strong in the manufacturing sector as firms expand existing operations research staffs in the face of growing foreign competition. More and more manufacturers are using mathematical models to study parts of the organization for the first time. For example, analysts will be needed to determine the best way to distribute finished products and to find out where sales offices should be based. In addition, increasing factory automation will require more operations research analysts to alter existing models or develop new ones for production layout, robotics installation, work schedules, and inventory control.

The Department of Defense and defense contractors employ many operations research analysts. For example, operations researchers helped plan the 1990 military deployment to Saudi Arabia. They determined the best air and water transport schedules to move the maximum amount of personnel and equipment in the shortest time, making optimal use of people, ships, aircraft, and fuel. Since defense expenditures are likely to be cut in the future, there will be fewer jobs available in the military and defense-related industries for these workers. However, high demand outside the military should more than offset reductions in defense-related demand.

Earnings

According to recruiters and national operations research associations, operations research analysts with a master's degree generally earned starting salaries of about $30,000 to $35,000 a year in 1990. Experienced operations research analysts earned about $50,000 a year in 1990, with top salaries exceeding $90,000.

Operations research analysts employed by the Federal Government averaged about $52,100 a year in 1991.

Related Occupations

Operations research analysts apply mathematical principles to organizational problems. Workers in other occupations that stress quantitative analysis include computer scientists, applied mathematicians, statisticians, and economists. Operations research is closely allied to managerial occupations in that its goal is improved organizational efficiency.

Sources of Additional Information

Information on career opportunities for operations research analysts is available from:

- The Operations Research Society of America, 428 East Preston St., Baltimore, MD 21202.
- The Institute for Management Science, 290 Westminster St., Providence, RI 02903.

For information on careers in the Armed Forces and Department of Defense, contact:

- Military Operations Research Society, 101 South Whiting St., Suite 202, Alexandria, VA 22304.

Physical Therapists

(D.O.T. 076.121-014)

Nature of the Work

Physical therapists improve the mobility, relieve the pain, and prevent or limit the permanent physical disabilities of patients suffering from injuries or disease. Their patients include accident victims and disabled individuals with such conditions as multiple sclerosis, cerebral palsy, nerve injuries, burns, amputations, head injuries, fractures, low back pain, arthritis, and heart disease.

Therapists evaluate a patient's medical history; test and measure each patient's strengths, weaknesses, range of motion, and ability to function; and develop written treatment plans. These plans describe the treatments to be provided, their purpose, and their anticipated outcomes. In some cases, plans are based on physicians' treatment orders. As treatment continues, they document progress, conduct periodic re-evaluations, and modify treatments, if necessary.

Treatment often includes exercise for patients who have been immobilized and lack flexibility. Using a technique known as passive exercise, therapists increase the patient's flexibility by stretching and manipulating stiff joints and unused muscles. Later in the treatment, they encourage patients to use their own muscles to further increase flexibility and range of motion before finally advancing to weights and other exercises to improve strength, balance, coordination, and endurance.

Physical therapists also use electricity, heat, or ultrasound to relieve pain or improve the condition of muscles or related tissues just as cold and water are used to reduce swelling and treat burns. They may also use traction or deep-tissue massage to relieve pain and restore function. Therapists also teach and motivate patients to use crutches, prostheses, and wheelchairs to perform day-to-day activities and show them therapies to do at home.

Physical therapists document evaluations, daily progress, medical team conferences, and reports to referring practitioners and insurance companies. Such documentation is used to track the patient's progress, identify areas requiring more or less attention, justify billings, and for legal purposes.

Some physical therapists treat a wide variety of problems; others specialize in such areas as pediatrics, geriatrics, orthopedics, sports physical therapy, neurology, and cardiopulmonary physical therapy.

Working Conditions

Physical therapists work in hospitals, clinics, and therapists' offices that have specially equipped facilities, or they treat patients in hospital rooms, homes, or schools.

Most physical therapists work a 40-hour week, which may include some evenings and weekends. The job can be physically demanding because therapists often have to stoop, kneel, crouch, lift, and stand for long periods of time. In addition, therapists move heavy equipment and lift patients or help them turn, stand, or walk. Work can be demanding and frustrating when patients do not improve.

Employment

Physical therapists held about 88,000 jobs in 1990; about 1 in 4 worked part time.

Hospitals employed one-third and offices of other health practitioners, including those of physical therapists, one-quarter of all salaried physical therapists in 1990. Other jobs were in offices of physicians, home health agencies, nursing homes, and schools. Some physical therapists are in private practice, providing services to individual patients or contracting to provide services in hospitals, rehabilitation centers, nursing homes, home health agencies, adult daycare programs, and schools. These self-employed therapists may be in solo practice or be part of a consulting group. Some physical therapists teach in academic institutions and conduct research.

Training, Other Qualifications, and Advancement

All States require physical therapists to pass a licensure exam after graduating from an accredited physical therapy program.

Entry level education in physical therapy is available in 78 bachelor's degree and 44 master's degree programs. Physical therapy education, however, is undergoing a transition. Experts are coming to believe that a master's degree is better for teaching a growing body of knowledge and for preparing students for independent practice. As a result, it is likely that most bachelor's degree programs will eventually be extended to master's degree programs, although for the next few years most graduates will continue to be from bachelor's degree programs.

The bachelor's degree curriculum usually starts with introductory science courses such as chemistry, anatomy, physiology, and neuroanatomy and then introduces specialized courses such as biomechanics, human growth and development, manifestations of disease and trauma, evaluation and assessment techniques, research, and therapeutic procedures. Besides classroom and laboratory instruction, students receive supervised clinical experience, mostly in hospitals, but also in rehabilitation centers, private practices, and schools.

Competition for entry to physical therapy programs is keen, so interested students should attain superior grades in high school and college, especially in science courses. Courses useful when applying to physical therapy programs include anatomy, biology, chemistry, social science, mathematics, and physics. Individuals wanting to know more about physical therapy should do volunteer work in the physical therapy department of a hospital or clinic. In fact, many education programs require such experience for admission.

Physical therapists should enjoy working with people and be patient, tactful, persuasive, resourceful, and emotionally stable to help patients understand the treatments and adjust to their disabilities. Similar traits are also needed to deal with the patient's family.

Physical therapists also need manual dexterity and physical stamina. Physical therapists should expect to continue to develop professionally by participating in continuing education courses and workshops from time to time throughout their careers. A number of States require continuing education for maintaining licensure.

Job Outlook

Employment of physical therapists is expected to grow much faster than the average for all occupations through the year 2005. Growth will occur as new medical technologies save more people, who then need therapy; as new technologies permit more disabling conditions to be treated; and as the population grows and ages.

The rapidly growing elderly population is particularly vulnerable to chronic and debilitating conditions that will require more therapeutic services. At the same time, the baby-boom generation will enter the prime age for heart attack and strokes, increasing the demand for cardiac and physical rehabilitation. More young people will also need physical therapy as medical advances save the lives of a larger proportion of newborns with severe birth defects. Future medical developments will also permit a higher percentage of trauma victims to survive, creating additional demand for rehabilitative care.

Growth will also result from advances in medical technology which permit treatment of more disabling conditions. In the past, for example, the development of hip and knee replacements for those with arthritis gave rise to employment for physical therapists to improve flexibility and strengthen weak muscles.

The widespread interest in health promotion should also increase demand for physical therapy services. A growing number of employers are using physical therapists to evaluate worksites, develop exercise programs, and teach safe work habits to employees in the hope of reducing injuries.

There have been shortages of physical therapists in recent years. However, this situation should ease somewhat as the number of physical therapy education programs increases and more students graduate.

Earnings

Physical therapists employed full-time in private hospitals averaged $17.01 an hour, excluding premium pay for overtime and for weekends, holidays, and late shifts in January 1991. Among metropolitan areas studied separately, earnings ranged from $14.83 in St. Louis to $20.52 in San Francisco.

Related Occupations

Physical therapists treat and rehabilitate persons with physical or mental disabilities. They may use general or specialized exercises, massage, heat, water, electricity, and various therapeutic devices to help their patients gain independence. Others who work in the rehabilitation field include occupational therapists, speech pathologists and audiologists, orthotists, prosthetists, respiratory therapists, chiropractors, acupuncturists, and athletic trainers.

Sources of Additional Information

Additional information on a career as a physical therapist and a list of accredited educational programs in physical therapy are available from:

- American Physical Therapy Association, 1111 North Fairfax St., Alexandria, VA 22314.

Physician Assistants

(D.O.T. 079.364-018)

Nature of the Work

As their title suggests, physician assistants (PA's) support physicians. However, they should not be confused with medical assistants (see elsewhere in this book). PA's are formally trained to perform many of the routine but time-consuming tasks physicians usually do. They take medical histories, perform physical examinations, order laboratory tests and X-rays, make preliminary diagnoses, and give inoculations. They also treat minor injuries by suturing, splinting, and casting. In 30 States and the District of Columbia, physician assistants may prescribe medications. PA's may have managerial duties too. Some order medical and laboratory supplies and equipment; others oversee technicians and assistants.

Physician assistants always work under the supervision of a physician. The proximity of supervision, however, depends upon the locality. For example, some PA's, working in rural or inner city clinics where a physician may be available just 1 or 2 days each week, may provide most of the health care needs for patients, consulting with the supervising physician by telephone. Other PA's may make "house calls" or go on "hospital rounds" to check on patients and report back to the physician.

PA's assist physicians in specialty areas, such as family practice, internal medicine, general and thoracic surgery, emergency medicine, and pediatrics. PA's specializing in surgery, also called surgeon's assistants, provide pre- and post-operative care and may work as first or second assistants during major surgery.

Working Conditions

Although PA's generally work in a climate-controlled, well-lighted environment, those in surgery often stand for long periods, and others do considerable walking.

The workweek and schedule vary according to practice setting and are often comparable to that of their supervising physician. A few emergency room PA's work 24-hour shifts twice weekly, and others work three 12-hour shifts each week. The workweek of PA's in physicians' offices may include weekends, night hours, or early morning hospital rounds to visit patients. PA's in clinics usually work a 5-day, 40-hour week.

Employment

Physician assistants held about 53,000 jobs in 1990. Most PA's work in physicians' offices and clinics. Others work in hospitals. The rest work for public health clinics, nursing homes, prisons, and rehabilitation centers.

About 30 percent of all PA's provide health care to communities having fewer than 50,000 residents and where physicians may be in limited supply, according to the American Academy of Physician Assistants.

Training, Other Qualifications, and Advancement

Almost all States require that new PA's complete an accredited, formal education program. In 1991, there were 55 such educational programs for physician assistants, including three programs for surgeon assistants. Thirty-seven of these programs offered a baccalaureate degree or a degree option. The rest offered either a certificate, an associate degree, or a master's degree.

Admission requirements vary, but many programs require 2 years of college and some work experience in the health care field. About half of all applicants hold a bachelor's or master's degree.

PA programs generally last 2 years. Most are located in medical schools, schools of allied health, or 4-year colleges; a few are in community colleges and in hospitals. Many accredited PA programs have clinical teaching affiliations with medical schools.

PA education includes classroom instruction in biochemistry, nutrition, human anatomy, physiology, microbiology, clinical pharmacology, clinical medicine, geriatric and home health care, disease prevention, and medical ethics. Students obtain supervised clinical training in several areas, including family medicine, inpatient and ambulatory medicine, general surgery, obstetrics and gynecology, geriatrics, emergency medicine, internal medicine, ambulatory psychiatry, and pediatrics. Sometimes, one or more of these "rotations" are served under the supervision of a physician who is seeking to hire a PA. Sometimes these rotations lead to a permanent employment.

PA postgraduate residency training programs, as yet unaccredited, are available in emergency medicine, gynecology, critical care medicine, surgery, pediatrics, neonatology, and occupational medicine. Candidates must be graduates of an accredited program and be certified by the National Commission on Certification of Physician Assistants.

As of 1990, 49 States, the District of Columbia, and Guam had legislation governing the qualifications or practice of physician assistants. Mississippi did not. Forty-five States required physician assistants to pass a certifying exam that is only open to graduates of an accredited educational program.

In some States, the duties of a physician assistant are determined by the supervising physician; in others, they are determined by the State's regulatory agency. There is variation in State practice laws and regulations; therefore, aspiring PA's should investigate the laws and regulations in the States where they wish to practice.

Physician assistants need to exhibit leadership, self-confidence, and emotional stability, and be willing to continue studying throughout their career to keep up with medical advances.

Some PA's pursue additional education in order to practice in a specialty area such as surgery, neonatology, or emergency medicine. Others—as they attain greater clinical knowledge and experience—advance to added responsibilities and higher earnings. However, by the very nature of the profession, individual PA's are always supervised by physicians.

Job Outlook

Employment opportunities are expected to be excellent for physician assistants, particulary in areas or settings, like rural and inner city clinics, that have difficulty attracting enough physicians.

Employment of PA's is expected to grow faster than the average for all occupations through the year 2005 due to anticipated expansion of the health services industry and an emphasis on cost containment. Physicians and institutions are expected to employ more PA's to provide primary care and assist with medical and surgical procedures, thus freeing physicians to perform more complicated and revenue generating tasks. The public and third party payers also seem to approve of PA's use. For example, Medicare now allows physicians to bill the government for services provided by their PA's to hospital and nursing home patients.

Besides the traditional office-based setting, PA's should find a growing number of jobs in institutional settings such as hospitals, academic medical centers, public clinics, and prisons. The growth of HMO's and group medical practices should also lead to more jobs since they use PA's for basic medical tasks because their salaries are lower than those of physicians.

Earnings

In 1990, the median salary for physician assistants working in hospitals and medical schools was about $33,971, according to a national survey conducted by the University of Texas Medical Branch.

According to the American Academy of Physician Assistants, the average salary for all physician assistants in 1991 was between $40,000 and $44,999.

The average salary for PA's working in the Federal government was $39,625 in 1991.

Related Occupations

Other health workers who provide direct patient care that requires a similar level of skill and training include nurse practitioners, physical therapists, occupational therapists, clinical psychologists, and speech and hearing clinicians.

Sources of Additional Information

A free brochure, *Physician Assistants, Partners in Health Care*, is available from:

- American Academy of Physician Assistants, 950 North Washington St., Alexandria, VA 22314.

For a list of accredited programs and for a catalog of individual PA training programs, contact:

- Association of Physician Assistant Programs, 950 North Washington St., Alexandria, VA 22313.

For eligibility requirements and a description of the Physician Assistant National Certifying Examination, write to:

- National Commission on Certification of Physician Assistants, Inc., 2845 Henderson Mill Rd. NE., Atlanta, GA 30341.

Physicians

(D.O.T. 070 and 071)

Nature of the Work

Physicians perform medical examinations, diagnose illnesses, and treat people suffering from injury or disease. They advise patients on diet, hygiene, and preventive health care. Those in private practices handle or oversee the business aspects of running an office.

There are two types of physicians: The M.D.—Doctor of Medicine—and the D.O.—Doctor of Osteopathic Medicine. M.D.'s are also known as allopathic physicians. While M.D.'s and D.O.'s may use all accepted methods of treatment, including drugs and surgery, D.O.'s place special emphasis on the body's musculoskeletal system. They believe that good health requires proper alignment of bones, muscles, ligaments, and nerves.

Most M.D.'s specialize. (See table 1.) Pediatricians, general and family practitioners, and general internists are often called primary care physicians since they are the first health professionals patients usually consult. They tend to see the same patients on a regular basis for a variety of ailments and preventive treatment. When appropriate, they refer patients to other specialists. D.O.'s tend to be primary care providers although they can be found in all specialties.

Working Conditions

Physicians often work long, irregular hours. Almost half work more than 60 hours a week, but one-fourth generally work a 40-hour week. Most specialists work fewer hours than general practitioners and family practitioners. In general, as doctors approach retirement age, they may accept fewer new patients and tend to work shorter hours.

Salaried physicians who are employees of Health Maintenance Organizations (HMO's) or group practices work about the same number of hours a week as self-employed physicians. However, salaried physicians spend fewer hours in direct patient care.

Employment

Physicians (M.D.'s and D.O.'s) held about 580,000 jobs in 1990. About 2 out of 3 were in office-based practice, including clinics and HMO's; about one-fifth were employed in hospitals; and most others practiced in the Federal Government.

While physicians have traditionally been solo practitioners, a growing number are partners or salaried employees of group practices. Organized as clinics, HMO's, or as groups of physi-

cians, medical groups can afford expensive medical equipment and realize other business advantages.

The Northeast has the highest ratio of physicians to population; the South, the lowest. D.O.'s tend to practice in small cities and towns and in rural areas. M.D.'s, on the other hand, tend to locate in urban areas, close to hospital and educational centers. Some rural areas remain underserved, although the situation is changing somewhat. Currently, more medical students are being exposed to practice in rural communities with the direct support of educational centers and hospitals in more populous areas.

Table 1. Distribution of M.D.'s by specialty, 1989

	Percent
Total.	100.0
General and family practice	11.7
Medical specialties:	
Allergy	0.2
Cardiovascular diseases	2.6
Dermatology	1.2
Gastroentrology	1.2
Internal medicine	16.2
Pediatrics	6.6
Pediatric allergy	0.1
Pediatric cardiology	0.1
Pulmonary diseases	1.0
Surgical specialties:	
Colon and rectal surgery	0.1
General surgery	6.4
Neurological surgery	0.7
Obstetrics and gynecology	5.5
Ophthalmology	2.7
Orthopedic surgery	3.1
Otolaryngology	1.3
Plastic surgery	0.7
Thoracic surgery	0.4
Other specialties:	
Aerospace medicine	0.1
Anesthesiology	4.2
Child psychiatry	0.7
Diagnostic radiology	2.5
Emergency medicine	2.3
Forensic pathology	0.1
General preventive medicine	0.2
Neurology	1.5
Nuclear medicine	0.2
Occupational medicine	0.5
Psychiatry	5.8
Public health	0.3
Physical medicine and rehabilitation	0.7
Pathology	2.7
Radiology	1.9
Radiation oncology	0.5
Urology	1.5
Other specialty	1.5
Unspecified/unknown	12.3

Source: *American Medical Association*

Osteopathic physicians are located chiefly in States that have osteopathic hospitals. In 1991, 4 out of 5 D.O.'s were practicing in 16 States. Michigan had the most D.O.'s, followed by Pennsylvania, Ohio, Florida, Texas, and New Jersey.

Training and Other Qualifications

All States, the District of Columbia, and U.S. territories require physicians to be licensed. Licensure requirements for both D.O.'s and M.D.'s include graduation from an accredited medical school (usually 4 years), completion of a licensing examination, and between 1 and 6 years of graduate medical education, that is, a residency for M.D.'s and an internship for D.O.'s. Although physicians licensed in one State can usually get a license to practice in another without further examination, some States limit reciprocity. Graduates of foreign medical schools can generally begin practice in the United States after completing a U.S. hospital residency training program.

The minimum educational requirement for entry to a medical or osteopathic school is 3 years of college; most applicants, however, have at least a bachelor's degree, and many have advanced degrees. A few medical schools offer a combined college and medical school program that lasts 6 years instead of the customary 8 years.

Required premedical study includes undergraduate work in physics, biology, and inorganic and organic chemistry. Students should also take courses in English, other humanities, mathematics, and the social sciences.

There are 141 medical schools in the United States—126 teach allopathic medicine and award a Doctor of Medicine (M.D.); 15 teach osteopathic medicine and award the Doctor of Osteopathic Medicine (D.O.). Acceptance to medical school is very competitive. Applicants must submit transcripts, scores from the Medical College Admission Test (MCAT), and letters of recommendation. An interview with an admissions officer may also be necessary. Character, personality, leadership qualities, and participation in extracurricular activities also are considered.

Students spend the first 2 years of medical school primarily in laboratories and classrooms taking courses such as anatomy, biochemistry, physiology, pharmacology, microbiology, pathology, medical ethics, and laws governing medicine. They also learn to take case histories, perform examinations, and recognize symptoms. During the last 2 years, students work with patients under the supervision of experienced physicians in hospitals and clinics to learn acute, chronic, preventive, and rehabilitative care. Through rotations in internal medicine, obstetrics and gynecology, pediatrics, psychiatry, and surgery, they gain experience in the diagnosis and treatment of illness.

Following medical school, almost all M.D.'s go directly on to graduate medical education, called a residency. The National Board of Medical Examiners (NBME) gives a standard examination for all students, including foreign medical school graduates, applying for an M.D. residency. All D.O.'s serve a 12-month rotating internship after graduation. The National Board of Osteopathic Medical Examiners gives an examination for internship application. Following their internship, many D.O.'s take a residency program in a specialty area, too.

M.D.'s and D.O.'s seeking board certification in a specialty may spend up to 6 years—depending on the specialty—in residency training. A final examination immediately after residency, or after 1 or 2 years of practice, is also necessary for board certification by the American Board of Medical Specialists (ABMS) or the American Osteopathic Association (AOA). Physicians can be board-certified in 24 different areas: Allergy and immunology; anesthesiology; colon and rectal surgery; dermatology; emergency medicine; family practice; internal medicine; neurological surgery; neurology; nuclear medicine; obstetrics and gynecology; ophthalmology; orthopaedic surgery; otolaryngology; pathology; pediatrics; physical medicine and rehabilitation; plastic surgery; preventative medicine; psychiatry; radiology; surgery; thoracic surgery; and urology. For those training in a subspecialty, another 1 to 2 years of residency is usual.

To teach or do research, physicians may acquire a master's or Ph.D. in such fields as biochemistry or microbiology. They may otherwise spend 1 year or more in research or in an advanced clinical training fellowship.

A physician's training is costly. In 1987-88, the annual tuition for public medical schools averaged approximately $13,100; for private medical schools it was approximately $25,600. Room, board, and other expenses are extra. While education costs have increased, student financial assistance has not. Scholarships have become harder to find. Loans are available, but subsidies to reduce interest rates are limited.

People who wish to become physicians must have a desire to serve the ill, be self-motivated, and be able to survive the pressures and long hours of premedical and medical education. For example, medical residents often work 24-hour shifts and 80 hours a week or more. Efforts, however, are being made to limit the hours residents work. Prospective physicians must also be willing to study throughout their career to keep up with medical advances. Physicians should have a good bedside manner, be emotionally stable, and be able to make decisions in emergencies.

Job Outlook

Employment of physicians is expected to grow faster than the average for all occupations through the year 2005 due to continued expansion of the health industry. The population is growing and aging, and health care needs increase sharply with age. In addition, new technologies permit physicians to do more tests, perform more procedures, and treat conditions previously regarded as untreatable. Despite efforts to control costs, the payment of most services through private insurance, Medicare, and Medicaid will continue to encourage growth. The need to replace physicians is lower than for most occupations because almost all physicians remain in the profession until they retire.

Job prospects are better for primary care physicians such as family practitioners and internists, and for geriatric and preventive care specialists, than for those in some nonprimary care specialties such as surgery and radiology. However, changes in Federal Medicare and Medicaid reimbursement, which are designed to encourage more physicians to provide primary care services, may equalize prospects.

There are shortages of physicians in some rural and low income areas. This is because physicians find these areas unattractive due to low earnings potential, isolation from medical colleagues, or other reasons, not because of any overall shortage.

Some health care analysts believe that there is, or that there will soon be a general oversupply of physicians; others disagree. In analyzing job prospects, it should be kept in mind that an oversupply may not necessarily limit the ability of physicians to find employment or to set up and maintain a practice. It could result in physicians performing more procedures than otherwise so as to keep up their incomes, or it could result in their providing more time to each patient, giving more attention to preventive care, and providing more services in rural and poor areas. It is also possible that where surpluses are due to specialty imbalances, physicians in surplus specialities would provide more services in shortage ones.

Unlike their predecessors, newly trained physicians face radically different choices of where and how to practice. Many new physicians are likely to avoid solo practice and take salaried jobs in group medical practices, clinics, and HMO's in order to have regular work hours and the opportunity for peer consultation. Others will take salaried positions simply because they cannot afford the high costs of establishing a private practice while paying off student loans.

Graduates of foreign medical schools have long been a source of physicians in the United States. It seems unlikely, however, that they will continue to augment the supply of U.S.-trained physicians to the extent they have had in the past. This is due to such factors as more difficult qualifying entrance exams for foreign-trained students seeking U.S. residencies and keener competition for a residency once having passed the exams.

Earnings

Physicians have among the highest earnings of any occupation. According to the American Medical Association, average income, after expenses, for all physicians was about $155,800 in 1989; those under 36 years of age averaged $113,300. Earnings vary according to specialty; the number of years in practice; geographic region; hours worked; and skill, personality, and professional reputation. Self-employed physicians—those who own or are part owners of their medical practice—had an average income of $175,300, while those who were employed by others earned an average of $119,200 a year.

As shown in table 2, average income of physicians, after expenses, varies by specialty.

Table 2. Average income of M.D.'s after expenses, 1989

All physicians	$155,800
Surgery	220,500
Radiology	210,500
Obstetrics/gynecology	194,300
Anesthesiology	185,800
Pathology	154,500
Internal medicine	146,500
Psychiatry	117,700
Pediatrics	104,700
General practice/family practice	95,900

Source: *American Medical Association*

Salaries of medical residents averaged $25,858 in 1990-91 for those in their first year of residency to $33,277 for those in their sixth year, according to the Association of American Medical Colleges.

Physicians who establish their own practice make a sizable financial investment to equip a modern office.

Related Occupations

Physicians work to prevent, diagnose, and treat diseases, disorders, and injuries. Professionals in other occupations that require similar kinds of skill and critical judgment include audiologists, chiropractors, dentists, optometrists, podiatrists, speech pathologists, and veterinarians.

Sources of Additional Information

For a list of allopathic medical schools, as well as general information on premedical education, financial aid, and medicine as a career, contact:

- American Medical Association, 515 N. State St., Chicago, IL 60610.
- Association of American Medical Colleges, Publications Department, 2450 N St. NW., Washington, DC 20037.

For general information on osteopathic medicine as a career, contact:

- American Osteopathic Association, Department of Public Relations, 142 East Ontario St., Chicago, IL 60611.
- American Association of Colleges of Osteopathic Medicine, 6110 Executive Blvd., Suite 405, Rockville, MD 20852.

Information on Federal scholarships and loans is available from the directors of student financial aid at schools of allopathic and osteopathic medicine.

Information on licensing is available from State boards of examiners.

Podiatrists

(D.O.T. 079.101-022)

Nature of the Work

The human foot is a complex structure, containing twenty-six bones, plus muscles, nerves, ligaments, and blood vessels, designed for balance and mobility. Podiatrists, also known as doctors of podiatric medicine (DPM's), diagnose and treat disorders and diseases of the foot and lower leg to keep this part of the body working properly.

Podiatrists treat the major foot conditions: Corns calluses, ingrown toenails, and bunions; as well as, hammertoes, ankle and foot injuries, and foot complaints associated with diseases such as diabetes. In treating these problems, podiatrists prescribe drugs, order physical therapy, and perform surgery. They also fit corrective inserts called orthotics and design custom-made shoes. Podiatrists may use a force plate to help design the orthotics and shoes. They have patients walk across the plate that is connected to a computer, which "reads" the patients' feet. From the computer readout, podiatrsts may order the correct design.

In diagnosing a foot problem, podiatrists may order X-rays and laboratory tests. Podiatrists refer patients to other health practitioners when they spot systemic diseases, such as arthritis, diabetes, and heart disease, of which first symtoms may appear in the foot. For example, diabetics are prone to foot ulcers and infections due to their poor circulation.

Most podiatrists are in private practice, which means that they run a small business. They handle administrative duties like hiring employees, ordering supplies, and overseeing recordkeeping.

Most podiatrists have a general practice. Some podiatrists

Job Outlook

Employment of respiratory therapists is expected to increase much faster than the average for all occupations through the year 2005 because of substantial growth of the middle-aged and elderly population, a development that is virtually certain to heighten the incidence of cardiopulmonary disease.

The elderly are the most common sufferers from respiratory ailments and cardiopulmonary diseases such as pneumonia, chronic bronchitis, emphysema, and heart disease. As their numbers increase, the need for respiratory therapists to care for them will increase as well. In addition, advances in treating victims of heart attacks, accident victims, and premature infants (many of whom may be dependent on a ventilator during part of their treatment) will require the services of respiratory care practitioners. Projected rapid growth in the number of patients with AIDS will also boost demand for respiratory care since lung disease so often accompanies AIDS.

Developments within the profession will affect the kids of skills in greatest demand. Neonatal care and cardiopulmonary care have already emerged as distinct specialities, and opportunities appear to be highly favorable for respiratory therapists with the requisite skills.

Very rapid growth is expected in home health agencies, equipment rental companies, and first that provide respiratory care on a contract basis. Technological advances and changes in third-party (Medicare and insurance companies) payments should allow more respiratory care to be provided at home. Because or reimbursement policies, especially strong growth is expected in durable medical equipment firms which rent respiratory equipment. However, it is important to bear in mind that the very rapidly growing field of home health care accounts for a relatively small share of respiratory therapy jobs. As in other occupations, most job openings will result from the need to replace workers who transfer to other jobs or stop working altogether.

Earnings

Respiratory therapists who work full-time in private hospitals averaged $12.60 an hour, excluding premium pay for overtime and for work on weekends, holidays, and late shifts in January 1991. Average hourly earnings ranged from $11.48 in Fort Worth-Arlington to $18.02 in San Francisco. Therapists who worked part-time averaged $13.01.

Related Occupations

Respiratory therapists, under the supervision of a physician, administrator respiratory care and life support to patients with heart and lung difficulties. Other workers who care for, treat, or train people to improve their physical condition include dialysis technicians, registered nurses, occupational therapists, physical therapists, and radiation therapy technologists.

Sources of Additional Information

Information concerning a career in respiratory care is available from:

- American Association for Respiratory Care, 11030 Ables Ln., Dallas, TX 75229.

Information on gaining credentials as a respiratory therapy practitioner can be obtained from:

- The National Board for Respiratory Care, Inc., 8310 Nieman Rd., Lenexa, KS 66214.

For the current list of CAHEA-accredited educational programs for respiratory therapy occupations, write:

- Joint Review Committee for Respiratory Therapy Education, 1701 W. Euless Blvd., Suite 200, Euless, TX 76040.

Secondary School Teachers

(D.O.T. 091.221-010, .227-010; 094.224-010, .227-010 through -022; 099.244-010, and .227-022)

Nature of the Work

Secondary school teachers help students delve more deeply into subjects introduced in elementary school and learn more about the world and about themselves. They specialize in a specific subject, such as English, Spanish, mathematics, history, or biology, in junior high or high school. They may teach a variety of related courses, for example, American history, contemporary American problems, and world geography.

Special education teachers instruct students with a variety of disabilities. Other teachers work with students who are very bright or "gifted," academically or economically disadvantaged, or who have limited English proficiency.

Teachers lecture and demonstrate to students, and may use films, slides, overhead projectors, and the latest technology in teaching, such as computers and video discs. Teachers must continually update their skills to utilize the latest technology in the classroom. They design their classroom presentations to meet student needs and abilities. They may also work with students individually. Teachers assign lessons, give tests, and maintain classroom discipline. Teachers increasingly are using new assessment methods, such as examining a portfolio of a student's artwork or writing, to analyze student achievement.

Science teachers supervise laboratory work, and vocational education teachers give students "hands-on" experience with instruments, tools, and machinery.

In addition to classroom activities, secondary school teachers plan and evaluate lessons, prepare tests, grade papers, prepare report cards, oversee study halls and homerooms, supervise extracurricular activities, and meet with parents and school staff. They also may help students deal with academic or personal problems and in their choice of courses, colleges, and careers. Teachers also participate in education conferences and workshops. In recent years, teachers have become more involved in curriculum design, such as choosing textbooks and evaluating teaching methods.

Working Conditions

Seeing students develop new skills and gain an appreciation of the joy of learning can be very rewarding. However, teaching may be frustrating when dealing with unmotivated and disrespectful students.

Including school duties performed outside the classroom, many teachers work more than 40 hours a week. Most teachers work the traditional 10-month school year with a 2-month vacation during the summer. Teachers on the 10-month schedule may teach in summer sessions or take other jobs. Many enroll in college courses or workshops in order to continue their education. Teachers in districts with a year-round schedule work 8 weeks, are on vacation for 1 week, and have a 5-week midwinter break.

Most States have tenure laws that prevent teachers from being fired without just cause and due process. Teachers may obtain tenure after they have satisfactorily completed a probationary period of teaching, normally 3 years. Tenure is not a guarantee of a job, but it does provide some security.

Employment

Secondary school teachers held about 1,280,000 jobs in 1990; more than 9 out of 10 were in public schools. In addition, some of the 332,000 special education teachers worked in secondary schools. Employment is distributed geographically much the same as the population.

Training, Other Qualifications, and Advancement

All 50 States and the District of Columbia require public secondary school teachers to be certified. Certification is generally for one or several related subjects. Usually certification is granted by the State board of education or a certification advisory committee.

Requirements for regular certificates vary by State. However, all States require a bachelor's degree and completion of an approved teacher training program with a prescribed number of subject and education credits and supervised practice teaching in a secondary school. Aspiring teachers either major in the subject they plan to teach while also taking education courses, or major in education and take subject courses. Some States require specific grade point averages for teacher certification.

Many States offer alternative teacher certification programs for people who have college training in the subject they will teach but do not have the necessary education courses required for a regular certificate. Alternative certification programs were originally designed to ease teacher shortages in certain subjects, such as mathematics and science. The programs have expanded to attract other people into teaching, including recent college graduates and mid-career changers. In some programs, individuals begin teaching immediately under provisional certification. After working under the close supervision of experienced educators for 1 or 2 years while taking education courses outside school hours, they receive regular certification if they have progressed satisfactorily. Under other programs, college graduates who do not meet certification requirements take only those courses that they lack, and then become certified. This may take from 1 to 2 semesters of full-time study. Aspiring teachers who need certification may also enter programs that grant a master's degree in education, as well as certification. States also issue emergency certificates to individuals who do not meet all requirements for a regular certificate when schools cannot hire enough teachers with regular certificates.

Almost all States require applicants for teacher certification to be tested for competency in basic skills, teaching skills, or subject matter proficiency. Almost all require continuing education for renewal of the teacher's certificate—some require a master's degree.

Many States have reciprocity agreements that make it easier for teachers certified in one State to become certified in another.

Secondary school teachers should be knowledgeable in their subject and able to communicate with and motivate students. With additional preparation and certification, teachers may move into positions as school librarians, reading specialists, curriculum specialists, or guidance counselors. Teachers may become administrators or supervisors, although the number of positions is limited. In some systems, well-qualified experienced teachers can become senior or mentor teachers, with higher pay and additional responsibilities. They guide and assist less experienced teachers while keeping most of their teaching responsibilities.

Job Outlook

Employment of secondary school teachers is expected to increase faster than the average for all occupations through the year 2005 as high school enrollments grow and class size declines. Job openings for secondary school teachers are expected to increase substantially by the end of the decade as the large number of teachers now in their 40's and 50's reach retirement age.

Employment of special education teachers is expected to increase much faster than the average for all occupations through the year 2005 due to recent Federal legislation emphasizing training and employment for individuals with disabilities; technological advances resulting in more survivors of accidents and illnesses; and growing public interest in individuals with special needs.

The supply of secondary school teachers is also expected to increase in response to reports of job opportunities, more teacher involvement in school policy, greater public interest in education, and higher salaries. In fact, enrollments in teacher training programs have already increased. In addition, more teachers should be available from alternative certification programs.

Some central cities and rural areas have difficulty attracting enough teachers, so job prospects should continue to be better in these areas than in suburban districts.

The number of teachers employed depends on State and local expenditures for education. Pressures from taxpayers to limit spending could result in fewer teachers than projected; pressures to spend more to improve the quality of education could mean more.

Earnings

According to the National Education Association, public secondary school teachers averaged about $33,700 a year in 1990-91. Earnings in private schools generally were lower.

Many public school teachers belong to unions, such as the American Federation of Teachers and the National Education Association, that bargain with school systems over wages, hours, and the terms and conditions of employment.

In some schools, teachers receive extra pay for coaching sports and working with students in extracurricular activities. Some teachers earn extra income during the summer working in the school system or in other jobs.

Related Occupations

Secondary school teaching requires a wide variety of skills and aptitudes, including organizational, administrative, and recordkeeping abilities; research and communication skills; the power to influence, motivate, and train others; patience; and creativity. Workers in other occupations requiring some of these aptitudes include school administrators, college and university faculty, counselors, trainers and employee development specialists, employment interviewers, librarians, public relations representatives, sales representatives, and social workers.

Sources of Additional Information

Information on certification requirements and approved teacher training institutions is available from local school systems and State departments of education.

Information on teachers' unions and education-related issues may be obtained from:

- American Federation of Teachers, 555 New Jersey Ave. NW., Washington, DC 20001.
- National Education Association, 1201 16th St. NW., Washington, DC 20036.

A list of institutions with teacher education programs accredited by the National Council for Accreditation of Teacher Education can be obtained from:

- National Council for Accreditation of Teacher Education, 2010 Massachusetts Ave. NW., 2nd Floor, Washington, DC 20036.

Social Workers

(D.O.T. 189.267-010, 195.107-010 through -046, .137-010, .164-010, .167-010, -014, -030, and -034, .267-018, and .367-026)

Nature of the Work

Social workers help individuals and families cope with problems such as homelessness or inadequate housing, unemployment, lack of job skills, financial mismanagement, serious illness, handicaps, substance abuse, unwanted pregnancy, or antisocial behavior. They also work with families that have serious conflicts, including those involving child or spousal abuse or divorce.

Through direct counseling, social workers help clients bring their real concerns into the open and help them to consider

solutions or find other resources. Often, social workers provide concrete information such as: Where to go for debt counseling; how to find childcare or eldercare; how to apply for public assistance or other benefits; or how to get an alcoholic or drug addict admitted to a rehabilitation program.

They may also pull together services in consultation with clients and then follow through to assure they are actually provided. They may review eligibility requirements, fill out forms and applications, arrange for services, visit clients on a regular basis, and step in during emergencies.

Most social workers specialize in one field such as child welfare and family services, mental health, medical social work, school social work, community organization, or clinical social work.

Social workers in child welfare or family services may counsel children and youth who have difficulty adjusting socially, advise parents on how to care for handicapped children, or arrange homemaker services during a parent's illness. If children have serious problems in school, child welfare workers may consult with parents, teachers, and counselors to identify underlying causes. Some social workers assist single parents, arrange adoptions, and help find foster homes for neglected or abandoned children. Child welfare workers also work in residential institu-

tions for children and adolescents.

Social workers in child or adult protective services investigate reports of abuse and neglect and intervene if necessary. They may institute legal action to remove victims from homes and place them temporarily in an emergency shelter or with a foster family.

Mental health social workers provide for the mentally disabled—services such as individual and group therapy, outreach, crisis intervention, social rehabilitation, and training in skills of everyday living. They may also help plan for supportive services to ease patients' return to the community. (Also see the statements on counselors and psychologists elsewhere in this book.)

Medical social workers help patients and their families cope with chronic, acute, or terminal illnesses and handle problems that may stand in the way of recovery or rehabilitation. They may organize support groups for families of patients suffering from cancer, AIDS, Alzheimer's disease, or other illnesses. They also advise family caregivers, and counsel patients and help plan for their needs after discharge by arranging for at-home services—from meals-on-wheels to oxygen equipment. Some work on interdisciplinary teams that evaluate certain kinds of patients—geriatric or transplant patients, for example.

School social workers diagnose students' problems and arrange needed services, counsel children in trouble, and integrate handicapped students into the general school population. School social workers deal with problems such as student pregnancy, misbehavior in class, and excessive absences. They also advise teachers on how to deal with problem students.

Social workers in criminal justice make recommendations to courts, do pre-sentencing assessments, and provide services for prison inmates. Probation and parole officers provide similar services to individuals sentenced by a court to probation or those on parole.

Industrial or occupational social workers, generally located in an employer's personnel department or health unit, offer direct counseling to employees, often those whose performance at work is affected by emotional or family problems or substance abuse. They also develop education programs and provide information about community resources.

Clinical or psychiatric social workers offer psychotherapy or counseling.

Some social workers specialize in gerontological services. They run support groups for family caregivers or for the adult children of aging parents; advise elderly people or family members about the choices in such areas as housing, transportation, and long-term care; and coordinate and monitor services.

Working Conditions

Most social workers have a standard 40-hour week. However, they may work some evenings and weekends to meet with clients, attend community meetings, and handle emergencies. Some, particularly in voluntary nonprofit agencies, work part time. They may spend most of their time in an office or residential facility, but may also travel locally to visit clients or meet with service providers.

The work, while satisfying, can be emotionally draining. Understaffing and large caseloads add to the pressure in some agencies.

Employment

Social workers held about 438,000 jobs in 1990. About 2 out of 5 jobs were in State, county, or municipal government agencies, primarily in departments of human resources, social services, child welfare, mental health, health, housing, education, and corrections. Most in the private sector were in voluntary social service agencies, community and religious organizations, hospitals, nursing homes, or home health agencies.

Although most social workers are employed in cities or suburbs, some work in rural areas.

Training, Other Qualifications, and Advancement

A bachelor's degree is the minimum requirement for most positions. Besides the bachelor's in social work (BSW), undergraduate majors in psychology, sociology, and related fields satisfy hiring requirements in some agencies, especially small community agencies. A master's degree in social work (MSW) is generally necessary for positions in health and mental health settings. Jobs in public agencies may also require an MSW. Supervisory, administrative, staff training positions usually require at least an MSW. College and University teaching positions and most research appointments normally require a doctorate in social work.

In 1990, the Council on Social Work Education accredited 394 BSW programs and 113 MSW programs. There were 45 doctoral programs for Ph.D. in Social Work and for DSW (Doctor of Social Work). BSW programs prepare graduates for direct service positions such as caseworker or group worker. They include courses in social work practice, social welfare policies, human behavior and the social environment, and social research methods. Accredited BSW programs require at least 400 hours of supervised field experience.

An MSW degree prepares graduates to perform assessments, to manage cases, and to supervise other workers. Master's programs usually last 2 years and include 900 hours of supervised field instruction, or internship. Entry into an MSW program does not require a bachelor's in social work, but courses in psychology, biology, sociology, economics, political science, history, social anthropology, urban studies, and social work are recommended. Some schools offer an accelerated MSW program for those with a BSW.

Social workers may advance to supervisor, program manager, assistant director, and finally to executive director of an agency or department. Advancement generally requires an MSW, as well as experience. Other career options for social workers are teaching, research, and consulting. Some help formulate government policies by analyzing and advocating policy positions in government agencies, in research institutions, and on legislators' staffs.

Some social workers go into private practice. Most private practitioners are clinical social workers who provide psychotherapeutic counseling. Private practitioners usually need an MSW and a network of contacts for referrals.

In 1990, 48 States and the District of Columbia had licensing, certification, or registration laws regarding social work practice and the use of professional titles. Voluntary certification is offered by the National Association of Social Workers (NASW), which grants the titled ACSW (Academy of Certified Social Workers) or ACBSW (Academy of Certified Baccalaureate Social Workers) to those who qualify. For clinical social workers, professional credentials include listing in the *NASW Register of Clinical Social Workers* or in the *Directory of American Board of Examiners in Clinical Social Work*. These credentials are particularly important for those in private practice: some health insurance providers require them for reimbursement.

Social workers should be emotionally mature, objective, and sensitive to people and their problems. They must be able to handle responsibility, work independently, and maintain good working relationships with clients and coworkers. Volunteer or paid jobs as a social work aide offer ways of testing one's interest in this field.

Job Outlook

Employment of social workers is expected to increase faster than the average for all occupations through the year 2005. The number of older people, who are more likely to need services, is growing rapidly. In addition, the need for and concern about services to the mentally ill, the mentally retarded, and individuals and families in crisis are expected to grow. The need to replace social workers who leave the occupation, however, will provide the most openings.

Employment in hospitals is projected to grow much faster than the average for the economy as a whole due to greater emphasis on discharge planning, which facilitates early discharge of patients by assuring that the necessary medical services and social supports are in place. Employment in private social service agencies is also projected to grow much faster than average. Employment in government is projected to grow only about as fast as average.

Opportunities for social workers in private practice will expand because of the anticipated availability of funding from health insurance and from public sector contracts. Also, with increasing affluence, people will be more willing to pay for professional help to deal with personal probleblems. The growing popularity of employee assistance programs is also expected to spur demand for private practitioners, some of whom provide social work services to corporations on a contract basis.

Employment in home health care services is growing, not only because hospitals are moving to release patients more quickly, but because a large and growing number of people have impairments or disabilities that make it difficult to live at home without some form of assistance.

Employment of school social workers is expected to grow, due to expanded efforts to respond to the adjustment problems of immigrants, children from single-parent families, and others in difficult situations. Moreover, continued emphasis on integrating handicapped children into the general school population—a requirement under the Education for All Handicapped Children Act—will probably lead to more jobs. The availability of State and local funding will dictate the actual increase in jobs in this setting, however.

Competition is stronger in cities where training programs for social workers abound; rural areas often find it difficult to attract and retain qualified staff.

Earnings

In January 1991, medical social workers in private hospitals who worked full-time averaged $14.73 per hour, excluding premium pay for overtime and for work on weekends, holidays, and late shifts.

Social workers employed by the Federal Government averaged $38,195 in 1991. According to limited data, social workers in all types of settings generally earned between $23,000 and $36,000 in 1990.

Related Occupations

Through direct counseling or referral to other services, social workers help people solve a range of personal problems. Workers in occupations with similar duties include the clergy, counselors, counseling psychologists, and vocational rehabilitation counselors.

Sources of Additional Information

For information about career opportunities in social work, contact:

- National Association of Social Workers, 7981 Eastern Ave., Silver Spring, MD 20910.

The Council on Social Work Education publishes an annual *Directory of Accredited BSW* and *MSW Programs*. Price and ordering information for this and other CSWE publications is available from:

- Council on Social Work Education, 1600 Duke St., Alexandria, VA 22314.

For information on doctoral programs in social work, contact:

- Dr. Sheila B. Kamerman, Chair for Group for the Advancement of Doctoral Education, c/o Columbia University, School of Social Work, 122 West 113rd St., New York, NY 10025.

Speech-Language Pathologists and Audiologists

(D.O.T. 076.101, .104, and .107)

Nature of the Work

Speech-language pathologists assess and treat persons with speech, language, voice, and fluency disorders, while audiologists assess and treat those with hearing and related disorders.

Speech-language pathologists work with people who can not make speech sounds, or can not make them clearly; those with speech rhythm and fluency problems, such as stuttering; people with speech quality problems, such as inappropriate pitch or harsh voice; and those with problems understanding and producing language. They may also work with people who have oral motor problems that cause eating and swallowing difficulties. Speech and language problems may result from causes such as hearing loss, brain injury or deterioration, cerebral palsy, stroke, cleft palate, voice pathology, mental retardation, or emotional problems. Speech-language pathologists use special instruments, as well as written and oral tests, to determine the nature and extent of impairment, and to record and analyze speech irregularities. For individuals with little or no speech, speech-language pathologists select alternative communication systems, including automated devices and sign language, and teach their use. They teach other patients how to make sounds, improve their voices, or increase their language skills.

Audiologists work with people who have hearing and related problems. They use audiometers and other testing devices to measure the loudness at which a person begins to hear sounds, their ability to distinguish between sounds, and other tests of the nature and extent of their hearing loss. Audiologists may coordinate these results with medical, educational, and psychological information, make a diagnosis, and determine a course of treatment. Treatment may include examining and cleaning the ear canal, the fitting of a hearing aid, auditory training, and instruction in speech or lip reading. They may also recommend use of amplifiers and alerting devices. Audiologists also test noise levels in workplaces and conduct hearing protection programs.

Most speech-language pathologists and audiologists provide direct clinical services to individuals with communication disorders. In speech, language, and hearing clinics, they may independently develop and carry out a treatment program. In medical facilities, they may work with physicians, social workers, psychologists, and other therapists to develop and execute a treatment plan. Speech-language pathology and audiology personnel in schools also develop individual or group programs, counsel parents, and assist teachers with classroom activities, to meet the needs of children with speech, language, or hearing disorders.

Speech-language pathologists and audiologists keep records on the initial evaluation, progress, and discharge of clients. This helps pinpoint problems, tracks client progress, and justifies the cost of treatment when applying for reimbursement. They counsel individuals and their families about communication disorders and how to cope with the stress and misunderstanding that often accompany them. They also work with family members to recognize and change behavior patterns that impede communication and treatment, and show them communication-enhancing techniques to use at home.

Some speech-language pathologists and audiologists conduct research on how people speak and hear. Others design and develop equipment or techniques for diagnosing and treating problems.

Working Conditions

Speech-language pathologists and audiologists spend most of their time at a desk or table in clean comfortable surroundings. The job is not physically demanding, but does require attention to detail and intense concentration. The emotional needs of clients and their families may be demanding and there may be frustration when clients do not improve. Speech-language pathologists and audiologists who work on a contract basis may spend a substantial amount of time traveling between facilities.

Employment

Speech-language pathologists and audiologists held about 68,000 jobs in 1990. About one-half provided services in preschools, elementary and secondary schools, or colleges and universities. More than 10 percent were in hospitals. Others were in offices of physicians; offices of speech-language pathologists and audiologists; speech, language, and hearing centers; home health care agencies; and other facilities. Some were in private practice, working either as solo practitioners or in a group practice.

Some experienced speech-language pathologists or audiologists contract to provide services in schools, hospitals, or nursing homes or work as consultants to industry.

Training, Other Qualifications, and Advancement

A master's degree in speech-language pathology or audiology is the standard credential in this field. Of the 40 States that license audiologists, and the 39 States that license speech-language pathologists, all require a master's degree or equivalent; 275 to 300 hours of supervised clinical experience; a passing score on a national examination; and 9 months of post-graduate professional experience. For licensure renewal, 20 states have continuing education requirements. Medicaid, Medicare, and private insurers generally require a license to qualify for reimbursement.

In schools, people with bachelor's degrees in speech-language pathology may work with children who have communication problems. They may have to be certified by the State educational agency, and may be classified as special education teachers rather than speech-language pathologists or audiologists. Recent Federal legislation requires speech-language pathologists in school systems to have a minimum of a master's degree or equivalent. All States require audiologists to hold a master's degree or equivalent.

About 230 colleges and universities offered master's programs in speech-language pathology and audiology in 1991. Courses cover anatomy and physiology of the areas involved in speech, language, and hearing; the development of normal speech, language, and hearing and the nature of disorders; acoustics; and psychological aspects of communication. Graduate students also learn to evaluate and treat speech, language, and hearing disorders and receive supervised clinical training in communication disorders.

Those with a master's degree can acquire the Certificate of Clinical Competence (CCC) offered by the American Speech-Language-Hearing Association. To earn the CCC, a person must have a master's degree, have 300 hours of supervised clinical experience, complete a 9-month post-graduate internship, and pass a national written examination.

Speech-language pathologists and audiologists should be able to effectively communicate test results, diagnoses, and proposed treatment in a manner easily understood by their clients. They also need to be able to approach problems objectively and provide support to clients and their families. Patience and compassion are important since a client's progress may be slow.

With experience, some salaried speech-language pathologists and audiologists enter private practice; others become directors or administrators of services in schools, hospitals, health departments, and clinics. Some become researchers.

Job Outlook

Employment of speech-language pathologists and audiologists is expected to increase faster than the average for all occupations through the year 2005. Their employment in the health care industry is projected to grow faster than the average for all occupations, while employment in education is expected to grow only as fast as the average.

Employment in the health care industry will increase as a result of several factors. Because hearing loss is strongly associated with older age, rapid growth in the population age 75 and over will cause the number of hearing-impaired persons to increase rapidly. In addition, baby boomers are now entering middle age, when the possibility of neurological disorders and their associated speech, language and hearing impairments, increases. Medical advances are also improving the survival rate of trauma victims, who then need treatment.

The number of speech-language pathologists and audiologists in private practice, though small, is likely to rise sharply by the year 2005. Encouraging this growth is the increasing use of contract services by hospitals, schools, and nursing homes.

Employment in schools will increase as elementary and secondary school enrollments grow. Recent Federal legislation guaranteeing special education and related services to all eligible children with disabilities, while originally designed for school-age children, was recently extended to include children from 3 to 5 years of age. This legislation will also increase employment in day care centers, rehabilitation centers, and hospitals.

Earnings

According to a 1990 survey by the American Speech-Language-Hearing Association, the median annual salary for speech-language pathologists with 1 to 3 years experience was about $25,000; for audiologists, it was about $26,000. Speech-language pathologists with 16 years or more experience earned a median annual salary of about $38,000, while experienced audiologists earned about $42,000. Salaries also vary according to geographic location.

Speech-language pathologists and audiologists in hospitals and medical schools earned a median annual salary of about $30,500, according to a 1990 survey conducted by the University of Texas Medical Branch.

Related Occupations

Speech-language pathologists and audiologists specialize in the prevention, diagnosis, and treatment of speech, language, and hearing problems. Workers in in other rehabilitation occupations include occupational therapists, physical therapists, recreational therapists, and rehabilitation counselors.

Sources of Additional Information

State departments of education can supply information on certification requirements for those who wish to work in public schools.

General information on speech-language pathology and audiology is available from:

- American Speech-Language-Hearing Association, 10801 Rockville Pike, Rockville, MD 20852.

Technicians and Related Support Occupations

Aircraft Pilots

(D.O.T. 196 except .163 and 621.261-018)

Nature of the Work

Pilots are highly trained people who fly airplanes and helicopters to carry out a wide variety of tasks. Most pilots transport passengers, cargo, and mail, while others dust crops, spread seed for reforestation, test aircraft, and take photographs. Helicopter pilots are involved in firefighting, police work, offshore exploration for natural resources, evacuation and rescue efforts, logging operations, construction work, and weather station operations; some also transport passengers.

Except on small aircraft, two pilots usually make up the cockpit crew. Generally, the most experienced pilot (called captain) is in command and supervises all other crew members. The copilot assists in communicating with air traffic controllers, monitoring the instruments, and flying the aircraft. Most large aircraft have a third pilot in the cockpit—the flight engineer—who assists the other pilots by monitoring and operating many of the instruments and systems, making minor inflight repairs, and watching for other aircraft. New technology can perform many flight tasks, however, and virtually all new aircraft now fly with only two pilots. New aircraft have computerized controls, requiring pilots to make more extensive use of video controls.

Before departure, pilots plan their flights carefully. They confer with flight dispatchers and aviation weather forecasters to find out about weather conditions enroute and at their destination. Based on this information, they choose a route, altitude, and speed that should provide the fastest, safest, and smoothest flight. When flying under instrument flight rules (procedures governing the operation of the aircraft when there is poor visibility), the pilot in command must file an instrument flight plan with air traffic control so that the flight can be coordinated with other air traffic.

Before taking off, pilots thoroughly check their planes to make sure that the engines, controls, instruments, and other systems are functioning properly. They also make sure that baggage or cargo has been loaded correctly.

Takeoff and landing are the most difficult and dangerous parts of the flight and require close coordination between the pilot and copilot. For example, as the plane accelerates for takeoff, the pilot concentrates on the runway while the copilot scans the instrument panel. To calculate the speed they must attain to become airborne, pilots consider the altitude of the airport, outside temperature, weight of the plane, and the speed and direction of the wind. The moment the plane reaches takeoff speed, the copilot informs the pilot, who then pulls back on the controls to raise the nose of the plane.

Unless the weather is bad, the actual flight is relatively easy. Pilots steer the plane along their planned route and are monitored by the air traffic control stations they pass along the way. They continuously scan the instrument panel to check their fuel supply, the condition of their engines, and the air-conditioning, hydraulic, and other systems. Pilots may request a change in altitude or route if circumstances

dictate. For example, if the ride is rougher than expected, they may ask air traffic control if pilots flying at other altitudes have reported better conditions. If so, they may request a change. This procedure also may be used to find a stronger tailwind or a weaker headwind to save fuel and increase speed. In addition, pilots monitor warning devices designed to help detect sudden shifts in wind conditions that can cause crashes.

If visibility is poor, pilots must rely completely on their instruments. Using the altimeter readings, they know how high above ground they are and can fly safely over mountains and other obstacles. Special navigation radios give pilots precise information which, with the help of special maps, tells them their exact position. Other very sophisticated equipment provides directions to a point just above the end of a runway and enables pilots to land completely "blind."

Once on the ground, pilots must complete records on their flight for their company and the Federal Aviation Administration (FAA).

Airline pilots have the services of large support staffs and consequently perform few nonflying duties. Pilots employed by businesses that use their own aircraft, however, usually are the businesses' only experts on flying and, consequently, have many other duties. They may load the plane, handle all passenger luggage to insure a balanced load, and supervise refueling. Other nonflying responsibilities include keeping records, scheduling flights, arranging for major maintenance, and performing minor maintenance and repair work on their planes.

Some pilots are instructors. They teach their students the principles of flight in ground-school classes and demonstrate how to operate aircraft in dual-controlled planes.

A few specially trained pilots employed by the airlines are "examiners" or "check pilots." They periodically fly with each airline pilot and copilot to make sure that they are proficient.

Working Conditions

By law, airline pilots cannot fly more than 100 hours a month or more than 1,000 hours a year. Most airline pilots fly an average of 75 hours a month and work an additional 120 hours a month performing nonflying duties. The majority of flights involve layovers away from home. When pilots are away from home, the airlines provide hotel accommodations, transportation between the hotel and airport, and an allowance for expenses. Airlines operate flights at all hours of the day and night, so work schedules often are irregular. Based on seniority, pilots generally have a choice of flights.

Pilots employed outside the airlines often have irregular schedules as well; they may fly 30 hours one month and 90 hours the next. Since these pilots frequently have many nonflying responsibilities, they have much less free time than airline pilots. Except for business pilots, most pilots employed outside the airlines do not remain away from home overnight. They may work odd hours, however. Instructors, for example, often give lessons at night or on weekends.

Airline pilots, especially those on international routes, often suffer jet lag—disorientation and fatigue caused by many hours

in a hospital, but sometimes also includes other settings.

L.P.N.'s should have a caring, sympathetic nature. They should be emotionally stable because work with the sick and injured can be stressful. As part of a health care team, they must be able to follow orders and work under close supervision.

Job Outlook

Employment of L.P.N.'s is expected to increase much faster than the average for all occupations through the year 2005, in response to the long-term care needs of a rapidly growing population of very old people and to the general growth of health care.

Nursing homes will offer the most new jobs for L.P.N.'s as the number of aged and disabled persons in need of long-term care rises rapidly. In addition to caring for the aged, nursing homes may be called on to care for the increasing number of patients who have been released from the hospital before they are fully recovered. Finally, recent State and Federal regulations require nursing homes to employ more L.P.N.'s.

Very rapid growth is also expected in such residential care facilities as board and care homes, old age homes, and group homes for the mentally retarded.

Employment of L.P.N.'s in hospitals is not expected to increase much, largely because the number of inpatients, with whom most work, is not expected to increase much. If hospitals continue to face a scarcity of R.N.'s, however, they may employ more L.P.N.'s than projected.

Employment is projected to grow very rapidly in physicians' offices and clinics, including health maintenance organizations—a fast-growing segment of the health care industry—and in the temporary help secsector. A growing number of licensed practical nurses will also provide home care. As in most other occupations, replacement needs will be the main source of job openings.

Job prospects depend on supply as well as demand. The number of people completing L.P.N. training dropped sharply during the mid 1980's, but has begun to increase again. Unless the number increases very sharply, job prospects should remain good.

Earnings

Median weekly earnings of L.P.N.'s who worked full time in 1990 were $377. The middle 50 percent earned between $312 and $456. The lowest 10 percent earned less than $267; the top 10 percent, more than $539.

L.P.N.'s in nursing homes had median earnings of $9.92 an hour in 1991, according to a survey by the Hospital Compensation Service, Hawthorne, NJ.

L.P.N.'s employed full-time in private hospitals averaged $10.21 an hour, excluding premium pay for overtime and for work on weekends, holidays, and late shifts in January 1991. Among 19 metropolitan areas studied separately, earnings ranged from $9.67 in Dallas to $14.43 in San Francisco. Part-time L.P.N.'s averaged $10.70 a hour.

Related Occupations

Other jobs that involve working closely with people while helping them include emergency medical technician, social service aide, human service worker, and teacher aide.

Sources of Additional Information

A list of State-approved training programs and information about practical nursing are available from:

- Communications Department, National League for Nursing, 350 Hudson St., New York, NY 10014.
- National Association for Practical Nurse Education and Service, Inc., 1400 Spring St., Suite 310, Silver Spring, MD 20910.

For information about a career in practical nursing, contact:

- National Federation of Licensed Practical Nurses, Inc., P.O. Box 1088, Raleigh, NC 27619.

Information about employment opportunities in Veterans Administration medical centers is available from local VA medical centers and also from:

- Title 38 Employment Division, (054D), Veterans Administration, 810 Vermont Ave. NW., Washington, DC 20420.

For information on nursing careers in hospitals, contact:

- American Hospital Association, Division of Nursing, 840 North Lake Shore Dr., Chicago, IL 60611.

For a copy of *Health Careers in Long-Term Care*, write:

- American Health Care Association, 1201 L St. NW., Washington, DC 20005.

Medical Record Technicians

(D.O.T. 079.367-014)

Nature of the Work

When you enter a hospital, you see a whirl of white coats of physicians, nurses, radiologic technologists, and others. Every time these health care personnel treat a patient, they record what they observed and did to the patient. This record includes information the patient provides about his or her symptoms and medical history, and also the results of examinations, reports of X-ray and laboratory tests, and diagnoses and treatment plans. Medical record technicians organize and evaluate these records for completeness and accuracy.

When assembling a patient's medical record, technicians first make sure that the medical chart is complete. They ensure that all forms are present and properly identified and signed, or that all necessary information is on a computer file. Sometimes, they talk to physicians or others to clarify diagnoses or get additional information.

Technicians assign a code to each diagnosis and procedure. They consult a classification manual and rely, too, on their knowledge of disease processes. Technicians may then use a packaged computer program to assign the patient to one of several hundred "diagnosis-related groups" or DRG's. The DRG determines the amount the hospital will be reimbursed if the patient is covered by Medicare or other insurance programs that use the DRG system. In large hospitals, technicians who specialize in coding are called medical record coders, coder/abstractors, or coding specialists.

Technicians may also tabulate and analyze data to help improve patient care, to control costs, to be used in legal actions, or to respond to surveys. Technicians known as registrars maintain registries showing occurrences of certain diseases, such as cancer.

Medical record technicians' duties vary with the size of the facility. In large to medium facilities, technicians may specialize in one aspect of medical records or supervise medical record clerks and transcriptionists while a *medical record administrator* manages the department (See statement on health services managers elsewhere in this book.). In small hospitals and many nursing homes, an accredited record technician may manage the department.

Working Conditions

Medical record technicians generally work a 40-hour week. Some overtime may be required. In hospitals where medical record departments are open 18-24 hours a day, 7 days a week, they may work on day, evening, and night shifts.

They work in pleasant and comfortable offices. Medical record technician is one of the few health occupations in which there is little or no contact with patients. Accuracy is essential, and this demands concentration and close attention to detail. Medical record technicians who work at video display terminals for prolonged periods may experience eyestrain and musculoskeletal pain.

Employment

Medical record technicians held about 52,000 jobs in 1990. Three out of five jobs were in hospitals. Most of the remainder were in nursing homes, medical group practices, health maintenance organizations, and clinics.

In addition, insurance, accounting, and law firms that deal in health matters employ medical record technicians to tabulate and analyze data from medical records. Public health departments hire technicians to supervise data collection from health care institutions and to assist in research.

Some self-employed medical record technicians are consultants to nursing homes and physicians' offices.

Training, Other Qualifications, and Advancement

Medical record technicians entering the field usually have formal training in a 2-year associate degree program offered at community and junior colleges. Courses include medical terminology and diseases, anatomy and physiology, legal aspects of medical records, coding and abstraction of data, statistics, databases, quality assurance methods, and computers as well as general education.

Technicians may also gain training through an Independent Study Program in Medical Record Technology offered by the American Medical Record Association (AMRA). Hospitals sometimes advance promising medical record clerks to jobs as medical record technicians, although this practice is becoming less common. Advancement generally requires 2-4 years of job experience and successful completion of the hospital's in-house training program.

Most employers prefer to hire Accredited Record Technicians (ART). Accreditation is obtained by passing a written examination offered by the American Medical Record Association. To take the examination, a person must be a graduate of a 2-year associate degree program accredited by the Committee on Allied Health Education and Accreditation (CAHEA) of the American Medical Association, or a graduate of the Independent Study Program in Medical Record Technology who has also obtained 30 semester hours of academic credit in prescribed areas. Technicians who have received training in non-CAHEA accredited programs or on the job are not eligible to take the examination. In 1989, CAHEA accredited 99 programs for medical record technicians.

Experienced medical record technicians generally advance in one of two ways—by specializing or managing. Many senior medical record technicians specialize in coding, particularly Medicare coding. Tumor registry is another specialty area.

In large medical record departments, experienced technicians may become section supervisors, overseeing the work of the coding, correspondence, or discharge sections, for example. Senior technicians with Accredited Record Technician credentials may become director or assistant director of a medical record department in a small facility. However, in larger institutions, they probably will need a bachelor's degree in medical record administration.

Job Outlook

The job prospects for formally trained technicians should be excellent. Employment of medical record technicians is expected to grow much faster than the average for all occupations through the year 2005 due to rapid growth in the number of medical tests, treatments, and procedures and because medical records will be increasingly scrutinized by third-party payers, courts, and consumers.

A change in Medicare reimbursement policies starting January 1990 has increased the need for detailed medical records in offices and clinics of doctors of medicine. This should translate into rapid growth in employment opportunities for medical record technicians in large group practices and offices of specialists. Rapid growth is also expected in health maintenance organizations, nursing homes, and home health agencies. Nonetheless, hospitals will continue to employ the most technicians, and most job openings will occur because of replacement needs.

Earnings

In January 1991, medical record technicians employed full-time in private hospitals earned an average of $9.70, excluding premium pay for overtime and for work on weekends. Average hourly earnings ranged from $8.70 in the Fort Worth-Arlington area to $13.08 in San Francisco. In 1991, medical record technicians employed by the Federal Government averaged $19,660. According to a 1989 survey by the American Medical Record Association, Accredited Record Technicans averaged $22,462.

Related Occupations

Medical record technicians need a strong clinical background to analyze the contents of medical records. Other occupations that require a knowledge of medical terminology, anatomy, and physiology without directly touching the patient are medical secretaries, medical transcriptionists, tumor registrars, medical writers, and medical illustrators.

Sources of Additional Information

Information on careers in medical record technology, including the Independent Study Program, is available from:
- American Medical Record Association, 919 N. Michigan Ave., Suite 1400, Chicago, IL 60611.

A list of CAHEA-approved programs for medical record technicians is available from:
- American Medical Association, Division of Allied Health Education and Accreditation, 535 N. Dearborn St., Chicago, IL 60610.

Nuclear Medicine Technologists

(D.O.T. 078.161-018 and .361-018)

Nature of the Work

Nuclear medicine is the branch of radiology that uses radionuclides—unstable atoms that emit radiation spontaneously—to diagnosis and treat disease. Radionuclides are purified and compounded like other drugs to form radiopharmaceuticals. Radiopharmaceuticals are administered to patients and then monitored to show the characteristics or functioning of those tissues or organs in which they localize. Abnormal areas show up as higher or lower concentrations of radioactivity than normal.

Nuclear medicine technologists perform these radioactive tests and procedures under the supervision of physicians, who in turn interpret the results. Like radiologic technologists, nuclear medicine technologists operate diagnostic imaging equipment. However, the equipment used in these two specialties relies on different principles, and job duties reflect this. Radiologic technologists create an image by shooting a beam of radiation, commonly called an X-ray, through the patient (See the statement on radiologic technologists elsewhere in this book.). Nuclear medicine technologists prepare and administer radiopharmaceuticals, then operate cameras that detect and map the radioactive drug in the patient's body to create an image.

Technologists first explain test procedures to patients and try to relieve any anxiety. Then nuclear medicine technologists calculate and prepare the correct dosage of the radiopharmaceutical and administer it by mouth, injection, or other means. In preparing radiopharmaceuticals, technologists apply laboratory skills while adhering to safety precautions to keep the radiation dose to workers and patients as low as possible.

Technologists position the patient and start the gamma scintillation camera, or scanner, which creates images of the distribution of the radiopharmaceutical as it passes through or localizes in the patient's body. Technologists produce the images on a computer screen or on film for the physician, who interprets the nuclear medicine study. Some studies, such as cardiac function studies, are processed with the aid of a computer. Technologists who specialize in computer processing may be called "nuclear medicine technology computer specialists."

Nuclear medicine technologists also perform clinical laboratory procedures called radioimmunoassay studies to assess the behavior of the radioactive substance inside the body instead of using a diagnostic image. For example, technologists may add radioactive substances to blood or serum to determine levels of hormones or therapeutic drug content.

Technologists insure that radiation safety procedures are carefully followed by all workers in the nuclear medicine laboratory and that complete and accurate records are kept. They keep patient records and record the amount and type of radionuclides received, used, and disposed of.

Working Conditions

Nuclear medicine technologists generally work a 40-hour week. This may include evening or weekend hours in departments which operate on an extended schedule. Opportunities for part-time and shift work are also available. In addition, technologists in hospitals may be on-call duty on a rotational basis.

Technologists are on their feet much of the day, and may lift or turn disabled patients. Therefore, physical stamina is important.

Although there is potential for radiation exposure in this field, exposure is kept to a minimum by the use of shielded syringes, gloves, and other protective devices. Technologists also wear badges that measure radiation levels while they are in the radiation area. The badge measurement rarely approaches or exceeds established safety levels because of safety programs and built-in safety devices.

Employment

Nuclear medicine technologists held about 10,000 jobs in 1990. About 9 out of 10 jobs were in hospitals. The rest were in physicians' offices and clinics, including imaging centers.

Training, Other Qualifications, and Advancement

Nuclear medicine technology programs range in length from 1 to 4 years and may lead to a certificate, associate degree, or bachelor's degree. Generally, certificate programs are offered in hospitals; associate programs in community colleges; and baccalaureate programs in 4 year-colleges and in universities. Courses cover physical sciences, the biological effects of radiation exposure, radiation protection and procedures, radiopharmaceuticals and their use with patients, imaging techniques, and computer applications. Associate and bachelor's programs also cover liberal arts.

One-year certificate programs are for health professionals or individuals with a previous science background, especially radiologic technologists and ultrasound technologists wishing to specialize in nuclear medicine. They also attract medical technologists, registered nurses, and others who wish to change fields or specialize.

People not already trained in one of the health occupations have three options: a 2-year certificate program, a 2-year associate program, or a 4-year baccalaureate program.

The Committee on Allied Health Education and Accreditation (CAHEA) accredits most formal training programs in this field. In 1990, there were 107 CAHEA-accredited programs in nuclear medicine technology.

All nuclear medicine technologists must meet the minimum Federal standards on the administration of radioactive drugs and the operation of radiologic equipment. In addition, about half of all States require technologists to be licensed. Technologists also may obtain voluntary professional certification or registration. Registration or certification is available from the American Registry of Radiologic Technologists (ARRT) and from the Nuclear Medicine Technology Certification Board (NMTCB). Many employers prefer to hire certified or registered technologists.

Technologists may advance to supervisor, then to chief technologist, and finally to department administrator or director. Some technologists specialize in a clinical area such as nuclear cardiology or computer analysis or leave patient care to take positions in research laboratories. Some become instructors or directors in nuclear medicine technology programs, a step that usually requires an associate or bachelor's degree in nuclear medicine technology. Others leave the occupation to work as sales or training representatives with health equipment or radiopharmaceutical manufacturing firms, or as radiation safety officers in regulatory agencies or hospitals, positions which build upon their background and experience.

Job Outlook

Employment of nuclear medicine technologists is expected to grow much faster than the average for all occupations through the year 2005. Substantial growth in the number of middle-aged and older persons will spur demand for diagnostic procedures, including nuclear medicine tests. Nuclear medicine is especially beneficial for bone, heart, and brain scans.

Furthermore, technological innovations seem likely to increase the diagnostic uses of nuclear medicine. One example is the use of radiopharmaceuticals in combination with monoclonal antibodies to detect cancer at far earlier stages than is customary today, and without resorting to surgery. Another is the use of radionuclides to examine the heart's ability to meet the body's need for blood. Some technologies are still on the drawing board. Presently large research institutes are using positron emission tomography (PET) imaging to observe metabolic and biochemical changes for neurology, cardiology and oncology procedures. However, the radiopharmaceuticals used in PET imaging have very short half-lives and have to be made on the premises in expensive machines called cyclotrons. Radiopharmaceutical companies are now researching ways for hospitals without cyclotrons to perform PET imaging.

Cost considerations will affect the speed with which new applications of nuclear medicine grow. Some promising nuclear medicine procedures, such as PET, are extremely costly, and hospitals contemplating them will have to consider equipment costs, reimbursement policies, and the number of potential users.

Employment prospects are excellent at present; reports of shortages are widespread. The long-run outlook is favorable, inasmuch as the supply of new graduates may not keep pace with demand. Enrollment in accredited training programs has declined in recent years. Unless enrollments increase, shortages should persist.

Earnings

According to a national survey by the University of Texas Medical Branch, the median salary for nuclear medicine technologists in hospitals and medical schools was $28,506 in 1990; the average minimum salary was $23,925, and the average maximum salary was $34,247.

Related Occupations

Nuclear medical technologists operate sophisticated equipment to help physicians and other health practitioners diagnose and treat patients, so do radiologic technologists, diagnostic medical sonographers, cardiology technologists, electroencephalographic technologists, clinical laboratory technologists, perfusionists, and respiratory therapists.

Sources of Additional Information

Additional information on a career as a nuclear medicine technologist is available from:

- The Society of Nuclear Medicine-Technologist Section, 136 Madison Ave., New York, NY 10016.

- American Society of Radiologic Technologists, 15000 Central Ave., Albuquerque, NM 87123.

For the current list of accredited programs in nuclear medicine technology, write to:

- Division of Allied Health Education and Accreditation, American Medical Association, 515 N. State St., Chicago, IL 60610.

Information on certification is available from:

- Nuclear Medicine Technology Certification Board, 2970 Clairmont Rd., Suite 610, Atlanta, GA 30329.
- The American Registry of Radiologic Technologists, 1255 Northland Dr., Mendota Heights, MN 55120.

Paralegals

(D.O.T. 119.267-022 and -026)

Nature of the Work

Not all legal work requires a law degree. Lawyers are often assisted in their work by paralegals—also called "legal assistants"—who perform many of the same tasks as lawyers, except for those tasks considered to be the practice of law.

Paralegals work directly under the supervision of a lawyer. While the lawyer assumes responsibility for the paralegal's work, a paralegal is often allowed to perform all the functions of a lawyer other than accepting clients, setting legal fees, giving legal advice, or presenting a case in court.

Paralegals generally do background work for lawyers. To help prepare a case for trial, a paralegal investigates the facts of the case to make sure that all relevant information is uncovered. The paralegal may conduct research to identify the appropriate laws, judicial decisions, legal articles, and other material that will be used to determine whether or not the client has a good case. After analyzing all the information, the paralegal may prepare a written report that is used by the attorney to decide how the case should be handled. Should the attorney decide to file a lawsuit on behalf of the client, the paralegal may assist in the preparation of legal arguments, draft pleadings to be filed with the court, obtain affidavits, and assist the attorney during the trial. The paralegal also may keep files of all documents and correspondence important to the case.

Besides litigation, paralegals may also work in areas such as bankruptcy, corporate law, criminal law, employee benefits, patent and copyright law, and real estate. They help draft documents such as contracts, mortgages, separation agreements, and trust instruments. They may help prepare tax returns and plan estates. Some paralegals coordinate the activities of the law office employees and keep the financial records for the office.

Paralegals who work for corporations help attorneys with such matters as employee contracts, shareholder agreements, stock option plans, and employee benefit plans. They may help prepare and file annual financial reports, maintain corporate minute books and resolutions, and help secure loans for the corporation. Paralegals may also review government regulations to make sure that the corporation operates within the law.

The duties of paralegals who work in government vary depending on the type of agency that employs them. Generally, paralegals in government analyze legal material for internal use, maintain reference files, conduct research for attorneys, collect and analyze evidence for agency hearings, and prepare informative or explanatory material on the law, agency regulations, and agency policy for general use by the agency and the public.

Paralegals employed in community legal service projects help the poor, the aged, and other persons in need of legal aid. They file forms, conduct research, and prepare documents. When authorized by law, they may represent clients at administrative hearings.

Some paralegals, usually those in small and medium-sized law firms, have varied duties. One day the paralegal may do research on judicial decisions on improper police arrests and the next day may help prepare a mortgage contract. This requires a general knowledge of many areas of the law.

Some paralegals work for large, departmentalized law firms, government agencies, and corporations and specialize in one area of the law. Some specialties are real estate, estate planning, family law, labor law, litigation, and corporate law. Even within specialties, functions often are broken down further so that a paralegal deals with one narrow area of the specialty. For example, paralegals who specialize in labor law may deal exclusively with employee benefits.

A growing number of paralegals are using computers in their work. Computer software packages are increasingly used to search legal literature stored in the computer and identify legal texts relevant to a specific subject. In litigation that involves many supporting documents, paralegals may use computers to organize and index the material. Paralegals may also use computer software packages to perform tax computations and explore the consequences of possible tax strategies for clients.

Working Conditions

Paralegals do most of their work at desks in offices and law libraries. Occasionally, they travel to gather information and perform other duties.

Paralegals employed by corporations and government work a standard 40-hour week. Although most paralegals work year round, some are temporarily employed during busy times of the year then released when work diminishes. Paralegals who work for law firms sometimes work very long hours when they are under pressure to meet deadlines. Some law firms reward such loyalty with bonuses and additional time off.

Paralegals handle many routine assignments, particularly when they are inexperienced. Some find that these assignments offer little challenge and become frustrated with their duties. However, paralegals usually assume more responsible and varied tasks as they gain experience. Furthermore, as new laws and judicial interpretations emerge, paralegals are exposed to many new legal problems that make their work more interesting and challenging.

Employment

Paralegals held about 90,000 jobs in 1990. Private law firms employed the vast majority; most of the remainder worked for various levels of government. Paralegals are found in nearly every Federal Government agency; the Departments of Justice, Treasury, Interior, and Health and Human Services, and the General Services Administration are the largest employers. State and local governments and publicly funded legal service projects employ paralegals as well. Banks, real estate development companies, and insurance companies also employ small numbers of paralegals.

Training, Other Qualifications, and Advancement

There are several ways to enter the paralegal profession. Employers generally require formal paralegal training; several types of training programs are acceptable. However, some employers prefer to train their paralegals on the job, promoting experienced legal secretaries or hiring persons with college education but no legal experience. Other entrants have experience in a technical field that is useful to law firms, such as a background in tax preparation for tax and estate practice or nursing or health administration for personal injury practice.

Over 600 formal paralegal training programs are offered by 4-year colleges and universities, law schools, community and junior colleges, business schools, and proprietary schools. In 1991, over 150 programs had been approved by the American Bar Association (ABA). Although this approval is neither required nor sought by many programs, graduation from an ABA-approved program can enhance one's employment opportunities. The requirements for admission to formal training programs vary widely. Some require some college courses or a bachelor's degree. Others accept high school graduates or persons with legal experience. A few schools require standardized tests and personal interviews.

Most paralegal programs are completed in 2 years, although some take as long as 4 years and award a bachelor's degree upon completion. Other programs take only a few months to complete, but require a bachelor's degree for admission. Programs typically include a combination of general courses on subjects such as the law and legal research techniques, and courses that cover specialized areas of the law, such as real estate, estate planning and probate, litigation, family law, contracts, and criminal law. Many employers prefer applicants with training in a specialized area of the law. Programs also increasingly include courses that introduce students to the legal applications of computers. Many paralegal training programs include an internship in which students gain practical experience by working for several months in a law office, corporate legal department, or government agency. Experience gained in internships is an asset when seeking a job after graduation. Depending on the program, graduates may receive a certificate, an associate degree, or, in some cases, a bachelor's degree.

The quality of paralegal training programs varies; the better programs generally emphasize job placement. Prospective students should examine the experiences of recent graduates of programs in which they are considering enrolling.

Paralegals need not be certified, but the National Association of Legal Assistants has established standards for voluntary certification which require various combinations of education and experience. Paralegals who meet these standards are eligible to take a 2-day examination given each year at several regional testing centers by the Certifying Board of Legal Assistants of the National Association of Legal Assistants. Persons who pass this examination may use the designation Certified Legal Assistant (CLA). This designation is a sign of competence in the field and may enhance employment and advancement opportunities.

Paralegals must be able to handle legal problems logically and effectively communicate, both orally and in writing, their findings and opinions to their supervising attorney. They must understand legal terminology and have good research and investigative skills. Familiarity with the operation and applications of computers in legal research and litigation support is increasingly important. Paralegals must always stay abreast of new developments in the law that affect their area of practice.

Because paralegals often deal with the public, they must be courteous and uphold the high ethical standards of the legal profession. A few States have established ethical guidelines that paralegals in the State must follow.

Experienced paralegals usually are given progressively more responsible duties and less supervision. In large law firms, corporate legal departments, and government agencies, experienced paralegals may supervise other paralegals and clerical staff and delegate work assigned by the attorneys. Advancement opportunities include promotion to managerial and other law-related positions within the firm or corporate legal department. However, some paralegals find it easier to move to another law firm when seeking increased responsibility or advancement.

Job Outlook

The number of job openings for paralegals is expected to increase significantly through the year 2005, but so will the number of persons pursuing this career. Thus, keen competition for jobs should continue as the growing number of graduates from paralegal training programs keeps pace with employment growth. Still, job prospects are generally expected to be good for graduates of highly regarded formal programs.

Employment of paralegals has grown tremendously since the emergence of this occupation in the late 1960's. Employment is expected to continue to grow much faster than the average for all occupations through the year 2005. The emphasis on hiring paralegals should continue in both legal and law-related fields so that the cost, availability, and efficiency of legal services can be improved. Besides jobs arising from growth in demand for paralegals, numerous job openings are expected to arise as persons leave the occupation for various reasons.

Private law firms will continue to be the largest employers of paralegals as a growing population sustains the need for legal services. The growth of prepaid legal plans also should contribute to the demand for the services of law firms. A growing array of other organizations, such as corporate legal departments, insurance companies, real estate and title insurance firms, and banks will also hire paralegals. Job opportunities are expected to expand throughout the private sector as more companies become aware that paralegals are able to do many legal tasks for lower salaries than lawyers.

Job opportunities for paralegals will expand even in the public sector. Community legal service programs—which provide assistance to the poor, the aged, minorities, and middle-income families—operate on limited budgets and will employ more paralegals to keep expenses down and serve the most people. Federal, State, and local government agencies, consumer organizations, and the courts also should continue to hire paralegals in increasing numbers.

To a limited extent, paralegal jobs are affected by the business cycle. During recessions, the demand for some discretionary legal services, such as planning estates, drafting wills, and handling real estate transactions, declines. Corporations are less inclined to initiate litigation when falling sales and profits lead to fiscal belt tightening. As a result, full time paralegals employed in offices adversely affected by a recession may be laid off or have their work hours reduced. On the other hand, during recessions, corporations and individuals are more likely to face other legal problems, such as bankruptcies, foreclosures, and divorces, that require legal solutions. Furthermore, the continuous emergence of new laws and judicial interpretations of existing laws creates new business for lawyers and paralegals without regard to the business cycle.

Earnings

Earnings of paralegals vary greatly. Salaries depend on the education, training, and experience the paralegal brings to the job, the type and size of employer, and the geographic location of the job. Generally, paralegals who work for large law firms or in large metropolitan areas earn more than those who work for smaller firms or in less populated regions.

Paralegals had an average annual salary of about $24,900 in 1991, according to a utilization and compensation survey by the National Association of Legal Assistants; the middle 50 percent earned between $20,000 and $29,000 a year. Starting salaries of paralegals averaged $20,900, while paralegals with from 3 to 5 years of experience averaged $24,200 a year. Salaries of paralegals with over 10 years of experience averaged $28,500 annually, according to the same survey. In addition to a salary, many paralegals received an annual bonus, which averaged $1,100 in 1991. Employers of the majority of paralegals provided life and health insurance benefits and contributed to a retirement plan on their behalf.

Paralegal Specialists hired by the Federal Government in 1991 started at about $17,000 or $21,000 a year, depending on their training and experience. The average annual salary of paralegals who worked for the Federal Government in 1990 was about $32,164.

Related Occupations

Several other occupations also call for a specialized understanding of the law and the legal system but do not require the extensive training of a lawyer. Some of these are abstractors, claim examiners, compliance and enforcement inspectors, occupational safety and health workers, patent agents, police officers, and title examiners.

Sources of Additional Information

General information on a career as a paralegal and a list of paralegal training programs approved by the American Bar Association may be purchased for a $5 fee from:

- Standing Committee on Legal Assistants, American Bar Association, 750 North Lake Shore Dr., Chicago, IL 60611.

For information on certification of paralegals, schools that offer training programs in a specific State, and standards and guidelines for paralegals, contact:

- National Association of Legal Assistants, Inc., 1601 South Main St., Suite 300, Tulsa, OK 74119.

Information on a career as a paralegal, schools that offer

training programs, and local paralegal associations can be obtained from:
- National Federation of Paralegal Associations, Suite 201, 104 Wilmot Rd., Deerfield, IL 60015-5195.
- National Paralegal Association, P.O. Box 406, Solebury, PA 18963.

Information on paralegal training programs may be obtained from:
- American Association for Paralegal Education, P.O. Box 40244, Overland Park, KS 66204.

General information about a career as a legal assistant manager is available from:
- Legal Assistant Management Association, P.O. Box 40129, Overland Park, KS 66204.

Radiologic Technologists

(D.O.T. 078.162-010, .361-034, .362-026 and .364-010)

Nature of the Work

Perhaps the most familiar use of the X-ray is the diagnosis of broken bones. However, medical uses of radiation go far beyond that. Radiation is used not only to produce images of the interior of the body, but to treat cancer as well. At the same time, the rapidly growing use of imaging techniques that do not involve X-rays is transforming the field, and the term "diagnostic imaging" embraces procedures such as ultrasound and magnetic resonance scans as well as the familiar X-ray.

Radiographers produce X-ray films (radiographs) of parts of the human body for use in diagnosing medical problems. They prepare patients for radiologic examinations by explaining the procedure, by removing any articles, such as jewelry, through which X-rays cannot pass, and by positioning the patients so that the correct parts of the body can be radiographed. To prevent unnecessary radiation exposure, technologists surround the exposed area with radiation protection devices, such as lead shields, or in some way limit the size of the X-ray beam. Radiographers position radiographic equipment at the correct angle and height over the appropriate area of a patient's body. Using instruments similar to a measuring tape, technologists measure the thickness of the section to be radiographed and set controls on the machine to produce radiographs of the appropriate density, detail, and contrast. They place the X-ray film under the part of the patient's body to be examined and make the exposure. Afterward, technologists remove the film and develop it.

Experienced radiographers may perform more complex imaging tests. For fluoroscopies, radiographers may prepare a solution of contrast medium for the patient to drink, allowing the radiologist, the physician who interprets X-rays, to see soft tissues in the body. For computed tomography scans (CTs), radiographers use a computer to enhance the X-ray. For magnetic resonance imaging (MRI), technologists use giant magnets and radio-waves rather than radiation to create an image.

Radiation therapy technologists prepare cancer patients for treatment and administer prescribed doses of ionizing radiation to specific body parts. Technologists operate many kinds of equipment, including high-energy linear accelerators with electron capabilities. They position patients under the equipment with absolute accuracy in order to expose affected body parts to treatment while protecting the rest of the body from radiation.

Technologists also check the patients reactions for radiation side effects such as nausea, hair loss, and skin irritation. They need to give clear instructions and explanations to patients who are likely to be very ill and may be dying. Radiation therapy technologists, in contrast to other areas in radiology, are likely to see the same patient on a daily basis throughout the course of treatment.

Sonographers, also known as ultrasound technologists, use non-ionizing, ultrasound equipment to transmit high frequency sound waves into areas of the patient's body, then collect reflected echoes to form an image. The image is viewed on a screen and may be recorded on a printout strip or photographed for use in interpretation and diagnosis by physicians. Sonographers explain the procedure, record additional medical history, and then position the patient for testing. Viewing the screen as the scan takes place, sonographers look for subtle differences between healthy and pathological areas, check for factors such as position, obstruction, or change of shape, and judge if the images are satisfactory for diagnostic purposes. Sonographers may specialize in neurosonography (the brain), vascular sonography, echocardiography (the heart), abdominal (the liver, kidneys, spleen, and pancreas), obstetrics/ gynecology, and opthalmology (the eye).

Radiologic technologists must precisely follow physicians' instructions and regulations concerning use of radiation to insure that they, patients, and co-workers are protected from its dangers.

In addition to preparing patients and operating equipment, radiologic technologists keep patient records and adjust and maintain equipment. They may also prepare work schedules, evaluate equipment purchases, or manage their department.

Working Conditions

Radiologic technologists generally work a 40-hour week that may include evening and weekend or on-call hours. Part-time work is widely available.

Technologists are on their feet for long periods and may lift or turn disabled patients. They work close to the machines. Some technologists travel in mobile imaging vans; however, most work in hospitals, physicians' offices, or imaging centers.

Radiation therapy technologists are prone to emotional "burn out" since they treat extremely ill and dying patients on a daily basis.

Although potential radiation hazards exist in this field, they have been minimized by the use of lead aprons, gloves, and other shielding devices, as well as by instruments that measure radiation exposure. Technologists wear badges that measure radiation levels in the radiation area, and detailed records are kept on their cumulative lifetime dose.

Employment

Radiologic technologists held about 149,000 jobs in 1990. Most technologists were radiographers. A small proportion were sonographers and radiation therapy technologists.

About 3 out of 5 jobs are in hospitals. The rest are in physicians' offices and clinics, including diagnostic imaging centers.

Training, Other Qualifications, and Advancement

Preparation for this field is offered in hospitals, colleges and universities, vocational-technical institutes, and the Armed Forces. Hospitals, which employ most radiologic technologists, prefer to hire those with formal training.

Formal training is offered in radiography, radiation therapy technology, and diagnostic medical sonography (ultrasound). Programs range in length from 1 to 4 years and lead to a certificate, associate degree, or bachelor's degree. Two-year programs are most prevalent.

Some 1-year certificate programs are for individuals from other health occupations such as medical technologists and registered nurses who want to change fields or experienced radiographers who want to specialize in radiation therapy technology or learn sonography. A bachelor's or master's degree in one of the radiologic technologies is desirable for supervisory, administrative, or teaching positions.

The Committee on Allied Health Education and Accreditation (CAHEA) accredits most formal training programs for this field. CAHEA accredited 672 radiography programs, 104 radiation therapy technology programs, and 38 diagnostic medical sonography programs in 1990.

Radiography programs require, at a minimum, a high school diploma or the equivalent. High school courses in mathematics, physics, chemistry, and biology are helpful. The programs provide both classroom and clinical instruction in anatomy and physiology, patient care procedures, radiation physics, radiation protection, principles of imaging, medical terminology, positioning of patients, medical ethics, radiobiology, and pathology.

For training programs in radiation therapy and diagnostic medical sonography, applicants with a background in science, or experience in one of the health professions, generally are preferred. Most programs consider applicants with liberal arts backgrounds, however, as well as high school graduates with courses in math and science.

Radiographers and radiation therapy technologists are covered by provisions of the Consumer Patient Radiation Health and Safety Act of 1981, which aims to protect the public from the hazards of unnecessary exposure to medical and dental radiation by making sure that operators of radiologic equipment are properly trained. The act requires the Federal Government to set standards that the States, in turn, may use for accrediting training programs and certifying individuals who engage in medical or dental radiography.

By 1990, 23 States required radiographers to be licensed, and 20 required radiation therapy technologists to be licensed. (Puerto Rico requires a license for the practice of either specialty.) One State, Utah, licenses diagnostic medical sonographers.

Voluntary registration is offered by the American Registry of Radiologic Technologists (ARRT) in both radiography and radiation therapy technology. The American Registry of Diagnostic Medical Sonographers (ARDMS) certifies the competence of sonographers. To become registered, technologists must be graduated from a CAHEA-accredited school or meet other prerequisites and have passed an examination. Many employers prefer to hire registered technologists.

With experience and additional training, staff technologists in large radiography departments may be promoted to clinical jobs performing special procedures including CT scanning, ultrasound, angiography, and magnetic resonance imaging.

Experienced technologists may also be promoted to supervisory positions such as supervisor, chief technologist, and—ultimately—department administrator or director. Depending on the institution, courses in business or a master's degree in health administration may be necessary for the director's position. Some technologists progress by becoming instructors or directors in radiologic technology programs; others take jobs as sales representatives or instructors with equipment manufacturers.

With additional education, available at major cancer centers, radiation therapy technologists can specialize and become medical radiation dosimetrists. Dosimetrists work with health physicists and oncologists (physicians who specialize in the study and treatment of tumors) to develop treatment plans.

Job Outlook

Employment in the field of radiologic technology is expected to grow much faster than the average for all occupations through 2005 because of the vast clinical potential of diagnostic imaging and therapeutic technology. Current as well as new uses of imaging equipment are virtually certain to sharply increase demand for radiologic technologists.

Technology will continue to evolve. New generations of diagnostic imaging equipment are expected to give even better information to physicians. Since it is non-invasive, it will be less risky and uncomfortable for the patient than the exploratory surgery of today. Computed tomography, magnetic resonance imaging, arteriography, and digital vascular imaging have taken hold very quickly. Applications of diagnostic ultrasound—already in wide use in cardiology and obstetrics/gynecology—are expected to grow.

In the treatment area, radiation therapy will continue to be used—alone or in combination with surgery or chemotherapy—to treat cancer. More treatment of cancer is anticipated due to the aging of the population, educational efforts aimed at early detection, and improved ability to detect malignancies through radiologic procedures such as mammography.

However, the speed with which institutions adopt new technologies depends largely on cost and reimbursement considerations. Although physicians ar are enthusiastic about the clinical benefits, the willingness of third-party payers (insurers) to pay for a particular procedure governs the facilities' decision to adopt costly technology. Some promising new technologies may not come into widespread use because they are too expensive, but on the whole, it appears that the benefits to physicians and patients are so great that new uses of radiologic procedures will continue to grow.

Hospitals will remain the principal employer of radiologic technologists. However, employment is expected to grow most rapidly in offices and clinics of physicians, including diagnostic imaging centers. Health facilities such as these are expected to grow very rapidly through 2005 due to the strong shift toward outpatient care, encouraged by third party payers and made possible by technological advances that permit more procedures to be performed outside the hospital.

Technologists are even working on the road. In response to rural needs, radiologic technologists travel in large vans equipped with sophisticated diagnostic equipment. This trend is likely to continue.

Most jobs will come from the need to replace technologists who leave the occupation. Turnover is relatively high in radiation therapy technology, because of the stress in treating patients who may be close to death.

Currently there are reports of a shortage of technologists, especially radiation therapy technologists. However, efforts by employers to fill vacancies—raising salaries and improving working conditions—could attract more people to radiology and eventually create a balance between jobseekers and openings.

Earnings

In January 1991, radiologic technologists working full-time in private hospitals averaged $12.75 an hour, excluding premium pay for overtime and for work on weekends, holidays, and late shifts. Average hourly earnings ranged from $11.83 in the Fort Worth-Arlington area to $19.11 in San Francisco. Radiologic technologists working part-time averaged $12.76 an hour. Diagnostic medical sonographers working full-time averaged $14.47 an hour; their average hourly earnings ranged from $13.38 in Denver to $18.06 in San Francisco. Those working part-time averaged $15.18 an hour.

According to a University of Texas Medical Branch survey of hospitals and medical schools, the median salary for radiation therapy technologists was $29,162 in 1990; the average minimum salary was $24,699, and the average maximum salary was $35,811.

Related Occupations

Radiologic technologists operate sophisticated equipment to help physicians, dentists, and other health practitioners diagnose and treat patients. Workers in related occupations include nuclear medicine technologists, cardiology technologists, cardiovascular technologists, perfusionists, respiratory therapists, clinical laboratory technologists, and electroencephalographic technologists.

Sources of Additional Information

For career information, enclose a stamped, self-addressed business-size envelope with your request to:

- American Society of Radiologic Technologists, 15000 Central Ave. SE., Albuquerque, NM 87123.
- Society of Diagnostic Medical Sonographers, 12225 Greenville Ave., Suite 434, Dallas, TX 75231.

Information about a career in radiation therapy technology is also available from your local chapter of the American Cancer Society.

For the current list of accredited education programs in radiography, radiation therapy technology, or diagnostic medical sonography, write to:

- Division of Allied Health Education and Accreditation, American Medical Association, 515 N. State St., Chicago, IL 60610.

For information on certification in radiologic technology, contact:

- American Registry of Radiologic Technologists, 1255 Northland Dr., Mendota, MN 55120.

For information on certification in sonography, contact:

- American Registry of Diagnostic Medical Sonographers, 2368 Victory Pky., Suite 510, Cincinnati, OH 45206.

Surgical Technologists

(D.O.T. 079.374-022)

Nature of the Work

Surgical technologists, also called operating room technicians, assist in operations under the supervision of surgeons or registered nurses. Before an operation, surgical technologists help set up the operating room with surgical instruments, equipment, sterile linens, and fluids such as saline (a salt solution), or glucose (a sugar solution). They also may "prep" (prepare) patients for surgery by washing, shaving, and disinfecting body areas where surgeons will operate. They transport patients to the operating room. cover them with special surgical "drapes," and help position them on the operating table.

During surgery, technologists pass instruments and other sterile supplies to surgeons and surgeons' assistants. They may hold retractors, cut sutures, and help count sponges, needles, supplies, and instruments. Surgical technologists help prepare, care for, and dispose of specimens taken for laboratory analysis and may help apply dressings. They may operate sterilizers, lights, or suction machines, and help operate diagnostic equipment.

After an operation, surgical technologists may help transfer patients to the recovery room and clean and restock the operating room.

Working Conditions

Surgical technologists work in clean, well-lighted, cool environments. They need stamina to be on their feet and must be alert and able to concentrate throughout operations that may last several hours.

Most surgery is performed during the day, but some workplaces, such as emergency surgical units, require 24-hour coverage. A 40-hour workweek is normal for surgical technologists, although they may be "on call" (available to work on short notice for emergencies) during weekends and evenings on a rotating basis.

Employment

Surgical technologists held about 38,000 jobs in 1990. Most surgical technologists are employed by hospitals. Others are employed in offices and clinics of physicians that have operating, delivery, and emergency room facilities. A few, known as private scrubs, are employed directly by surgeons who have special surgical teams like those for liver transplants.

Training, Other Qualifications, and Advancement

Surgical technologists receive their training in formal programs offered by community and junior colleges, vocational and technical institutes, or hospitals. In 1991, the Committee on Allied Health Education and Accreditation (CAHEA) of the American Medical Association recognized 117 accredited programs. High school graduation normally is required for admission. Programs last 1 to 2 years and lead to a certificate or associate degree.

Programs provide classroom education and supervised clinical experience. Required study includes anatomy, physiology, microbiology, pharmacology, and medical terminology. Other studies cover care and safety of patients during surgery, aseptic techniques, and surgical care procedures. Students also learn to sterilize instruments; prevent and control infection; and handle special drugs, solutions, supplies, and equipment.

Hospital-based programs last from 6 months to 1 year. The shorter programs are for licensed practical nurses, who already have some medical background. Some surgical technologists are trained in the Armed Forces. Surgical technologists are expected to keep abreast of new developments in the field.

Idaho is the only State that requires surgical technologists to be licensed. But technologists may obtain voluntary professional certification from the Liaison Council on Certification by passing a national certification examination. Technologists wishing to become certified after 1993 must also have been graduated from a formal program. Continuing education or reexamination is required to maintain certification, which must be renewed every 6 years. Many employers prefer to hire certified technologists.

Surgical technologists need manual dexterity because they must handle instruments quickly. They also must be conscientious, orderly, and emotionally stable to handle the demands of surgeons. Technologists must respond quickly and have a knowledge of procedures so that they may have instruments ready for surgeons without having to be told. Recommended high school courses include health, biology, chemistry, and mathematics.

Career advancement for surgical technologists is limited. Technologists may work as scrub technologists, cleaning and handing instruments to surgeons . They may also work as circulating technologists. A circulating technologist is the "unsterile" member of the surgical team who prepares patients; helps with anesthesia; gets, opens, and holds packages for the "sterile" person during the procedure; interviews the patient before surgery; and answers the surgeon's questions about the patient during the surgery. Some technologists advance to first assistants, who help with retracting, sponging, suturing, cauterizing bleeders, and assisting in closing and treating wounds. With additional training, they can work with lasers and assist in the more complex procedures such as open heart surgery. However, other health personnel like surgeons' assistants may perform the first assistant functions instead of technologists. Surgical technologists may leave the operating room to manage central supply departments. Some technologists leave health facilities to take positions with insurance companies, sterile supply services, or operating equipment firms. Others become instructors in surgical technology training programs.

Job Outlook

Employment of surgical technologists is expected to grow much faster than the average for all occupations through the year 2005, as the volume of surgery increases and operating room staffing patterns change.

The number of surgical procedures is expected to rise as the population grows and ages. Older people require more surgical procedures. Technological advances, such as fiber optics and laser technology, will also permit new surgical procedures.

In addition, operating room staffing patterns are changing. Some employers are substituting technologists for operating room nurses to reduce costs and because in some areas they have difficulty hiring operating room nurses. However, some facilities and States limit the work that surgical technologists can do, so surgical technologists will never totally replace operating room nurses.

Hospitals will continue to be the primary employer of surgical technologists. Nonetheless, the shift to outpatient or ambulatory surgery will create faster growth for technologists in offices and clinics of physicians, including "surgicenters."

Earnings

In January 1991, surgical technologists working full-time in private hospitals averaged $10.03 an hour, excluding premiums for overtime and for work on weekends, holidays, and late shifts. Average hourly earnings ranged from $9.46 in St. Louis to $13.03 in San Francisco.

Related Occupations

Other health occupations requiring approximately 1 year of training after high school are licensed practical nurses, respiratory therapy technicians, medical laboratory assistants, medical assistants, dental assistants, optometric assistants, and physical therapy aides.

Sources of Additional Information

Additional information on a career as a surgical technologist and on certification is available from:
- Association of Surgical Technologists, 7108-C S. Alton Way, Englewood, CO 80112.

For a list of CAHEA accredited programs, contact:
- American Medical Association, Division of Allied Health Education and Accreditation, 515 North State St., Chicago, IL 60610.

Marketing and Sales Occupations

Counter and Rental Clerks

(D.O.T. 216.482-030; 249.362-010; .366-010; 295.357-010, -014 and -018; .367-010, -014, and -026; .467-010, -014, and -018; .477-010; 299.367-018; 369.367-010 and -014; .477-014; and .677-010)

Nature of the Work

Whether choosing a video tape, dropping off clothes to be drycleaned, or renting a car, we rely on counter and rental clerks to handle these transactions efficiently. Although specific duties vary by establishment, counter and rental clerks are responsible for answering questions, taking orders, receiving payments, and accepting returns. At times, they may also sell items.

Regardless of where they work, counter and rental clerks must be knowledgeable about the company's services, policies, and procedures. Often, customers are not sure what they want. To assist them, counter and rental clerks may explain what is available, its cost, the rental provisions, and any promotions that are in effect. For example, in the car rental industry, they inform customers about the types of automobiles available and the daily and weekly rental costs.

When taking orders, counter and rental clerks use various types of equipment. In some establishments, they write out tickets and order forms. However, computers and bar code scanners are quickly becoming the norm. Most computer systems are user friendly and usually require very little data entry. Scanners "read" the product code and display a description of the item on a computer screen. Clerks must insure, however, that the data on the screen match the actual product.

Counter and rental clerks also note any special instructions and check the condition of the merchandise. In drycleaning establishments for example, they inform the customer when the items will be ready. In rental agencies, they ensure that customers meet any age or other requirements and state when and in what condition the item must be returned. When customers come to retrieve their clothing or return rented merchandise, counter and rental clerks calculate the fee and accept payment. They may also inspect the item to insure the merchandise has not been damaged.

Counter and rental clerks' duties also vary by the industry in which they are employed. Those employed in supermarkets and grocery stores may help customers select fresh flowers, delicatessen or bakery products, or cosmetics. In shops that rent formal wear, they may fit and measure garments; in video stores, they often make suggestions about which movie the customer might enjoy.

Working Conditions

Because firms employing counter and rental clerks generally operate at the convenience of their customers, these workers often work night and weekend hours. However, because of this, many employers offer flexible schedules. Many counter and rental clerks work a 40-hour week but nearly one-half are on part-time schedules—usually during rush periods, such as weekends, evenings, and holidays.

Working conditions are usually pleasant; most stores and service establishments are clean, well-lighted, and temperature controlled. However, clerks are on their feet much of the time and may be confined behind a small counter area. This job requires constant interaction with the public and can be taxing—especially when things go wrong.

Employment

Counter and rental clerks held about 215,000 jobs in 1990. About 1 clerk in 3 worked for a laundry or drycleaning establishment. Other large employers included automobile rental firms, equipment rental firms and leasing services, grocery stores, and video rental stores.

Counter and rental clerks are employed throughout the country but are concentrated in metropolitan areas where renting and leasing services are in greater demand.

Training, Other Qualifications, and Advancement

Counter and rental clerk jobs are primarily entry level and require little or no experience and little formal education. However, many employers prefer high school graduates for these positions.

In most companies, counter and rentental clerks are trained on the job. Clerks usually learn how to operate the equipment and become familiar with the establishment's policies and procedures under the observation of a more experienced worker. However, some employers have formal classroom training programs lasting from a few hours to a few weeks. Topics covered in this training usually include a description of the industry and the company, company policies and procedures, equipment operation, sales techniques, and customer service.

Persons who want to become counter and rental clerks should enjoy working with people and have the ability to deal tactfully with difficult customers. In addition, good oral and written communication skills are essential.

Advancement opportunities vary depending on the size and type of company. However, jobs as counter and rental clerks offer good opportunities for workers to learn about their company's products and business practices. These jobs can be steppingstones to more responsible positions, because it is common in many establishments to promote counter and rental clerks into assistant manager positions.

Job Outlook

Employment in this occupation is expected to increase faster than the average for all occupations through the year 2005 due to anticipated employment growth in the industries where they are concentrated. Despite this growth, however, most job openings will arise from the need to replace experienced workers who transfer to other occupations or leave the labor force.

In recent years, employment in rental and leasing services has skyrocketed—creating thousands of new jobs for counter and rental clerks. Like many other occupations in retail trade and food service, workers under the age of 25 traditionally have filled many of the openings in this occupation. This age group which shrank in numbers during the decade of the 1980's, will rebound but accounts for a slightly smaller share of the 2005 workforce than in 1990. Thus employers can be expected to improve efforts to attract and retain

Interviewing and new accounts clerks 250,000
Reservation and transportation ticket agents and
     travel clerks 150,000
Hotel desk clerks. 118,000

These workers are employed throughout the economy, but are concentrated in lodging establishments, offices of physicians, hospitals, banks, firms providing business services, and firms in the transportation industry. This type of work lends itself to flexible working arrangements—much more prevalent for receptionists, interviewing and new accounts clerks, and hotel and motel desk clerks than for reservation agents—and almost 1 of every 3 information clerks works part time.

Training, Other Qualifications, and Advancement

Although hiring requirements vary from industry to industry, a high school diploma or its equivalent usually is required. However, some high school students work part time as information clerks outside of school hours. For some jobs, such as airline reservation and ticket agents, some college education is preferred.

With the exception of airline reservation and other passenger transportation agents, orientation and training for information clerks is generally given on the job. Hotel and motel desk clerk job orientation is usually brief, and includes an explanation of the job duties and information about the establishment, such as room location and available services. They start work on the job under the guidance of a supervisor or an experienced clerk. They may need additional training in data processing or office machine operations to use computerized reservation, room assignment, and billing systems.

Receptionists and interviewing clerks also receive their training on the job. They learn good interviewing techniques and telephone etiquette; they learn how their employers keep records and become familiar with the kinds of business forms used. These workers also may learn to operate duplicating machines, calculators, word processors, and personal computers.

Most airline reservation agents learn their skills through formal company programs. They spend a few days in a classroom setting, learning company and industry policies that cover ticketing procedures and other matters related to the airline. They learn to use the computer to obtain information on schedules, seat availability, and fares; to reserve space for passengers; and to plan passenger itineraries. They must learn airport and airline code designations, and are tested on this knowledge. To maximize their productivity, reservation agents are expected to limit the time spent on each call without, of course, alienating customers. Thus, learning how to carry on a conversation in an organized, yet pleasing manner is an important part of their training. After completing classroom instruction, new agents work under supervisors or experienced agents for a short period of time. In contrast, automobile clubs train their travel clerks on the job, without formal classes.

Many information clerks continue to receive instruction after their initial training ends, with employers keeping them informed about new procedures and changes in company policies.

Because information clerks must deal directly with the public, a good appearance and a pleasant personality are essential, as are problem-solving ability and good interpersonal skills. A good speaking voice is essential because these employees frequently use the telephone or public address systems. Courses useful to persons wanting to enter these occupations include basic math and English, geography, U.S. history, psychology, and public speaking. Typing ability and computer literacy often are needed.

Some employers may require applicants to take a typing test to gauge their skills. It also may be helpful for those in the lodging industry to be able to speak a foreign language.

Advancement for information clerks comes about either by transfer to a more responsible job or by promotion to a supervisory position. For example, receptionists, interviewers, and new accounts clerks with typing or other clerical skills may advance to a better paying job as a secretary, administrative assistant, or bookkeeper. In the airline industry, a ticket agent may advance to supervisory positions or may become a field sales agent. Additional training frequently is helpful in preparing information clerks for promotion. In the lodging industry, for example, clerks can improve their chances for advancement by taking home or group study courses in lodging management such as those sponsored by the Educational Institute of the American Hotel and Motel Association. Regardless of job setting, a college degree frequently is required for advancement to the management ranks.

Job Outlook

Overall employment of information clerks is expected to increase much faster than the average for all occupations through the year 2005. In addition to the many openings that will occur as businesses and organizations expand, numerous jobs for information clerks will result from the need to replace experienced workers who transfer to other occupations or leave the labor force. Replacement needs will create an exceptionally large number of job openings, for the occupation is large and turnover is higher than average. Many young people work as information clerks for a few years before switching to other, better paying jobs. This work is well suited to flexible work schedules, and many opportunities for part-time work will continue to be available.

Economic growth and general business expansion are expected to stimulate demand for these workers. Employment of receptionists, hotel and motel desk clerks, interviewing clerks and reservation and transportation ticket agents and travel clerks should grow more rapidly than that of new accounts clerks. The slower growth projected for new accounts clerks reflects slower than average growth among commercial banks and savings institutions, where employment is heavily concentrated.

Earnings

In 1990, median weekly earnings of full-time information clerks were about $290. The middle 50 percent earned between $235 and $370. The bottom 10 percent earned less than $190, while the top 10 percent earned more than $480. Earnings vary widely by occupation. Salaries of reservation and ticket agents tend to be significantly higher than for other clerks, while hotel and motel desk clerks tend to earn quite a bit less, as the following tabulation of median weekly earnings shows.

Reservation and transportation ticket agents and
     travel clerks. $390
Interviewing and new accounts clerks 300
Receptionists 270
Hotel and motel clerks. 230

In 1991, the Federal Government paid beginning information receptionists with a high school diploma or 6 months' experience $12,400 a year. The average salary for all information receptionists employed by the Federal Government was $16,800 a year in 1991.

Earnings of hotel and motel desk clerks depend on the location, size, and type of establishment in which they work. Large luxury hotels and those located in metropolitan and resort areas generally pay clerks more than less expensive ones and those located in less populated areas. In general, hotels pay higher salaries than motels or other types of lodging establishments.

In addition to their hourly wage, full-time information clerks usually receive the same package of fringe benefits as other workers in the organization. Typical benefits include health and life insurance, vacation and sick leave, paid holidays, and a pension plan. Those who work evenings, nights, weekends, or holidays also may receive a shift differential. Some employers offer educational assistance to their employees. Reservation and transportation ticket agents and travel clerks receive free or very low cost travel on their company's carriers for themselves and their immediate family and, in some companies, free uniforms.

About 1 in 4 reservation and transportation ticket agents and travel clerks belongs to a labor union. Five unions cover most of the or organized agents and clerks: The Amalgamated Transit Union; the International Association of Machinists and Aerospace Workers; the Transportation Communications Union; the International Brotherhood of Teamsters, Chauffeurs, Warehousemen and Helpers of America; and the Transport Workers Union of America.

Related Occupations

A number of other workers deal with the public, receive and provide information, or direct people to others who can assist them. Among these are customer-service representatives, dispatchers, and telephone operators.

Sources of Additional Information

State employment service offices can provide information about job openings for information clerks.

Legal Secretaries

(D.O.T. 201)

Nature of the Work

Most organizations employ secretaries to perform and coordinate office activities and to ensure that information gets disseminated in a timely fashion to staff and clients. Managers, professionals, and other support staff rely on them to keep administrative operations under control. Their specific duties depend upon their level of responsibility and the type of firm in which they are employed.

Secretaries are responsible for a variety of administrative and clerical duties that are necessary to run and maintain organizations efficiently. They schedule appointments, give information to callers, organize and maintain files, fill out forms, and take dictation. They may also type letters, make travel arrangements, or contact clients. Secretaries also operate office equipment like facsimile machines, photocopiers, and telephones with voice mail capabilities.

In today's automated offices, secretaries increasingly use personal computers to run spreadsheet, word processing, data base management, desktop publishing, and graphics programs—tasks previously handled by managers and professionals. Secretaries sometimes work in clusters of three or four so that they can help each other. Because they are relieved from dictation and typing, for example, they can support several members of the professional staff.

Executive secretaries or administrative assistants perform fewer clerical tasks than lower level secretaries. As well as receiving visitors, arranging conference calls, and answering letters, they may handle more complex responsibilities such as doing research, preparing statistical reports, and supervising and training other clerical staff.

In addition to general administrative duties, some secretaries do highly specialized work. Knowledge of technical terminology and procedures is required for these positions. Further specialization in various types of law is common among legal secretaries. They prepare correspondence and legal papers such as summonses, complaints, motions, and subpoenas under the supervision of an attorney. They also may review legal journals and assist in other ways with legal research. Medical secretaries transcribe dictation, prepare correspondence, and assist physicians or medical scientists with reports, speeches, articles, and conference proceedings. They record simple medical histories, arrange for patients to be hospitalized, or order supplies. They may also need to know insurance rules, billing practices, and be familiar with hospital or laboratory procedures. Other technical secretaries assist engineers or scientists. They may prepare much of the correspondence, maintain the technical library, and gather and edit materials for scientific papers.

Working Conditions

Secretaries usually work in offices with other professionals or in schools, hospitals, or doctors' offices. Their jobs often involve sitting for long periods. If they spend a lot of time typing, particularly at a video display terminal, they may encounter problems of eyestrain, stress and repetitive motion problems such as carpal tunnel syndrome.

Secretaries generally work a standard 40-hour week. In some cities, especially in the Northeast, the scheduled workweek is 37 hours or less.

Office work lends itself to alternative or flexible working arrangements, like telecommuting, and 1 secretary in 6 works part time. In addition, a significant number of secretaries work as temporaries. A few participate in job-sharing arrangements in which two people divide responsibility for a single job.

Employment

Secretaries held 3,576,000 jobs in 1990, making this one of the largest occupations in the U.S. economy. The following tabulation shows the distribution of employment by secretarial specialty.

Legal secretaries	80,000
Medical secretaries	232,000
All other secretaries	3,064,000

Secretaries are employed in organizations of every description. About one-half of all secretaries are employed in firms providing services, ranging from education and health to legal and business services. Others work for firms that engage in manufacturing, construction, wholesale and retail trade, transportation, and communications. Banks, insurance companies, investment firms, and real estate firms are important employers, as are Federal, State, and local government agencies.

Training, Other Qualifications, and Advancement

High school graduates may qualify for secretarial positions provided they have basic office skills. Today, however, knowledge of word processing, spreadsheet, and database management programs is increasingly important and most employers require it. Secretaries must be proficient in keyboarding and good at spelling, punctuation, grammar, and oral communication. Shorthand is necessary for some positions.

The skills needed for a secretarial job can be acquired in various ways. Formal training, especially for computer skills, may lead to higher paying jobs. Secretarial training ranges from high school vocational education programs that teach office practices, shorthand, and keyboarding skills to 1- to 2-year programs in secretarial science offered by business schools, vocational- technical institutes, and community colleges. Specialized training programs also are available for students planning to become medical or legal secretaries or office automation specialists.

Employers also look for communication and interpersonal skills, since secretaries must be tactful in their dealings with many different people. Discretion, judgment, organizational ability, and initiative are important for higher level secretarial positions.

As office automation continues to evolve, retraining and continuing education will remain an integral part of many jobs. Continuing changes in the office environment, for instance, have increased the demand for secretaries who are adaptable and versatile. Secretaries may have to attend classes to learn to operate new office equipment such as word processing equipment, information storage systems, personal computers, or new updated software packages.

The majority of openings for secretaries are filled by people who have not been working. Although some of these entrants have been in school or between jobs, many have been full-time homemakers, and some transfer from another clerical job. The majority of entrants are between 25 and 54 years of age. Many positions are filled by persons who have completed some college coursework.

Testing and certification for entry-level office skills is available through the Office Proficiency Assessment and Certification (OPAC) program offered by Professional Secretaries International (PSI). As secretaries gain experience, they can earn the designation Certified Professional Secretary (CPS) by passing a series of examinations given by the Institute for Certifying Secretaries, a department of PSI. This designation is recognized by a growing number of employers as the mark of excellence for senior- level office professionals. Similarly, those without experience who want to be certified as a legal support professional may be certified as an Accredited Legal Secretary (ALS) by the Certifying Board of the National Association of Legal Secretaries. They also administer an examination to certify a legal secretary with 3 years' experience as a Professional Legal Secretary (PLS).

Advancement for secretaries generally comes about by promotion to a more responsible secretarial position. Qualified secretaries who broaden their knowledge of their company's operations may be promoted to other positions such as senior or executive secretary, clerical supervisor, or office manager.

Secretaries with word processing experience can advance to jobs as word processing trainers, supervisors, or managers within their own firms or in a secretarial or word processing service bureau. They also can get jobs with manufacturers of word processing or computer equipment in positions such as instructor or sales representative.

Job Outlook

Employment of secretaries is expected to grow about as fast as the average for all occupations through the year 2005 in line with the general growth of the economy. Despite productivity gains made possible by office automation, there will continue to be strong demand for secretaries. Many employers currently complain of a shortage of first-rate secretaries. As a result, well-qualified and experienced secretaries will continue to be in great demand and should find many job opportunities.

In addition to job openings resulting from growth in demand for secretaries, an exceptionally large number of job openings will arise due to replacement needs. Every year several hundred thousand secretaries transfer to other occupations or leave the labor force. In this occupation, as in most, replacement needs are the main source of jobs.

Demand for secretaries will rise as the labor force grows and as more workers are employed in offices. The trend toward having secretaries assume more responsibilities traditionally reserved for managers and professionals also will stimulate demand.

Productivity, gained with the use of new office technologies, will moderate employment growth, however. In firms that have invested in electronic typewriters, word processors, or personal computers, secretaries can turn out significantly more work than when they used electric or manual typewriters. New office technologies such as electronic mail, facsimile machines, and voice message systems are used in a growing number of organizations. These and other sophisticated computer software capabilities are expected to be used more widely in the years ahead and may limit demand for secretaries.

Widespread use of automated equipment is already changing the workflow in many offices. Administrative duties are being reassigned and the functions of entire departments are being restructured. Large firms are experimenting with different methods of staffing their administrative support operations. In some cases, such traditional secretarial duties as typing or keyboarding, filing, copying, and accounting are being assigned to workers in other units or departments. In some law offices and physicians' offices, paralegals and medical assistants are taking over some tasks formerly done by secretaries. Professionals and managers increasingly do their own word processing rather than submit the work to secretaries and other support staff, as they did previously. In addition, there is a trend in many offices for groups of professionals and managers to "share" secretaries, as opposed to the traditional practice of having one secretary work for only one professional or manager.

Developments in office technology are certain to continue, and they will bring about further changes in the secretary's work environment. However, many of a secretary's job duties are of a personal interactive nature—such as scheduling conferences, receiving clients, and transmitting staff instructions—and hence not easily automated. Because automated equipment cannot substitute for the personal skills that are essential to the job, the need for secretaries will continue to grow.

Earnings

The average annual salary for all secretaries was $24,100 in 1990. Salaries vary a great deal, however, reflecting differences in skill, experience, and level of responsibility, ranging from $20,500 to $32,900.

Salaries in different parts of the country also vary; earnings generally are lowest in southern cities and highest in northern and western cities. In 1990, for example, secretaries averaged $25,400 a year in the Northeast, $23,700 in the Midwest, $25,000 in the West, and $22,000 in the South.

In addition, salaries vary by industry. Salaries of secretaries tend to be highest in transportation, legal services, and public utilities and lowest in retail trade and finance, insurance, and real estate.

The starting salary for inexperienced secretaries in the Federal Government was $15,200 a year in 1991. Secretaries emploployed by the Federal Government in 1990 averaged about $20,500.

Related Occupations

A number of other workers type, record information, and process paperwork. Among these are bookkeepers, receptionists, stenographers, personnel clerks, typists, legal assistants, medical assistants, and medical record technicians.

Sources of Additional Information

For career information, contact:

- Professional Secretaries International, 10502 NW Ambassador Dr., Kansas City, MO 64195-0404. (Phone: 1-816-891-6600.)

Persons interested in careers as legal secretaries can request information from:

- National Association of Legal Secretaries (International), 2250 East 73rd St., Suite 550, Tulsa, OK 74136.

State employment offices can provide information about job openings for secretaries.

Medical Secretaries

(D.O.T. 201)

Nature of the Work

Most organizations employ secretaries to perform and coordinate office activities and to ensure that information gets disseminated in a timely fashion to staff and clients. Managers, professionals, and other support staff rely on them to keep administrative operations under control. Their specific duties depend upon their level of responsibility and the type of firm in which they are employed.

Secretaries are responsible for a variety of administrative and clerical duties that are necessary to run and maintain organizations efficiently. They schedule appointments, give information to callers, organize and maintain files, fill out forms, and take dictation. They may also type letters, make travel arrangements, or contact clients. Secretaries also operate office equipment like facsimile machines, photocopiers, and telephones with voice mail capabilities.

In today's automated offices, secretaries increasingly use personal computers to run spreadsheet, word processing, data base management, desktop publishing, and graphics programs—

tasks previously handled by managers and professionals. Secretaries sometimes work in clusters of three or four so that they can help each other. Because they are relieved from dictation and typing, for example, they can support several members of the professional staff.

Executive secretaries or administrative assistants perform fewer clerical tasks than lower level secretaries. As well as receiving visitors, arranging conference calls, and answering letters, they may handle more complex responsibilities such as doing research, preparing statistical reports, and supervising and training other clerical staff.

In addition to general administrative duties, some secretaries do highly specialized work. Knowledge of technical terminology and procedures is required for these positions. Further specialization in various types of law is common among legal secretaries. They prepare correspondence and legal papers such as summonses, complaints, motions, and subpoenas under the supervision of an attorney. They also may review legal journals and assist in other ways with legal research. Medical secretaries transcribe dictation, prepare correspondence, and assist physicians or medical scientists with reports, speeches, articles, and conference proceedings. They record simple medical histories, arrange for patients to be hospitalized, or order supplies. They may also need to know insurance rules, billing practices, and be familiar with hospital or laboratory procedures. Other technical secretaries assist engineers or scientists. They may prepare much of the correspondence, maintain the technical library, and gather and edit materials for scientific papers.

Working Conditions

Secretaries usually work in offices with other professionals or in schools, hospitals, or doctors' offices. Their jobs often involve sitting for long periods. If they spend a lot of time typing, particularly at a video display terminal, they may encounter problems of eyestrain, stress and repetitive motion problems such as carpal tunnel syndrome.

Secretaries generally work a standard 40-hour week. In some cities, especially in the Northeast, the scheduled workweek is 37 hours or less.

Office work lends itself to alternative or flexible working arrangements, like telecommuting, and 1 secretary in 6 works part time. In addition, a significant number of secretaries work as temporaries. A few participate in job-sharing arrangements in which two people divide responsibility for a single job.

Employment

Secretaries held 3,576,000 jobs in 1990, making this one of the largest occupations in the U.S. economy. The following tabulation shows the distribution of employment by secretarial specialty.

Legal secretaries	280,000
Medical secretaries	232,000
All other secretaries	3,064,000

Secretaries are employed in organizations of every description. About one-half of all secretaries are employed in firms providing services, ranging from education and health to legal and business services. Others work for firms that engage in manufacturing, construction, wholesale and retail trade, transportation, and communications. Banks, insurance companies, investment firms, and real estate firms are important employers, as are Federal, State, and local government agencies.

Training, Other Qualifications, and Advancement

High school graduates may qualify for secretarial positions provided they have basic office skills. Today, however, knowledge of word processing, spreadsheet, and database management programs is increasingly important and most employers require it. Secretaries must be proficient in keyboarding and good at spelling, punctuation, grammar, and oral communication. Shorthand is necessary for some positions.

The skills needed for a secretarial job can be acquired in various ways. Formal training, especially for computer skills, may lead to higher paying jobs. Secretarial training ranges from high school vocational education programs that teach office practices, shorthand, and keyboarding skills to 1- to 2-year programs in secretarial science offered by business schools, vocational- technical institutes, and community colleges. Specialized training programs also are available for students planning to become medical or legal secretaries or office automation specialists.

Employers also look for communication and interpersonal skills, since secretaries must be tactful in their dealings with many different people. Discretion, judgment, organizational ability, and initiative are important for higher level secretarial positions.

As office automation continues to evolve, retraining and continuing education will remain an integral part of many jobs. Continuing changes in the office environment, for instance, have increased the demand for secretaries who are adaptable and versatile. Secretaries may have to attend classes to learn to operate new office equipment such as word processing equipment, information storage systems, personal computers, or new updated software packages.

The majority of openings for secretaries are filled by people who have not been working. Although some of these entrants have been in school or between jobs, many have been full-time homemakers, and some transfer from another clerical job. The majority of entrants are between 25 and 54 years of age. Many positions are filled by persons who have completed some college coursework.

Testing and certification for entry-level office skills is available through the Office Proficiency Assessment and Certification (OPAC) program offered by Professional Secretaries International (PSI). As secretaries gain experience, they can earn the designation Certified Professional Secretary (CPS) by passing a series of examinations given by the Institute for Certifying Secretaries, a department of PSI. This designation is recognized by a growing number of employers as the mark of excellence for senior-level office professionals. Similarly, those without experience who want to be certified as a legal support professional may be certified as an Accredited Legal Secretary (ALS) by the Certifying Board of the National Association of Legal Secretaries. They also administer an examination to certify a legal secretary with 3 years' experience as a Professional Legal Secretary (PLS).

Advancement for secretaries generally comes about by promotion to a more responsible secretarial position. Qualified secretaries who broaden their knowledge of their company's operations may be promoted to other positions such as senior or executive secretary, clerical supervisor, or office manager.

Secretaries with word processing experience can advance to jobs as word processing trainers, supervisors, or managers within their own firms or in a secretarial or word processing service bureau. They also can get jobs with manufacturers of word processing or computer equipment in positions such as instructor or sales representative.

Job Outlook

Employment of secretaries is expected to grow about as fast as the average for all occupations through the year 2005 in line with the general growth of the economy. Despite productivity gains made possible by office automation, there will continue to be strong demand for secretaries. Many employers currently complain of a shortage of first-rate secretaries. As a result, well-qualified and experienced secretaries will continue to be in great demand and should find many job opportunities.

In addition to job openings resulting from growth in demand for secretaries, an exceptionally large number of job openings will arise due to replacement needs. Every year several hundred thousand secretaries transfer to other occupations or leave the labor force. In this occupation, as in most, replacement needs are the main source of jobs.

Demand for secretaries will rise as the labor force grows and as more workers are employed in offices. The trend toward having secretaries assume more responsibilities traditionally reserved for managers and professionals also will stimulate demand.

Productivity, gained with the use of new office technologies, will moderate employment growth, however. In firms that have invested in electronic typewriters, word processors, or personal computers, secretaries can turn out significantly more work than when they used electric or manual typewriters. New office technologies such as electronic mail, facsimile machines, and voice message systems are used in a growing number of organizations. These and other sophisticated computer software capabilities are expected to be used more widely in the years ahead and may limit demand for secretaries.

Widespread use of automated equipment is already changing the workflow in many offices. Administrative duties are being reassigned and the functions of entire departments are being restructured. Large firms are experimenting with different methods of staffing their administrative support operations. In some cases, such traditional secretarial duties as typing or keyboarding, filing, copying, and accounting are being assigned to workers in other units or departments. In some law offices and physicians' offices, paralegals and medical assistants are taking over some tasks formerly done by secretaries. Professionals and managers increasingly do their own word processing rather than submit the work to secretaries and other support staff, as they did previously. In addition, there is a trend in many offices for groups of professionals and managers to "share" secretaries, as opposed to the traditional practice of having one secretary work for only one professional or manager.

Developments in office technology are certain to continue, and they will bring about further changes in the secretary's work environment. However, many of a secretary's job duties are of a personal interactive nature—such as scheduling conferences, receiving clients, and transmitting staff instructions—and hence not easily automated. Because automated equipment cannot substitute for the personal skills that are essential to the job, the need for secretaries will continue to grow.

Earnings

The average annual salary for all secretaries was $24,100 in 1990. Salaries vary a great deal, however, reflecting differences in skill, experience, and level of responsibility, ranging from $20,500 to $32,900.

Salaries in different parts of the country also vary; earnings generally are lowest in southern cities and highest in northern and western cities. In 1990, for example, secretaries averaged $25,400 a year in the Northeast, $23,700 in the Midwest, $25,000 in the West, and $22,000 in the South.

In addition, salaries vary by industry. Salaries of secretaries tend to be highest in transportation, legal services, and public utilities and lowest in retail trade and finance, insurance, and real estate.

The starting salary for inexperienced secretaries in the Federal Government was $15,200 a year in 1991. Secretaries employed by the Federal Government in 1990 averaged about $20,500.

Related Occupations

A number of other workers type, record information, and process paperwork. Among these are bookkeepers, receptionists, stenographers, personnel clerks, typists, legal assistants, medical assistants, and medical record technicians.

Sources of Additional Information

For career information, contact:
- Professional Secretaries International, 10502 NW Ambassador Dr., Kansas City, MO 64195-0404. (Phone: 1-816-891-6600.)

Persons interested in careers as legal secretaries can request information from:
- National Association of Legal Secretaries (International), 2250 East 73rd St., Suite 550, Tulsa, OK 74136.

State employment offices can provide information about job openings for secretaries.

Reservation and Transportation Ticket Agents and Travel Clerks

(D.O.T. 214.362-030; 238.167-010 and -014, .362-014, 67 except -022; and 248.382-010)

Nature of the Work

Each year, millions of Americans travel by plane, train, ship, bus, and automobile. Because so many people travel, it often is necessary to make reservations and plan trips well in advance. Reservations and transportation ticket agents and travel clerks are some of the workers who help people do this. These workers facilitate passenger travel in a variety of ways. They help passenger plan their trips by answering questions and offering suggestions on travel arrangements such as routes, time schedules, rates, and types of accommodation. They make and confirm transportation and hotel reservations, calculate expenses, and write and sell tickets. When passengers are about to embark on their trip, these agents and clerks check their baggage, direct them to the point of departure, and help them to board.

Reservation agents usually work in large central office answering customer telephone inquiries and booking reservations. Most agents have access to computer terminals and, by typing instructions on the keyboard, can quickly obtain the necessary information and make the reservations. Agents also can change or cancel reserva-

tions at the customer's request, simply by modifying the record on the computer. After the reservation has been and the ticket has been purchased, ticketing clerks compile and record the information, such as dates of travel and method of payment. The tickets then are sent to or picked up by the passenger.

Ticket agents are sometimes referred to by other titles, such as passenger agent, passenger-booking clerk, reservation clerk, ticket clerk, and ticket seller. In addition to selling tickets, they answer inquiries, check baggage, examine passport and visas, ensure passenger seating, and check in animals. Other ticket agents, more commonly known as gate agents, work in airports assisting passenger when boarding. Their duties include directing passengers to the correct boarding area, checking flight tickets, making boarding announcements, and assisting elderly, disabled, or young passengers when they board or depart the airplane.

Passenger rate clerks work for bus companies. They arrange trips by planning travel routes, computing rate, selling fares, and keeping customers informed of appropriate details. They also may arrange travel accommodations for tourists.

Most travel clerks are employed by automobile clubs. These workers, often called travel counselors, plan trips and offer travel suggestions for club members. Using a road map, they show the best route from the point of origin to the destination, as well as the return. They indicate the points of interest, restaurants, hotels, or other housing accommodations along the route and explain what emergency repair services are available during the trip. They make reservations for club members and calculate mileage.

Travel clerks also work in other settings, such as for hotels and motel, business firms, and government agencies. When guests or employees are planning trips, travel clerks assist them by providing them with the appropriate literature and information, answering questions, and offering suggestions. They make reservations, pick up and deliver tickets, arrange for visas, and make any other arrangements necessary for a safe and enjoyable trip.

Regardless of setting, reservation and transportation ticket agents and travel clerks must be knowledgeable about their companies' policies and procedures. They must be aware of the availability of special promotions and services and be able to answer any questions their customers may have.

Working Conditions

Those clerks who greet customers and visitors usually work in areas that are highly visible and carefully designed and furnished to make a good impression. Working conditions usually are pleasant; work stations are clean, well lighted, and relatively quiet. Reservation agents generally work away from the public, in work spaces where a number of agents sit, so the work space can be noisy.

Although most clerks work a standard 40-hour week, a sizable number work irregular schedules. Some jobs—those in the transportation industry, in particular—may require working evenings, late night shifts, weekends, and holidays. Employees with the least seniority usually are assigned the least desirable shifts.

For most clerks, the work in not physically demanding, although the repetitious nature of the job may be tiring. For example, reservation agents may spend all day answering telephone inquiries and entering reservations into a computer system. Prolonged expose to a video display terminal may lead to eye and musculoskeletal strain as well as complications to pregnancy.

Ticket agents are on their feet most of the time, and ticket agents may have to lift heavy baggage. During holidays and other busy periods, these clerks may find the work hectic due to the large number of guests or travelers who must be served. When service does not flow smoothly—because of cancelled flights or mishandled reservations, for example—these clerks act as a buffer between the establishment and its customers. Trying to pacify angry customers can be emotionally draining.

Employment

Reservation and transportation ticket agents and travel clerks held about 150,000 jobs in 1990. Nearly 7 of every 10 of these workers were employed by the airlines. Others worked for automobile clubs, hotels and other lodging places, railroad companies, and other companies that provide transportation services.

Although agents and clerks are found throughout the country, most work in downtown ticket and reservation offices and at large metropolitan transportation terminals, where most passenger business originates. The remainder work in smaller communities often served only by intercity bus or railroad lines.

Training, Other Qualifications, and Advancement

Although hiring requirements vary from industry to industry, a high school diploma or its equivalent usually is required. However, some high school students work part time as clerks outside of school hours. For some jobs, such as airline reservation and ticket agents, some college education is preferred.

With the exception of airline reservation and other passenger transportation agents, orientation and training for clerks is generally given on the job. They start work on the job under the guidance of a supervisor or an experienced clerk. They may need additional training in data processing of office machine operations to use computerized reservation and billing systems.

Most airline reservation agents learn their skills through formal company programs. They spend a few days in a classroom settings, learning company and industry policies that cover ticketing procedures and other matters related to the airline. They learn to use the computer to obtain information on schedules, seat availability, and fares; to reserve space for passengers; and to plan passenger itineraries. They must learn airport and airline code designations, and are tested on this knowledge. To maximize their productivity, reservation agents are expected to limit the time spend on each call without, of course, alienating customers. Thus, learning how to carry on a conversation in an organized, yet pleasing manner is an important part of their training. After completing classroom instruction, new agents work under supervisors or experienced agents for a short period of time. In contrast, automobile clues train their travel clerks on the job, without formal classes.

Many clerks continue to receive instruction after their initial training ends, with employers keeping them informed about new procedures and changes in company policies.

Because clerks must deal directly with the public, a good appearance and a pleasant personality are essential, as are problem-solving ability and good interpersonal skills. A good speaking voice is essential because these employees frequently use the telephone or public address systems. Courses useful to persons wanting to enter these occupations include basic math and English, geography, U.S. history, psychology, and public speaking. Typing ability and computer literacy often are needed.

Some employers may require applicants to take a typing test to gauge their skills. It also may be helpful for those in the lodging industry to be able to speak a foreign language.

Advancement for clerks comes about either by transfer to a more responsible job or by promotion to a supervisory position. In the airline industry, a ticket agent may advance to supervisory positions or may become a field sales agent. Additional training frequently is helpful in preparing information clerks for promotion.

Job Outlook

Employment of reservation and transportation ticket agents and travel clerks is expected to increase faster than the average for all occupations through the year 2005. Business travel, a significant contributor to airline, bus, rail, and automobile travel, will likely remain strong and spur employment growth. Increases in the number of two-earner families, as well as smaller families and delayed childbearing, should raise discretionary income and allow for more travel, also contributing to demand for these workers.

In addition, job openings will become available as workers transfer to other occupations, retire, or leave the labor force for other reasons. However, the number of openings will be smaller than that of other information clerks because turnover among reservation and transportation ticket agents and travel clerks is the lowest of all information clerks.

Applicants are likely to encounter considerable competition for openings, not only due to the relatively low turnover, but because he supply of qualified applicants far outstrips demand. Many people satisfy the entry requirements, and airline jobs, in particular, attract many applicants because of the travel benefits and glamour associated with the industry. Employment of reservation and transportation ticket agents and travel clerks is sensitive to cyclical swings in the economy.

During recessions, discretionary passenger travel declines, and transportation service companies are less likely to hire and may even lay off or demote agents and clerks.

Earnings

In 1990, medial weekly earnings of full-time information clerks were about $290. The middle 50 percent earned between $235 and $370. The bottom 10 percent earned less than $190, while the top percent earned more than $480. Earnings vary widely by occupation. Salaries of reservation and ticket agents tend to be significantly higher than for other clerks, while hotel and motel desk clerks tend to earn quite a bit less, as the following tabulation of median weekly earnings shows.

Reservation and transportation ticket agents
   and travel clerks. $390
Interviewing and new accounts clerks 300
Receptionists 270
Hotel and motel clerks. 230

In 1991, the Federal Government paid beginning information receptionists with a high school diploma or 6 months' experience $12,400 a year. The average salary for all information receptionists employed by the Federal Government was $16,800 a year in 1991.

In addition to their hourly wage, full-time information clerks usually receive the same package of fringe benefits as other workers in the organization. Typical benefits include health and life insurance, vacation and sick leave, paid holidays, and a pension plan. Those who work evenings, weekends, or holidays also may receive a shift differential. Some employers offer educational assistance to their employees. Reservation and transportation ticket agents and travel clerks receive free or very low cost travel on their company's carriers for themselves and their immediate family and, in some companies, free uniforms.

About 1 in 4 reservation and transportation ticket agents and travel clerks belongs to a labor union. Five unions cover most of the organized agents and clerks: The Amalgamated Transit Union; the International Association of Machinists and Aerospace Workers; the Transportation Communications Union; the International Brotherhood of Teamsters, Chauffeurs, Warehousemen and Helpers of America; and the Transport Workers Union of America.

Related Occupations

A number of other workers deal with the public, receive and provide information, or direct people to others who can assist them. Among these are customer service representatives, dispatchers, and telephone operators.

Sources of Additional Information

For information about job opportunities as reservation and transportation ticket agents and travel clerks, write the personnel manager of individual transportation companies. Address of airlines are available from:

- Air Transport Association of America, 1709 New York Ave. NW., Washington, DC 20006.

A brochure describing airline jobs is available from:

- Air Line Employees Association, 5600 South Central Ave., Chicago, IL 60638-3797.

Teacher Aides

(D.O.T. 099.327-010; 219.467-010; 249.367-074, -086)

Nature of the Work

Teacher aides, also called paraprofessionals, help classroom teachers in a variety of ways to give them more time for teaching. They help and supervise students in the classroom, cafeteria, schoolyard, or on field trips. They record grades, set up equipment, or help prepare materials for instruction. They also tutor and assist children in learning class material.

Aides' responsibilities vary greatly. Some teacher aides just handle routine nonteaching and clerical tasks. They grade tests and papers, check homework, keep health and attendance records, type, file, and duplicate materials. They may also stock supplies, operate audiovisual equipment, and keep classroom equipment in order. Other aides instruct children, under the direction and guidance of teachers. They work with students individually or in small groups—listening while students read, reviewing class work, or helping them find information for reports. Many aides have a combination of instructional and clerical duties, designed to most

effectively assist classroom teachers. Sometimes, aides take charge of special projects and prepare equipment or exhibits—for a science demonstration, for example.

Working Conditions

About half of all teacher aides work part time during the school year. Most work the traditional 9- to 10-month school year, usually in a classroom setting. Aides may also work outdoors supervising recess when weather allows and spend much of their time standing, walking, or kneeling. Seeing students develop and gain appreciation of the joy of learning can be very rewarding. However, working closely with students can be both physically and emotionally tiring.

Employment

Teacher aides held about 808,000 jobs in 1990. About 8 out of 10 worked in elementary and secondary schools, mostly in the lower grades. A significant number assisted special education teachers in working with children who have disabilities. Most of the others worked in child daycare centers and religious organizations.

Training, Other Qualifications, and Advancement

Educational requirements for teacher aides range from a high school diploma to some college training. Those aides with teaching responsibilities usually require more training than those who don't have teaching tasks. Increasingly, employers prefer aides who have some college training.

A number of 2-year and community colleges offer associate degree programs that prepare graduates to work as teacher aides. However, most teacher aides receive on-the-job training. Aides who tutor and review lessons with students must have a thorough understanding of class materials and instructional methods, and must be familiar with the organization and operation of a school. Aides must also know how to operate audiovisual equipment, keep records, and prepare instructional materials.

Teacher aides should enjoy working with children and be able to handle classroom situations with fairness and patience. Preference in hiring may be given to those with previous experience in working with children. Aides also must demonstrate initiative and a willingness to follow a teacher's directions. They must have good oral and writing skills and be able to communicate effectively with students and teachers. Clerical skills may also be necessary.

Some States have established certification and training requirements for general teacher aides. To qualify, an individual may need a high school diploma or general equivalency degree (G.E.D.), or even some college training.

Advancement for teacher aides, usually in the form of higher earnings or increased responsibility, comes primarily with experience or additional education. Some school districts provide time away from the job so that aides may take college courses. Aides who earn bachelor's degrees may become certified teachers.

Job Outlook

Employment of teacher aides is expected to grow faster than the average for all occupations through the year 2005. In addition, many jobs will become available because a relatively high proportion of workers transfer to other occupations or leave the labor force for family responsibilities, to return to school, or for other reasons.

In recent years, an increasing number of teacher aides have

been hired to assist teachers, and this trend is expected to continue. In addition, many teacher aides work in special education, a field that is expected to grow rapidly through the year 2005, further contributing to overall employment growth of teacher aides. However, teacher aide employment is sensitive to changes in State and local expenditures for education. Pressures on education budgets are greater in some States and localities than in others. A number of teacher aide positions, such as Head Start assistant teachers, are financed through Federal programs, which may also be affected by budget constraints.

Earnings

According to the Educational Research Service, aides involved in teaching activities earned an average of $7.77 an hour in 1990- 91; those performing only nonteaching activities averaged $7.43 an hour. Earnings varied by region and by work experience and academic qualifications. Many aides are covered by collective bargaining agreements and have health and pension benefits similar to those of the teachers in their schools.

Related Occupations

Teacher aides who instruct children have duties similar to those of preschool, elementary, and secondary school teachers and librarians. However, teacher aides do not have the same level of responsibility or training. The support activities of teacher aides and their educational backgrounds are similar to those of childcare workers, library technicians, and library assistants.

Sources of Additional Information

Information on teacher aides as well as on a wide range of education-related subjects, including teacher aide unionization, can be obtained from:

- American Federation of Teachers, Organizing Department, 555 New Jersey Ave. NW., Washington, DC 20001.

School superintendents and State departments of education can provide details about employment requirements.

course for admission. Some private vocational schools offer 4-
to 6-month courses in dental assisting, but these are not accredited by the Commission on Dental Accreditation.

Certification is available through the Dental Assisting National Board. Certification is an acknowledgment of an
assistant's qualifications and professional competpetence, but
usually is not required for employment. In several States that
have adopted standards for dental assistants who perform radiologic procedures, completion of the certification examination
meets those standards. Candidates may qualify to take the certification examination by graduating from an accredited training
program or by having 2 years of full-time experience as a dental
assistant. In addition, applicants must have taken a course in
cardiopulmonary resuscitation.

Without further education, advancement opportunities are
limited. Some dental assistants working the front office become
office managers. Others, working chairside, go back to school to
become dental hygienists.

Job Outlook

Employment of dental assistants is expected to grow faster
than the average for all occupations through the year 2005.
Population growth, higher incomes, more dental insurance,
and greater retention of natural teeth by middle-aged and older
people will fuel demand for dental services. Also, in the
future, dentists are likely to employ more assistants, for several reasons. Older dentists, who are less likely to employ
assistants, will leave and be replaced by recent graduates, who
are more likely to use one, or even two. In addition, as the
current surplus of dentists abates, dentists' workloads will
increase. As this happens, they are expected to hire more
assistants to perform routine tasks, so they may use their own
time for more profitable procedures.

Opportunities should be good for people entering the occupation. The slow growth in the youth labor force—traditionally the
principal source of supply for dental assisting—means that relatively fewer young adults will be available for entry level jobs
such as this. Qualified applicants should have little trouble
locating a job, while employers may find it necessary to raise
wages, offer better benefits, or try to attract older workers.

Most job openings for dental assistants will arise from the
need to replace assistants who leave the occupation. Each year
many assistants leave the job to take on family responsibilities,
return to school, or transfer to another occupation.

Earnings

In 1990, median weekly earnings for dental assistants working full time were about $300. According to the American Dental
Association, the average hourly wage in 1989 for all dental
assistants was $8.90. For chairside dental assistants without
experience, the average was $6.90 an hour.

Related Occupations

Dental assistants perform a variety of duties that do not
require the dentist's professional knowledge and skill. Workers
in other occupations supporting health practitioners include
medical assistants, chiropractor assistants, ophthalmic medical
assistants, optometric assistants, podiatric assistants, and veteri-
nary technicians.

Sources of Additional Information

Information about career opportunities, scholarships, accred-
ited dental assistant programs, and requirements for certification
is available from:
- American Dental Assistants Association, 919 N. Michigan
  Ave., Suite 3400, Chicago, IL 60611.
- Commission on Dental Accreditation, American Dental Asso-
  ciation, 211 E. Chicago Ave., Suite 1814, Chicago, IL 60611.
- Dental Assisting National Board, Inc., 216 E. Ontario St.,
  Chicago, IL 60611.

Flight Attendants

(D.O.T. 352.367-010)

Nature of the Work

Flight attendants are aboard almost all passenger planes to
look after the passengers' flight safety and comfort.

At least 1 hour before each flight, attendants are briefed by
the captain on such things as expected weather conditions and
special passenger problems. The attendants see that the passenger cabin is in order, that supplies of food, beverages, blankets,
and reading material are adequate, and that first aid kits and other
emergency equipment are aboard and in working order. As
passengers board the plane, attendants greet them, check their
tickets, and assist them in storing coats and carry-on luggage.

Before the plane takes off, attendants instruct passengers in the
use of emergency equipment and check to see that all passengers
have their seat belts fastened and seat backs forward. In the air, they
answer questions about the flight, distribute magazines and pillows,
and help care for small children and elderly and handicapped
persons. They may administer first aid to passengers who become
ill. Attendants also serve cocktails and other refreshments and, on
many flights, heat and distribute precooked meals. After the plane
has landed, the flight attendants assist passengers as they leave the
plane. They then prepare reports on medications given to passengers, lost and found articles, and cabin equipment conditions. Some
flight attendants straighten up the plane's cabin.

Assisting passengers in the rare event of an emergency is the
most important function of attendants. This may range from
reassuring passengers during occasional encounters with strong
turbulence to opening emergency exits and inflating evacuation
chutes following an emergency landing.

Lead or first flight attendants aboard planes oversee the work
of the other attendants while performing most of the same duties.

Working Conditions

Since airlines operate around the clock year round, attendants
may work at night and on holidays and weekends. They usually fly
75 to 85 hours a month. In addition, they generally spend about 75
to 85 hours a month on the ground preparing planes for flight,
writing reports following completed flights, and waiting for planes
that arrive late. Because of variations in scheduling and limitations
on flying time, many attendants have 11 or more days off each
month. Attendants may be away from their home bases at least
one-third of the time. During this period, the airlines provide hotel
accommodations and an allowance for meal expenses.

The combination of free time and discount air fares provides flight attendants the opportunity to travel and see new places. However, the work can be strenuous and trying. Short flights require speedy service if meals are served. A rough flight can make serving drinks and meals difficult. Attendants stand during much of the flight and must remain pleasant and efficient regardless of how tired they are or how demanding passengers may be. Flight attendants are susceptible to injury because of the job demands in a moving aircraft.

Employment

Flight attendants held about 101,000 jobs in 1990. Commercial airlines employed the vast majority of all flight attendants, most of whom were stationed in major cities at the airlines' home bases. A small number of flight attendants worked for large companies that operate their own aircraft for business purposes.

Training , Other Qualifications, and Advancement

The airlines like to hire poised, tactful, and resourceful people who can deal comfortably with strangers. Applicants usually must be at least 19 to 21 years old, but some airlines have higher minimum age requirements. Flight attendants must have excellent health, good vision, and the ability to speak clearly.

Applicants must be high school graduates. Those having several years of college or experience in dealing with the public are preferred. Flight attendants for international airlines generally must speak an appropriate foreign language fluently.

Most large airlines require that newly hired flight attendants complete 4 to 6 weeks of intensive training in their own schools. The airlines that do not operate schools generally send new employees to the school of another airline. Transportation to the training centers and an allowance for board, room, and school supplies may be provided. Trainees learn emergency procedures such as evacuating an airplane, operating an oxygen system, and giving first aid. Attendants also are taught flight regulations and duties, and company operations and policies. Trainees receive instruction on personal grooming and weight control. Trainees for the international routes get additional instruction in passport and customs regulations and dealing with terrorism. Towards the end of their training, students go on practice flights. Attendants must receive 12 to 14 hours of training in emergency procedures and passenger relations annually.

After completing initial training, flight attendants are assigned to one of their airline's bases. New attendants are placed in "reserve status" and are called on either to staff extra flights or fill in for attendants who are sick or on vacation. Reserve attendants on duty must be available on short notice. Attendants usually remain on reserve for at least 1 year; at some cities, it may take 5 years or longer to advance from reserve status. Advancement takes longer today than in the past because experienced attendants are remaining in this career for more years than they used to. Attendants who no longer are on reserve bid for regular assignments. Because these assignments are based on seniority, usually only the most experienced attendants get their choice of base and flights.

Some attendants transfer to flight service instructor, customer service director, recruiting representative, or various other administrative positions.

Job Outlook

Employment of flight attendants is expected to grow much faster than the average for all occupations through the year 2005. Growth in population and income is expected to increase the number of airline passengers. Airlines enlarge their capacity by increasing the number and size of planes in operation. Since Federal Aviation Administration safety rules require one attendant for every 50 seats, more flight attendants will be needed.

Despite this above average growth, competition for jobs as flight attendants is expected to remain very keen because the number of applicants is expected to greatly exceed the number of job openings. The glamour of the airline industry and the opportunity to travel and meet people attract many applicants. Those with at least 2 years of college and experience in dealing with the public have the best chance of being hired.

As more career-minded people enter this occupation, job turnover—which traditionally has been very high—will decline. Nevertheless, most job openings are expected from the need to replace attendants who stop working or transfer to other occupations.

Employment of flight attendants is sensitive to cyclical swings in the economy. During recessions, when the demand for air travel declines, many flight attendants are put on part-time status or laid off. Until demand increases, few new attendants are hired.

Earnings

Beginning flight attendants had median earnings of about $13,000 a year in 1990, according to data from the Association of Flight Attendants. Flight attendants with 6 years of flying experience had median annual earnings of about $20,000, while some senior flight attendants earned as much as $35,000 a year. Flight attendants receive extra compensation for overtime and for night and international flights. In addition, flight attendants and their immediate families are entitled to reduced fares on their own and most other airlines.

Many flight attendants belong to the Association of Flight Attendants. Others are members of the Transport Workers Union of America or several other unions.

Flight attendants are required to buy uniforms and wear them while on duty. Uniform replacement items are usually paid for by the company. The airlines generally provide a small allowance to cover cleaning and upkeep of the uniforms.

Related Occupations

Other jobs that involve helping people and require the ability to be pleasant even under trying circumstances include tour guide, gate agent, host or hostess, waiter or waitress, and camp counselor.

Sources of Additional Information

Information about job opportunities in a particular airline and the qualifications required may be obtained by writing to the personnel manager of the company. For addresses of airline companies and information about job opportunities and salaries, contact:

- Future Aviation Professionals of America, 4959 Massachusetts Blvd., Atlanta, GA 30337. (This organization may be called toll free at 800-Jet-Jobs.)

Gardeners and Groundskeepers

(D.O.T. 406.381-010, .683-010, .684-010, -014,- 018, .687-010; 408.161-010, .684-010, and .687-014)

Nature of the Work

Attractively designed, healthy, and well-maintained lawns, gardens, trees, and shrubbery create a positive first impression, establish a peaceful mood, and increase property values. A growing number of individuals and organizations rely on gardeners and groundskeepers to care for them.

Some gardeners work on large construction projects, such as office buildings and shopping malls. Following the plans drawn up by the landscape architect, gardeners plant trees, hedges, and flowering plants and apply mulch for protection. For residential customers, gardeners terrace hillsides, build retaining walls, and install patios, as well as plant trees and shrubs.

Gardeners working for homeowners, estates, and public gardens feed, water, and prune the flowering plants and trees and mow and water the lawn. Some landscape gardeners, called lawn service workers, specialize in maintaining lawns and shrubs for a fee. A growing number of residential and commercial clients, such as managers of office buildings, shopping malls, multiunit residential buildings, and hotels and motels favor this full-service landscape maintenance. These workers perform a full range of duties, including mowing, edging, trimming, fertilizing, dethatching, and mulching. Those working for chemical lawn service firms are more specialized. They inspect lawns for problems and apply fertilizers, weed killers, and other chemicals.

Groundskeepers on athletic fields, golf courses, cemeteries, or parks have more varied duties, doing the work of a maintenance mechanic, as well. Groundskeepers who care for athletic fields keep natural and artificial turf fields in top condition and mark out boundaries and paint team logos and names before events. Groundskeepers must make sure the underlying soil on natural turf fields has the proper consistency to sustain new sod. They generally resod the entire field once a year in order to provide the best possible footing for the athletes. They regularly mow, water, fertilize, and aerate the fields and control insects, weeds, and crabgrass with chemicals and apply fungicides to prevent diseases. Groundskeepers vacuum and disinfect synthetic turf after use in order to prevent growth of harmful bacteria. They also periodically remove the turf and replace the cushioning pad.

Greenskeepers maintain golf courses. They do many of the same things athletic turf groundskeepers do. In addition, greenskeepers periodically relocate the holes on putting greens to eliminate uneven wear of the turf and add interest and challenge to the game. Greenskeepers also keep canopies, benches, ball washers, and tee markers repaired and freshly painted.

Cemetery workers prepare graves and maintain cemetery grounds. They dig graves to specified depth, generally using a back-hoe. They may place concrete slabs on the bottom and around the sides of the grave to line it for greater support. When readying a site for the burial ceremony, they position the casket-lowering device over the grave, cover the immediate area with an artificial grass carpet, erect a canopy, and arrange folding chairs to accommodate mourners. They regularly mow grass, prune shrubs, plant flowers, and remove debris from graves. They also must periodically build the ground up around new gravesites to compensate for settling.

Groundskeepers in parks and recreation facilities care for lawns, trees, and shrubs, maintain athletic fields and playgrounds, clean buildings, and keep parking lots, picnic areas, and other public spaces free of litter. They may also remove snow and ice from roads and walkways, erect and dismantle snow fences, and maintain swimming pools. These workers inspect buildings, and equipment, make needed repairs, and keep everything freshly painted.

Gardeners and groundskeepers use handtools such as shovels, rakes, pruning saws, saws, hedge and brush trimmers, and axes, as well as power lawnmowers, chain saws, snow blowers, and electric clippers. Some use equipment such as tractors and twin-axle vehicles. Park, school, cemetery, and golf course groundskeepers may use sod cutters to harvest sod that will be replanted elsewhere. Athletic turf groundskeepers use magnetic sweepers and vacuums and other devices to remove water from athletic fields. In addition, some workers in large operations use spraying and dusting equipment.

Working Conditions

Many of the jobs for gardeners and groundskeepers are seasonal, mainly in the spring and summer, when cleanup, planting, and mowing and trimming take place. Gardeners and groundskeepers work outdoors in all kinds of weather. They frequently are under pressure to get the job completed, especially when they are preparing for scheduled events, such as athletic competitions or burials.

They may work with pesticides, insecticides, and other chemicals and must exercise safety precautions to prevent exposure. They also work with dangerous equipment and tools such as power lawnmowers, chain saws, and electric clippers.

Employment

In 1990, gardeners and groundskeepers held about 874,000 jobs. About 3 out of 10 worked for lawn and garden services. About 1 out of 10 worked for private households and estates. Many worked for firms that operate real estate; for local government, including parks departments, and recreational facilities such as golf courses, race tracks, and amusement parks. Others were employed by schools, hospitals, cemeteries, hotels, retail nurseries, and garden stores.

Approximately 1 out of 5 was self-employed, providing landscape maintenance directly to customers on a contract basis.

About 1 out of 3 gardeners and groundskeepers worked part time, most likely students working their way through school. Others working part time were older workers who might have been cutting back their hours as they approached retirement.

Training , Other Qualifications, and Advancement

Entrance requirements for gardeners and groundskeepers are modest. Most entrants are high school graduates, but a high school diploma is not necessary for many jobs. Some people gain experience as a home gardener or by working in a nursery, a sod production operation, or for a tree service. High school students may gain experience in the Future Farmers of America.

There are no national standards for gardeners and groundskeepers, but some States require certification for workers who use chemicals extensively. Certification requirements vary, but usually include passing a test on the proper and safe use of insecticides, pesticides, and fungicides.

Employers prefer applicants with a good driving record and

some experience driving a truck. Workers who deal directly with customers must get along well with people. Employers also look for responsible, self-motivated individuals, since many gardeners and groundskeepers work with little supervision.

Courses in agronomy, horticulture, and botany are helpful for advancement. There are many 2- and 4-year programs in landscape management, interiorscape, and ornamental horiculture. Courses include turfgrass management, equipment use and care, landscape design, plant biology, and irrigation. There are cooperative education programs in which students work alternate semesters or quarters for a lawn care or landscape contractor. Generally, a gardener or groundskeeper can advance to supervisor after several years of progressively responsible experience, including the demonstrated ability to deal effectively with both coworkers and customers. Supervisors can advance to grounds manager or superintendent for a golf course or other athletic facility, a cemetery, a campus, a school system, or manager of a lawn maintenance firm. Many gardeners and groundskeepers become landscape contractors.

The Professional Grounds Management Society offers certification to those managers who have a combination of 8 years of experience and formal education beyond high school.

Job Outlook

Employment of gardeners and groundskeepers is expected to increase much faster than the average for all occupations through the year 2005 in response to increasing demand for gardening and landscaping services. Despite this growth, most job openings are expected to result from the need to replace workers who transfer to other occupations or leave the labor force.

Expected growth in the construction of commercial and industrial buildings, shopping malls, homes, highways, and parks and recreational facilities should stimulate demand for these workers. Developers are increasingly using landscaping services, both interior and exterior, to attract prospective buyers and tenants. In addition, owners of many existing buildings and facilities are upgrading their landscaping. Also, a growing number of homeowners are ue using lawn maintenance and landscaping services to enhance the beauty and value of their property as well as to conserve their leisure time. Growth in the number of parks, athletic fields, golf courses, cemeteries, and similar facilities also can be expected to add to the demand for these workers.

Job openings should be plentiful because the occupation is large and turnover is high. This occupation attracts many young people who are not committed to the occupation. Some take gardening or groundskeeping jobs to earn money for school, others only take these jobs until a better paying job is found. Because wages for beginners are low and the work is physically demanding, many employers have difficulty attracting enough workers to fill all openings.

Earnings

Median weekly earnings of gardeners and groundskeepers were about $270 in 1990; the middle 50 percent earned between $200 and $330. The lowest 10 percent earned less than $170, and the top 10 percent earned more than $450 a week.

According to a survey conducted by Lawn Care Industry Magazine, those who worked for chemical lawn care firms averaged between $7.20 and $8.50 an hour in 1990. In 1990, according to The Professional Grounds Management Society, seasonal laborers averaged $6.10 an hour; permanent, year-round laborers, $7.33; and supervisors $9.40. Managers, who generally had a 4 year degree, averaged $34,292 a year.

Related Occupations

Gardeners and groundskeepers perform the most of their work outdoors. Others whose jobs may be performed outdoors are construction workers, nursery workers, farmers, horticultural workers, tree surgeon helpers, tree trimmers and pruners, and forest conservation workers.

Sources of Additional Information

For career information, contact:
- Associated Landscape Contractors of America, Inc., 405 N. Washington St., Suite 104, Falls Church, VA 22046.
- National Landscape Association, 1250 I St. NW., Washington, DC 20005.

For career and certification information, contact:
- Professional Grounds Management Society, 10402 Ridgland Rd., Suite 4, Cockeysville, MD 21030.

Guards

(D.O.T. 372.563, .567-010, .667-010, -014, and -030 through -038; 376.667-010; and 379.667-010)

Nature of the Work

Guards, also called security officers, patrol and inspect property to protect against fire, theft, vandalism, and illegal entry. Their duties vary with the size, type, and location of their employer.

In office buildings, banks, hospitals, and department stores, guards protect records, merchandise, money, and equipment. In department stores, they often work with undercover detectives to watch for theft by customers or store employees.

At ports, airports, and railroads, guards protect merchandise being shipped as well as property and equipment. They screen passengers and visitors for weapons, explosives, and other contraband. They ensure that nothing is stolen while being loaded or unloaded, and watch for fires, prowlers, and trouble among work crews. Sometimes they direct traffic.

Guards who work in public buildings, such as museums or art galleries, protect paintings and exhibits. They also answer routine questions from visitors and sometimes guide tours.

In factories, laboratories, government buildings, data processing centers, and military bases where valuable property or information—such as information on new products, computer codes, or defense secrets—must be protected, guards check the credentials of persons and vehicles entering and leaving the premises. University, park, or recreation guards perform similar duties and also may issue parking permits and direct traffic. Golf course patrollers prevent unauthorized persons from using the facility and help keep play running smoothly.

At social affairs, sports events, conventions, and other public gatherings, guards provide information, assist in crowd control, and watch for persons who may cause trouble. Some guards work as "bouncers" and patrol places of entertainment such as nightclubs to preserve order among customers and to protect property.

Armored car guards protect money and valuables during transit. Bodyguards protect individuals from bodily injury, kidnapping, or invasion of privacy.

In a large organization, a security officer often is in charge of the guard force; in a small organization, a single worker may be responsible for all security measures. Patrolling usually is done on foot, but if the property is large, guards may make their rounds by car or motor scooter. As more businesses purchase advanced electronic security systems to protect their property, more guards are being assigned to stations where they monitor perimeter security, environmental functions, communications, and other systems. In many cases, these guards maintain radio contact with other guards patrolling on foot or in motor vehicles. Some guards use computers to store information on matters relevant to security—for example, visitors or suspicious occurrences—during their hours on duty.

As they make their rounds, guards check all doors and windows, see that no unauthorized persons remain after working hours, and ensure that fire extinguishers, alarms, sprinkler systems, furnaces, and various electrical and plumbing systems are working properly. They sometimes set thermostats or turn on lights for janitorial workers.

Guards usually are uniformed and may carry a nightstick and gun, although the use of guns is decreasing. They also may carry a flashlight, whistle, two-way radio, and a watch clock—a device that indicates the time at which they reach various checkpoints.

Correction officers—guards who work in prisons and other correctional institutions—are discussed separately in this section of the book.

Working Conditions

Guards work indoors and outdoors patrolling buildings, industrial plants, and grounds. Indoors, they may be stationed at a guard desk to monitor electronic security and surveillance devices or to check the credentials of persons entering or leaving the premises. They also may be stationed at gate shelters or may patrol grounds in all weather.

Because guards often work alone, there may be no one nearby to help if an accident or injury occurs. Some large firms, therefore, use a reporting service that enables guards to be in constant contact with a central station outside the plant. If they fail to transmit an expected signal, the central station investigates. Guard work is usually routine, but guards must be constantly alert for threats to themselves and to the property that they are protecting. Guards who work during the day may have a great deal of contact with other employees and members of the public.

Many guards work alone at night; the usual shift lasts 8 hours. Some employers have three shifts, and guards rotate to divide daytime, weekend, and holiday work equally. Guards usually eat on the job instead of taking a regular break.

Employment

Guards held about 883,000 jobs in 1990. Industrial security firms and guard agencies employed over one-half of all guards. These organizations provide security services on contract, assigning their guards to buildings and other sites as needed. The remainder were in-house guards, employed in large numbers by banks; building management companies; hotels; hospitals; retail stores; restaurants and bars; schools, colleges, and universities; and Federal, State, and local governments.

Although guard jobs are found throughout the country, most are located in metropolitan areas.

Training, Other Qualifications, and Advancement

Most employers prefer guards who are high school graduates. Applicants with less than a high school education also can qualify if they pass reading and writing tests and demonstrate competence in following written and oral instructions. Some jobs require a driver's license. Employers also seek people who have had experience in the military police or in State and local police departments. Most persons who enter guard jobs have prior work experience, although it is usually unrelated. Because of limited formal training requirements and flexible hours, this occupation attracts some persons seeking a second job. For some entrants, retired from military careers or other protective services, guard employment is a second career.

Applicants are expected to have good character references, no police record, good health—especially in hearing and vision— and good personal habits such as neatness and dependability. They should be mentally alert, emotionally stable, and physically fit in order to cope with emergencies. Some employers require applicants to take a polygraph examination or a written test of honesty, attitudes, and other personal qualities. Most employers require applicants and experienced workers to submit to drug screening tests as a condition of employment.

Virtually all States and the District of Columbia have licensing or registration requirements for guards who work for contract security agencies. Registration generally requires that employment of an individual as a guard be reported to the licensing authorities—the State police department or other State licensing commission. To be granted a license as a guard, individuals generally must be 18 years old, have no convictions for perjury or acts of violence, pass a background examination, and complete classroom training in such subjects as property rights, emergency procedures, and seizure of suspected criminals. In 1990, only about five States and the District of Columbia had licensing requirements for in-house guards.

Candidates for guard jobs in the Federal Government must have some experience as a guard and pass a written examination. Armed Forces experience also is an asset. For most Federal guard positions, applicants must qualify in the use of firearms.

The amount of training guards receive varies. Training requirements generally are increasing as modern, highly sophisticated security systems become more commonplace. Many employers give newly hired guards instruction before they start the job and also provide several weeks of on-the-job training. Guards receive training in protection, public relations, report writing, crisis deterrence, first aid, drug control, and specialized training relevant to their particular assignment. Guards employed at establishments that place a heavy emphasis on security usually receive extensive formal training. For example, guards at nuclear power plants may undergo several months of training before being placed on duty under close supervision. Guards may be taught to use firearms, administer first aid, operate alarm systems and electronic security equipment, and spot and deal with security problems. Guards who are authorized to carry firearms may be periodically tested in their use according to State or local laws. Some guards are periodically tested for strength and endurance.

Although guards in small companies receive periodic salary increases, advancement is likely to be limited. However, most large organizations use a military type of ranking that offers advancement in position and salary. Higher level guard experience may enable persons to transfer to police jobs that offer higher pay and greater opportunities for advancement. Guards with some college education may advance to jobs that involve administrative duties or the prevention of espionage and sabotage. A few guards with management skills open their own contract security guard agencies.

Job Outlook

Job openings for persons seeking work as guards are expected to be plentiful through the year 2005. High turnover in this large occupation ranks it among those providing the greatest number of job openings in the entire economy. Many opportunities are expected for persons seeking full-time employment, as well as for those seeking part-time or second jobs at night or on weekends. However, some competition is expected for in-house guard positions. Compared to contract security guards, in-house guards enjoy higher earnings and benefits, greater job security, and more advancement potential, and are usually given more training and responsibility.

Employment of guards is expected to grow faster than the average for all occupations through the year 2005. Increased concern about crime, vandalism, and terrorism will heighten the need for security in and around plants, stores, offices, and recreation areas. The level of business investment in increasingly expensive plant and equipment is expected to rise, resulting in growth in the number of guard jobs. Demand for guards will also grow as private security firms increasingly perform duties—such as monitoring crowds at airports and providing security in courts—formerly handled by government police officers and marshals. Because engaging the services of a security guard firm is easier and less costly than assuming direct responsibility for hiring, training, and managing a security guard force, job growth is expected to be concentrated among contract security guard agencies.

Guards employed by industrial security and guard agencies occasionally are laid off when the firm at which they work does not renew its contract with their agency. Most are able to find employment with other agencies, however. Guards employed directly by the firm at which they work are seldom laid off because a plant or factory must still be protected even when economic conditions force it to close temporarily.

Earnings

Guards working in 23 urban areas averaged an estimated $6.28 an hour in 1990. Those working in the Midwestern States earned more than the average, while guards employed in the South earned somewhat less. Hourly wages of guards were estimated to average $10.63 in public utilities and transportation; $11.83 in manufacturing; $8.45 in wholesale trade; $8.78 in banking, finance, insurance, and real estate; $6.96 in retail trade; and $5.61 in the various service industries, including security and guard agencies. Guards with specialized training or some supervisory responsibilities averaged $9.37 an hour, while those with less training and responsibility averaged $5.99 an hour. Guards employed by industrial security and guard agencies generally started at or slightly above the minimum wage, which was $4.25 an hour in 1991.

Unionized in-house guards tend to earn more than the average. Many guards are represented by the United Plant Guard Workers Of America. Other guards belong to the International Union of Guards or the International Union Of Security Officers.

Depending on their experience, newly hired guards in the Federal Government earned between $13,500 and $15,200 a year in 1991. Guards employed by the Federal Government averaged about $19,200 a year in 1990. These workers usually receive overtime pay as well as a wage differential for the second and third shifts.

Related Occupations

Guards protect property, maintain security, and enforce regulations for entry and conduct in the establishments at which they work. Related security and protective service occupations include: Bailiffs, border guards, correction officers, deputy sheriffs, fish and game wardens, house or store detectives, police officers, and private investigators.

Sources of Additional Information

Further information about work opportunities for guards is available from local employers and the nearest State employment service office.

Information about registration and licensing requirements for guards may be obtained from the State licensing commission or the State police department. In States where local jurisdictions establish licensing requirements, contact a local government authority such as the sheriff, county executive, or city manager.

Information about Federal Government contract guard job requirements is presented in the *Contract Guard Information Manual*, GPO Publication No. 022-00-00192-2, which may be purchased from the U.S. Government Printing Office, Washington, DC 20402.

Homemaker-Home Health Aides

(D.O.T. 079.224-010; 309.354-010; and 354.377-014)

Nature of the Work

Homemaker-home health aides help elderly, disabled, and ill persons live in their own homes instead of in a institution. Some homemaker-home health aides work with families in which a parent is incapacitated and small children need care. Others help discharged hospital patients who have relatively short-term needs. Most homemaker-home health aides, however, work with elderly or disabled clients who require more extensive care than spouse, family, or friends can or are willing to provide informally. These workers sometimes are called home care aides and personal care attendants or aides, too.

Homemaker-home health aides provide housekeeping services, personal care, and emotional support for their clients. They perform light housekeeping chores: Cleaning a client's room, kitchen, and bathroom; doing the laundry; and changing bed linens. Aides may also plan meals (including special diets), shop for food, and cook.

Home health aides provide personal care services, also known as "hands on" care because they physically touch the patient. These aides may assist clients with bathing, toileting, hair care, and moving from bed to a chair or another room. They may also check pulse, temperature, and respiration; help with simple prescribed exercises; and assist with medication routines. Occasionally, they may change nonsterile dressings, use special equipment such as a hydraulic lift, or assist with braces or artificial limbs.

Homemaker-home health aides also provide instruction and psychological support. For example, they may assist in toilet training a severely mentally handicapped child or just listen to clients talk about their problems.

In home care agencies, homemaker-home health aides are supervised by a registered nurse, a physical therapist, or a social worker, who assigns them specific duties. Aides report changes in the client's condition to the supervisor or case manager. Homemaker- home health aides also participate in reviews of clients' cases by the team caring for the client—registered nurses, therapists, and other health professionals.

Working Conditions

The homemaker-home health aide's daily routine may vary. A job can entail going to the same home every day for months or even years. More commonly, however, aides work with a number of different clients, each job lasting from a few hours, days, or weeks. Aides often go to four or five clients on the same day.

Surroundings differ from case to case. Some homes are neat and pleasant, while others are untidy or depressing. Some clients are angry, abusive, depressed, or otherwise difficult; others are pleasant and cooperative.

Homemaker-home health aides generally work on their own with periodic visits by their supervisor. They have detailed instructions explaining when to visit clients and what services to perform.

Most aides generally travel by public transportation, but some need an automobile. In any event, they are responsible for getting to the client's home. Aides may spend a good portion of the working day traveling from one client to another.

Employment

Homemaker-home health aides held about 391,000 jobs in 1990. Most aides are employed by homemaker-home health agencies, home health agencies, visiting nurse associations, hospitals, public health and welfare departments, and temporary help firms. Self-employed aides have no agency affiliation or supervision, and accordingly accept clients, set fees, and arrange work schedules on their own.

Training , Other Qualifications, and Advancement

Training requirements for homemaker-home health aides are changing. The Federal Goverment has enacted guidelines for home health aides whose employers receive reimbursement from Medicare. The Federal law requires home health aides to pass a competency test covering 12 areas: Communication skills; observation, reporting, and documentation of patient status and the care or services furnished; reading and recording vital signs; basic infection control procedures; basic elements of body function and changes; maintenance of a clean, safe, and healthy environment; recognition of and procedures for emergencies; the physical, emotional, and developmental characteristics of the patients served; personal hygiene and grooming; safe transfer techniques; normal range of motion and positioning; and basic nutrition. A home aide may also take training before taking the competency test. The Federal law requires at least 75 hours of classroom and practical training supervised by a registered nurse. Training and testing programs may be offered by the employing agency, but they must meet the approval of the Health Care Financing Administration. Training programs may vary depending upon State regulations. Thirteen States have specific laws on personnel care services.

The National HomeCaring Council, part of The Foundation for Hospice and Home Care, offers a National Homemaker-Home Health Aide certification. The certification is a voluntary demonstration that the individual has met industry standards.

Successful homemaker-home health aides like to help people and do not mind hard work. They have a sense of responsibility, compassion, emotional stability, and a cheerful disposition. Aides should be tactful, honest, and discreet since they work in private homes.

Homemaker-home health aides must be in good health. A physical examination including State regulated tests like for tuberculosis may be required.

Advancement is limited. In some agencies, workers start out performing homemaker duties, such as cleaning. With experience and training, they may take on personal care duties. The most experienced aides may assist with medical equipment such as ventilators, which help patients breathe.

Job Outlook

Employment of homemaker-home health aides is expected to grow much faster than the average for all occupations through the year 2005. Changing demographics will play a major role in this growth. The number of people in their seventies and beyond is projected to rise substantially. This age group is characterized by mounting health problems that require some assistance. Also, there will be an increasing reliance on home care for patients of all ages. This trend reflects several developments: Efforts to contain costs by moving patients out of hospitals as quickly as possible; the realization that treatment can be more effective in familiar surroundings rather than clinical surroundings; and the development of portable medical equipment for in-home treatment.

The extent to which these growth factors are translated into jobs for home care workers will depend on the availability of public and private funds for in-home services; willingness of family, friends, and neighbors to provide care; and the role of alternative arrangements, including adult day care and life care communities.

Job prospects will be excellent for people seeking work as homemaker-home health aides. In addition to jobs created by the increase in demand for these workers, replacement needs are expected to produce numerous openings. Turnover is high, a reflection of the relatively low skill requirements, low pay, and high emotional demands of the work. Persons who are interested in this work and suited for it should have no trouble finding and keeping a job, particularly those with experience or training as homemaker-home health aides or nursing aides. Although only a small number of men currently are employed in the occupation, more are needed to care for men who prefer a male aide. The demand for male homemaker-home health aides is increasing with the spread of AIDS.

Earnings

Earnings for homemaker-home health aides vary considerably. Some earn the Federal minimum wage—$4.25 an hour. Howevwever, employers may pay workers younger than 20 a lower training wage for up to 6 months. Homemaker-home health aides in large cities that have high living costs generally have the highest wages, up to $10 an hour. Most employers give slight pay increases with experience and added responsibility.

Aides usually are paid only for the time worked in the home. They normally are not paid for travel time between jobs.

Benefits vary even more than wages. Some employers offer a full package of vacation and sick leave, health and life insurance, and a retirement plan. Others hire only "on-call" hourly workers, with no benefits.

Related Occupations

Homemaker-home health aide is a service occupation that combines duties of health workers and social service workers. Workers in related occupations that involve personal contact to help or instruct others include attendants in children's institutions, childcare attendants in schools, child monitors, companions, nursing aides, nursery school attendants, occupational therapy aides, nursing aides, physical therapy aides, playroom attendants, and psychiatric aides.

Sources of Additional Information

General information about training and referrals to State and local agencies about opportunities for homemaker-home health aides, a list of relevant publications, and information on national certification are available from:

- Foundation for Hospice and Homecare/National HomeCaring Council, 519 C St. NE., Washington, DC 20002.

Medical Assistants

(D.O.T. 079.364-010, and -014, .367-010, and .374-018, 355.667-010)

Nature of the Work

Medical assistants help physicians examine and treat patients and perform routine tasks to keep offices running smoothly. Medical assistants should not be confused with physician assistants, who examine, diagnose, and treat patients, under the direct supervision of a physician. Physician assistants are discussed elsewhere in this book.

The duties of medical assistants vary from office to office, depending on the location and size of the practice and the physician's specialty. In small practices, medical assistants are usually "generalists," handling both clerical and clinical duties and reporting directly to the office manager or physician. Those in large practices tend to specialize in a particular area under the supervision of department administrators.

Medical assistants perform many clerical duties. They answer telephones, greet patients, update and file patient medical records, fill out insurance forms, handle correspondence, schedule appointments, arrange for hospital admission and laboratory services, and handle billing and bookkeeping.

Clinical duties vary according to State law and include taking and recording vital signs and medical histories; explaining treatment procedures to patients; preparing patients for examination; and assisting during the examination. Medical assistants collect and prepare laboratory specimens or perform basic laboratory tests on the premises; dispose of contaminated supplies; and sterilize medical instruments. They instruct patients about medication and special diets, prepare and administer medications as directed by a physician, authorize drug refills as directed, telephone prescriptions to a pharmacy, draw blood, prepare patients for X-rays, take EKG's, remove sutures, and change dressings.

Medical assistants may also arrange examining room instruments and equipment, purchase and maintain supplies and equipment, and keep waiting and examining rooms neat and clean.

Assistants who specialize have additional duties. *Podiatric medical assistants* make castings of feet, expose and develop X-rays, and assist podiatrists at surgery. *Ophthalmic medical assistants* help ophthalmologists provide medical eye care. They use precision instruments to administer diagnostic tests, measure and record vision, and test the functioning of eyes and eye muscles. They also show patients how to use eye dressings, protective shields, and safety glasses, and insert, remove, and care for contact lenses. Under the direction of the physician, they may administer medications, including eye drops. They also maintain optical and surgical instruments and assist the ophthalmologist in surgery.

Working Conditions

Medical assistants work in a well-lighted, clean environment. They constantly interact with other people, and may have to handle several responsibilites at once.

Most full-time medical assistants work a regular 40-hour week. Some work evenings and weekends.

Employment

Medical assistants held about 165,000 jobs in 1990. Three out of five were employed in physicians' offices, and about 1 in 5 worked in offices of other health practitioners such as chiropractors, optometrists, and podiatrists. Others worked in hospitals, nursing homes, and other health care facilities.

Training , Other Qualifications, and Advancement

Medical assisting is one of the few health occupations open to individuals with no formal training. Although education in medical assisting is available at both the secondary and postsecondary levels, such training—while generally preferred—is not always required. It is still sometimes the case that medical assistants are trained on the job. Applicants usually need a high school diploma or the equivalent. High school courses in mathematics, health, biology, typing, bookkeeping, computers, and office skills are helpful. Volunteer experience in the health care field may also be helpful.

Formal programs in medical assisting are offered in vocational- technical high schools, postsecondary vocational schools, community and junior colleges, and in colleges and universities. College-level programs usually last 1 to 2 years and lead to an associate degree. Vocational programs can take up to 1 year and lead to a diploma or certificate. Courses cover anatomy, physiology, and medical terminology as well as typing, transcription, recordkeeping, accounting, and insurance processing. Students learn laboratory techniques, clinical and diagnostic procedures, pharmaceutical principles and medication administration, and first aid. They are also instructed in office practices, patient relations, and medical law and ethics. Accredited programs may include an externship that provides practical experience in physicians' offices, hospitals, or other health care facilities.

Two agencies recognized by the U.S. Department of Education accredit programs in medical assisting: The American Medical Association's Committee on Allied Health Education and Accreditation (CAHEA) and the Accrediting Bureau of Health Education Schools (ABHES). In 1991, there were 186 medical assisting programs accredited by CAHEA and 127 accredited by ABHES. The Joint Review Committee for Opthalmic Medical Personnel has approved 12 programs in opthalmic medical assisting.

Although there is no licensing for medical assistants, some States require a test or a short course before performing procedures such as taking x-rays, drawing blood, or giving injections. Employers prefer to hire experienced workers or certified applicants who have passed a national examination, indicating that certain standards of competence have been met. The American Association of Medical Assistants awards the Certified Medical Assistant credential; the American Medical Technologists awards the Registered Medical Assistant credential; the American Society of Podiatric Medical Assistants awards the Podiatric Medical Assistant Certified credential; and the Joint Commission on Allied Health Personnel in Ophthalmology awards the Ophthalmic Medical Assistant credential at three levels: Certified Ophthalmic Assistant, Certified Ophthalmic Technician, and Certified Ophthalmic Medical Technologist.

Because medical assistants deal with the public, a neat, well-groomed appearance and a courteous, pleasant manner are needed. Medical assistants must be good at putting patients at ease, listening to to them, and explaining physicians' instructions. Conscientiousness and respect for the confidential nature of medical information are required. Clinical duties require a reasonable level of manual dexterity and visual acuity.

Medical assistants may be able to advance to office manager or become ward clerks, medical record clerks, phlebotomists, or EKG technicians in hospitals. Medical assistants may qualify for a wide variety of administrative support occupations, or may teach medical assisting. Some, with additional schooling, enter other health occupations such as nursing and medical technology.

Job Outlook

Employment of medical assistants is expected to grow much faster than the average for all occupations through the year 2005 as the health services industry expands.

Employment growth will be driven by the increased medical needs of an aging population, growth in the number of health practitioners, more diagnostic testing, and the increased volume and complexity of paperwork. Most job openings, however, will result from the need to replace experienced assistants who leave the occupation.

In view of the high turnover as well as the preference of many physicians for trained personnel, job prospects should be excellent for medical assistants with formal training or experience, particularly those with formal certification.

Earnings

The earnings of medical assistants vary widely, depending on experience, skill level, and location. According to a survey conducted by the Committee on Allied Health Education and Accreditation, the average starting salary for graduates of the medical assistant programs they accredit was about $14,000 a year in 1990. According to limited information, experienced medical assistants averaged several thousand dollars more.

Related Occupations

Workers in other medical support occupations include medical secretaries, hospital admitting clerks, pharmacy helpers, medical record clerks, dental assistants, occupational therapy aides, and physical therapy aides.

Sources of Additional Information

Information about career opportunities, CAHEA-accredited educational programs in medical assisting, and requirements for the Certified Medical Assistant exam is available from:

- The American Association of Medical Assistants, 20 North Wacker Dr., Suite 1575, Chicago, IL 60606.

Information about career opportunities and requirements for taking the Registered Medical Assistant certification exam are available from:

- Registered Medical Assistants of American Medical Technologists, 710 Higgins Rd., Park Ridge, IL 60068.

For a list of ABHES-accredited educational programs in medical assisting, write:

- Accrediting Bureau of Health Education Schools, Oak Manor Office, 29089 U.S. 20 West, Elkhart, IN 46514.

Information about career opportunities, training programs, and requirements to become a Certified Ophthalmic Assistant is available from:

- Joint Commission on Allied Health Personnel in Ophthalmology, 2025 Woodlane Dr., St. Paul, MN 55125-2995.

Information about careers for podiatric assistants is available from:

- American Society of Podiatric Medical Assistants, 2124 S. Austin Blvd., Cicero, IL 60650.

Nursing Aides and Psychiatric Aides

(D.O.T. 354.374-010, .377-010, and .677-010; 355.377- 014 and -018, .674-014, -018, and -026)

Nature of the Work

Nursing aides and psychiatric aides help care for physically or mentally ill, injured, disabled, or infirm individuals confined to hospitals, nursing or residential care facilities, and mental health settings. (Homemaker-home health aides, whose duties are similar but who work in clients' homes, are discussed elsewhere.) Nursing aides, also known as nursing assistants or hospital attendants, work under the supervision of nursing and medical staff. They answer patients' call bells, deliver messages, serve meals, make beds, and feed, dress, and bathe patients. Aides may also give massages, provide skin care to patients who cannot move, take temperatures, pulse, respiration, and blood pressure, and help patients get in and out of bed and walk. They may also escort patients to operating and examining rooms, keep patients' rooms neat, set up equipment, or store and move supplies. Aides observe patients' physical, mental, and emotional conditions and report any change to the nursing or medical staff.

Nursing aides employed in nursing homes are sometimes called geriatric aides. They are often the principal caregivers in nursing homes, having far more contact with residents than other members of the staff do. Since residents may stay in a nursing home for months or even years, aides are expected to develop ongoing relationships with them and respond to them in a positive, caring way.

Psychiatric aides are also known as mental health assistants, psychiatric nursing assistants, or ward attendants. They care for mentally impaired or emotionally disturbed individuals. They work under a team that may include psychiatrists, psychologists, psychiatric nurses, social workers, and therapists. In addition to helping patients dress, bathe, groom, and eat, psychiatric aides

CLUSTER Subgroup Occupation	Est. Emplmt. 1990[1]	Percent Change Emplmt. 1990-2005[1]	Number Change Emplmt. 1990-2005[1]	Employment prospects
Foresters and conservation scientists	29,000	12	3,600	Budgetary constraints in government, where employment is highly concentrated, will result in slower than average overall growth. However, State governments and private owners of timberland may employ more foresters due to increased interest in environmental protection and land management. Overall, job opportunities should be more favorable than in the past due to an expected wave of retirements and recent declines in the number of graduates in forestry and related fields.
Physical Scientists				
Chemists	83,000	16	13,000	Very good employment opportunities are expected because the number of graduates with degrees in chemistry is not expected to increase enough to meet future demand. Employment should increase about as fast as average. Job opportunities will be best in pharmaceuticals and biotechnology, where Ph.D. chemists are expected to be in strong demand.
Geologists and geophysicists	48,000	22	11,000	Environmental protection and regulation are becoming important fields of work for those with the appropriate training. When oil and gas exploration activities increase, geologists and geophysicists should have excellent opportunities. Average growth is expected.
Meteorologists	5,500	30	1,600	The National Weather Service, which employs many meterologists, plans to increase employment to improve its short-term and local forecasts. This should result in faster than average growth.
Physicists and astronomers	20,000	5	1,000	Although slower than average growth is expected, job opportunities for Ph.D.'s should be good in the late 1990's when many physics and astronomy professors become eligible for retirement.
Lawyers and judges	633,000	34	217,000	The demand for legal services caused by population growth and economic expansion will create faster than average employment growth. Competition is expected to ease somewhat for salaried attorney positions, but remain intense for judgeships.
Social Scientists and Urban Planners				
Economists and marketing research analysts	37,000	21	8,000	Employment is expected to increase as fast as average, reflecting increased reliance on quantitative methods to analyze business trends, forecast sales, and plan purchasing and production. For economists, master's and doctoral degree holders will have the best opportunities. Bachelor's degree holders face competition; those skilled in quantitative techniques have the best prospects. For marketing research positions, those with an advanced degree in marketing or a related field have the best prospects.

CLUSTER Subgroup Occupation	Est. Emplmt. 1990[1]	Percent Change Emplmt. 1990-2005[1]	Number Change Emplmt. 1990-2005[1]	Employment prospects
Computer systems analysts	463,000	79	366,000	Employment is expected to grow much faster than average as organizations attempt to maximize efficiency by networking their computer systems for office and factory automation, communications capability, and scientific research. Job prospects will be very good for college graduates who combine courses in programming and systems analysis with training and experience in applied fields.
Mathematicians	22,000	9	2,000	Employment is expected to grow more slowly than average. However, the continuing shortage of Ph.D.'s will result in favorable opportunities for mathematicians, especially those with doctorates in applied mathematics. Those with a master's or bachelor's degree who have strong backgrounds in computer science, electrical or mechanical engineering, or operations research should also have good job opportunities.
Operations research analysts	57,000	73	42,000	As computer costs fall and competitive pressures grow, more organizations will turn to operations research to aid decision making, resulting in much faster than average growth. Opportunities will be especially favorable in manufacturing, trade, and service firms.
Statisticians	16,000	12	1,800	Although employment is expected to grow more slowly than average, job opportunities should remain favorable, especially for people with advanced degrees. Graduates with a bachelor's degree in statistics and a strong background in mathematics or computer science should have the best prospects of finding jobs related to their field of study.
Life Scientists				
Agricultural scientists	25,000	27	6,600	Good employment prospects are expected because enrollments in agricultural science curriculums have dropped considerably over the last few years and because employment should grow faster than average. Animal and plant scientists with a background in molecular biology, microbiology, genetics, or biotechnology; soil scientists; and food technologists will probably have the best opportunities.
Biological scientists	62,000	34	21,000	Increased demand for genetic and biological research, because of efforts to preserve and clean up the environment, should result in faster than average growth. Most new jobs will be in the private sector; employment in government is expected to grow slowly.

1 Nearly all estimates are from the BLS industry-occupation matrix.

CLUSTER Subgroup Occupation	Est. Emplmt. 1990[1]	Percent Change Emplmt. 1990-2005[1]	Number Change Emplmt. 1990-2005[1]	Employment prospects
Recreation workers	194,000	24	47,000	Employment is expected to increase as fast as average. Programs for special groups and greater interest in fitness and health will underlie expansion. Competition is expected for full-time career positions. Opportunities for seasonal jobs will be excellent.
Religious Workers				
Protestant ministers	255,000	(4)	(4)	While the increasing cost of operating a church will moderate demand for ministers, slower growth in the number of ordained ministers will result in less competition. The most favorable opportunities are for rural and part-time positions, but opportunities vary by denomination.
Rabbis	2,700[5]	(4)	(4)	Opportunities are expected to be good, especially in small communities and nonmetropolitan areas since more rabbis prefer to serve in large, urban areas.
Roman Catholic priests	53,000[5]	(4)	(4)	The continuing decline in seminary enrollments coupled with an expected increase in retirements should intensify the shortage of ordained priests.
Teachers, Librarians, and Counselors				
Adult education teachers	517,000	29	152,000	Overall employment is expected to grow faster than average as demand for adult education programs continues to rise. Many openings will arise from the need to replace workers who leave the occupation, particularly given the large number of part-time workers and high turnover in the occupation.
Archivists and curators	17,000	21	3,700	Employment will increase as fast as average, continuing past trends. Competition for jobs will remain keen, however, given the small number of job openings and large supply of workers.
College and university faculty	712,000	19	134,000	Average employment growth is expected as enrollments increase. Beginning in the late 1990's, job opportunities should improve due to an expected wave of faculty retirements. Job prospects are best with business, engineering, computer, and science faculties because of the availability of high-paying jobs outside academe.
Counselors	144,000	34	49,000	Employment is expected to grow faster than average, due to increasing school enrollments, greater use of third party payments to counselors, and the expanded responsibilities of counselors. Job openings should increase by the year 2005 as the large number of counselors now in their 40's and 50's reach retirement age.

CLUSTER Subgroup Occupation	Est. Emplmt. 1990[1]	Percent Change Emplmt. 1990-2005[1]	Number Change Emplmt. 1990-2005[1]	Employment prospects
Psychologists	125,000	64	79,000	Much faster than average growth is anticipated due to increased attention being paid to the expanding elderly population, the maintenance of mental health, and the testing and counseling of children. Ph.D.'s with training in applied areas, such as clinical or counseling psychology, and in quantitative research methods will have the best prospects. Among master's degree holders, specialists in school psychology should have the best prospects, while bachelor's degree holders will have very few opportunities in this field.
Sociologists	(4)	(4)	(4)	Opportunities will be best for Ph.D.'s and master's degree holders with strong quantitative research skills and training in applied areas such as clinical sociology, gerontology, criminology, or demography. Bachelor's degree holders have very few opportunities in this field.
Urban and regional planners	23,000	19	4,400	Increased demand for planning related to the environment, the economy, transportation, and energy production should result in average employment growth. Opportunities will be best in rapidly growing areas, older areas undergoing preservation and redevelopment, and States that have mandated planning. Graduates of institutions with accredited planning programs have the best prospects.
Social and Recreation Workers				
Human services workers	145,000	71	103,000	Employment is expected to grow much faster than average due to the expansion of facilities and programs for the elderly and disabled and greater services for families in crisis. Prospects are excellent for qualified applicants, who are avidly sought because of the demanding nature of the work, the relatively low pay, and the subsequent high turnover.
Social workers	438,000	34	150,000	Faster than average growth is expected in response to the needs of a growing and aging population, as well as increasing concern about services for the mentally ill, the mentally retarded, and families in crisis. Employment in hospitals is expected to grow due to greater emphasis on discharge planning. Employment prospects in private practice are favorable due to funding from health insurance.

1 Nearly all estimates are from the BLS industry-occupation matrix.
4 Estimates not available.
5 Includes only those who served congregations

CLUSTER Subgroup Occupation	Est. Emplmt. 1990[1]	Percent Change Emplmt. 1990-2005[1]	Number Change Emplmt. 1990-2005[1]	Employment prospects
Kindergarten and elementary school teachers	1,521,000	23	350,000	Average employment growth is expected as enrollments increase and class size declines. The number of job openings should increase substantially after the mid-1990's, as the large number of teachers now in their 40's and 50's reach retirement age.
Librarians	149,000	11	17,000	Employment is expected to grow more slowly than average, continuing the limited employment growth of librarians during the 1980's. The decline in the number of graduates of library science programs in the 1980's, however, should result in favorable job prospects for such graduates.
Secondary school teachers	1,280,000	34	437,000	Employment is expected to increase faster than average as enrollments grow and class size declines. Job openings will increase substantially after the mid-1990's as the large number of teachers now in their 40's and 50's reach retirement age.
Health Diagnosing Occupations				
Chiropractors	42,000	(4)	(4)	Employment is expected to rise because of the rapidly growing older population, with its greater likelihood of physiological problems, and as the awareness of chiropractic services grows.
Dentists	174,000	12	21,000	Job prospects should continue to improve because the number of dental school graduates has declined since the early 1980's and is not likely to increase much. Despite a growing demand for dental services, employment is projected to grow more slowly than average. Dentists should respond to growing demand by working more hours and relying on dental hygienists and assistants to provide more services.
Optometrists	37,000	20	7,600	Employment is expected to grow as fast as average in order to meet the needs of a population that is larger, older, and more aware of the need for proper eye care. Job opportunities should be good, even though replacement needs are low.
Physicians	580,000	34	196,000	Employment is expected to grow faster than average due to a growing and aging population and technological improvements that encourage expansion of the health industry. Job prospects should be better in internal medicine, family practice, geriatrics, and preventive medicine than in other specialities.
Podiatrists	16,000	46	7,300	Employment is expected to grow much faster than average due to the rising demand for podiatric services, in particular by older people and fitness enthusiasts. Establishing a new podiatric practice will be toughest in areas surrounding the seven colleges of podiatric medicine since podiatrists are concentrated in these locations.
Veterinarians	47,000	31	14,000	Employment is expected to grow faster than average due to growth in the animal population and the willingness of pet owners to pay for more intensive care than in the past. The outlook for specialists — such as toxicologists, laboratory veterinarians, and pathologists — will be extremely good.
Health Assessment and Treating Occupations				
Dietitians and nutritionists	45,000	24	11,000	Employment is expected to grow about as fast as average in order to meet the expanding needs of nursing homes, hospitals, and social service programs and the growing interest and emphasis on dietary education.
Occupational therapists	36,000	55	20,000	Much faster than average growth is expected, reflecting anticipated growth in demand for rehabilitation services due to the increased survival rate of accident victims and the rising number of people in their 40's, an age when the risk of heart disease and stroke increases. The rapidly growing aged population will also increase demand for long-term care services. In addition, therapists will be needed for disabled students.
Pharmacists	169,000	21	35,000	Spurred by the pharmaceutical needs of a larger and older population and by scientific advances that will bring more drugs onto the market, employment is expected to grow as fast as average. Excellent job prospects are anticipated in both community and clinical settings; if current trends continue, demand is likely to outstrip supply in some places.
Physical therapists	88,000	76	67,000	Much faster than average job growth is expected due to the expansion of rehabilitation and long-term care. The shortage of physical therapists should ease somewhat as the number of physical therapy education programs increases and more students graduate.
Physician assistants	53,000	34	18,000	Employment is expected to grow faster than average due to the expansion of the health services industry and the increased emphasis on cost containment. Excellent prospects are anticipated, especially in areas that have difficulty attracting physicians.

1 Nearly all estimates are from the BLS industry-occupation matrix.
4 Estimates not available

CLUSTER Subgroup Occupation	Est. Emplmt. 1990[1]	Percent Change Emplmt. 1990-2005[1]	Number Change Emplmt. 1990-2005[1]	Employment prospects[1]
Writers and editors	232,000	26	60,000	Increased demand for salaried writers in publishing, public relations, communications, and advertising should cause employment to rise faster than average. Keen competition is expected to continue. Opportunities will be best with business, trade, and technical publications.
Visual Arts Occupations				
Designers	339,000	26	89,000	Continued emphasis on the quality and visual appeal of products will prompt faster than average growth for designers, especially industrial designers. Designers in most specialties will face competition throughout their careers because of the abundant supply of talented, highly qualified people attracted to this field. Finding a job in floral design should be relatively easy due to the relatively low pay and limited advancement opportunities.
Photographers and camera operators	120,000	23	28,000	Average overall growth is expected in response to the growing importance of visual images in education, communications, and entertainment. Faster than average growth is expected for camera operators. Jobseekers may face competition or keen competition, especially in commercial photography and photojournalism.
Visual artists	230,000	32	73,000	Strong demand for art, illustration, and design by advertising agencies, publishing firms, and other businesses will stimulate faster than average growth for graphic artists. Competition for jobs among fine artists will continue to be keen.
Performing Arts Occupations				
Actors, directors, and producers	95,000	41	39,000	Employment is expected to grow much faster than average as cable television, home movie rentals, and television syndication fuel a growing demand for productions. Still, continued overcrowding in this field will cause keen competition for jobs.
Dancers and choreographers	8,600	38	3,300	Employment is expected to grow much faster than average. Nonetheless, dancers seeking professional careers will continue to exceed the number of job openings, causing keen competition.
Musicians	252,000	9	24,000	Employment is expected to grow more slowly than average, reflecting the increasing use of synthesizers instead of multi-piece bands and orchestras. Also, a growing number of small clubs and dining establishments are hiring smaller bands than they have in the past. Competition will be extremely keen.

CLUSTER Subgroup Occupation	Est. Emplmt. 1990[1]	Percent Change Emplmt. 1990-2005[1]	Number Change Emplmt. 1990-2005[1]	Employment prospects[1]
Recreational therapists	32,000	39	13,000	Employment is expected to grow much faster than average, chiefly because of anticipated growth in the need for long-term care, rehabilitation, and services for the developmentally disabled. Job prospects should be favorable for those with a strong clinical background.
Registered nurses	1,727,000	44	767,000	Much faster than average growth is expected, due to the overall growth in health care and the number of complex medical technologies. Hospitals in many parts of the country report shortages of RN's. However, increasing enrollments in nursing programs may result in a balance between job seekers and openings.
Respiratory therapists	60,000	52	31,000	Much faster than average growth is expected because of the substantial growth of the middle-aged and elderly population, which is more likely to suffer from cardiopulmonary diseases. Hospitals will continue to be the primary employer, but employment will grow fastest in home health care services.
Speech-language pathologists and audiologists	68,000	34	23,000	Faster than average growth is likely in the health care industry because the number of older people will grow rapidly and the baby-boom generation will enter an age bracket when the possibility of stroke-induced hearing and speech loss increases. Average growth is expected in educational services.
Communications Occupations				
Public relations specialists	109,000	19	21,000	Average growth is expected as organizations increasingly recognize the need for good internal and external relations. Keen competition for these jobs is likely to persist among recent college graduates with communications degrees; people without the appropriate education or experience will face the toughest obstacles in acquiring these jobs.
Radio and television announcers and newscasters	57,000	20	11,000	Average growth is expected as new radio and TV stations are licensed and the number of cable TV stations continues to grow. Competition for beginning jobs will be very strong because the broadcasting field attracts many more jobseekers than there are jobs. Jobs will be easier to find in radio than in television because more radio stations hire beginners.
Reporters and correspondents	67,000	20	14,000	Employment is expected to grow about as fast as average. Writers who can handle highly specialized scientific or technical subjects will be at an advantage in the job market. The best opportunities are likely to be found on newspapers and magazines in small towns and suburbs.

1 Nearly all estimates are from the BLS industry-occupation matrix.

CLUSTER Subgroup Occupation	Est. Emplmt. 1990[1]	Percent Change Emplmt. 1990-2005[1]	Number Change Emplmt. 1990-2005[1]	Employment prospects
Medical record technicians	52,000	54	28,000	Greater use of medical records for financial management and quality control will produce much faster than average job growth with excellent job prospects for graduates of accredited programs in medical record technology.
Nuclear medicine technologists	10,000	53	5,500	Employment is expected to grow much faster than average to meet the health care needs of a growing and aging population. Technological innovations will also increase the diagnostic use of nuclear medicine. Job prospects are excellent.
Radiologic technologists	149,000	70	103,000	Employment is expected to grow much faster than average due to the growth and aging of the population and the greater role radiologic technologies are playing in the diagnosis and treatment of disease. Job prospects for graduates of accredited programs are excellent.
Surgical technologists	38,000	55	21,000	Much faster than average growth is expected as a growing population and technological advances increase the number of surgical procedures performed. Growth will be fastest in clinics and offices of physicians due to increases in outpatient surgery; however, most jobs will be in hospitals.
Technicians Except Health				
Aircraft pilots	90,000	34	31,000	Due to an expected shortage of qualified applicants, opportunities should be excellent in the coming years. Faster than average employment growth and the large number of expected retirements will provide many job openings. Job prospects with major airlines are best for college graduates who have a commercial pilot's license or a flight engineer's license and experience flying jets.
Air traffic controllers	32,000	7	2,200	Despite growth in the number of aircraft in service, productivity gains stemming from laborsaving air traffic control equipment will result in slower than average employment growth. Keen competition for job openings is expected because the occupation's relatively high pay and liberal retirement program attract many applicants.
Broadcast technicians	33,000	4	1,200	Because of laborsaving advances, such as computer-controlled programming and remote-controlled transmitters, employment is expected to show little or no change.
Computer programmers	565,000	56	317,000	Employment is expected to grow much faster than average as the number of computer applications continues to increase. Job prospects will be best for college graduates who majored in computer science or a related area and have experience or training in fields such as accounting, management, engineering, or science.

CLUSTER Subgroup Occupation	Est. Emplmt. 1990[1]	Percent Change Emplmt. 1990-2005[1]	Number Change Emplmt. 1990-2005[1]	Employment prospects
TECHNICIANS AND RELATED SUPPORT OCCUPATIONS				
Health technologists and technicians				
Clinical laboratory technologists	258,000	24	63,000	Although the number of medical tests will greatly increase, advances in laboratory automation should boost productivity, resulting in average employment growth. Many jobs will be in hospitals, but the fastest growth will be in commercial laboratories and doctors' offices due to changes in technology and business strategy. Job prospects are favorable.
Dental hygienists	97,000	41	40,000	Employment should grow much faster than average. Stimulating demand will be population growth, the tendency for middle-aged and elderly people to retain their teeth, and greater awareness of the importance of dental care along with the ability to pay for it. Also, dentists are expected to rely on hygienists to provide more services. Dental hygienists should have little trouble finding jobs.
Dispensing opticians	64,000	37	24,000	Employment is expected to grow much faster than average in response to rising demand for corrective lenses as the population ages. Opportunities should be very good for graduates of formal training programs.
EEG technologists	6,700	57	3,800	Much faster than average growth is expected, reflecting the increased numbers of neurodiagnostic tests performed. Job prospects should be excellent for formally trained technologists.
EKG technicians	16,000	-5	-800	Employment is expected to decline, despite the anticipated rise in the number of cardiology tests performed. Advances in technology have substantially raised EKG technicians' productivity and also have allowed registered nurses and other health personnel to perform the test.
Emergency medical technicians	89,000	30	26,000	Faster than average job growth is projected. Opportunities should be excellent in hospitals and private ambulance services, where pay and benefits generally are low. Competition will be keen in fire, police, and rescue squads because of attractive pay and benefits and good job security.
Licensed practical nurses	644,000	42	269,000	Employment is expected to grow much faster than average in response to the long-term care needs of a rapidly growing aged population and growth in health care in general. The job outlook should remain good unless the number of people completing L.P.N. training increases substantially.

1 Nearly all estimates are from the BLS industry-occupation matrix.

CLUSTER Subgroup Occupation	Est. Emplmt. 1990[1]	Percent Change Emplmt. 1990-2005[1]	Number Change Emplmt. 1990-2005[1]	Employment prospects
Drafters	326,000	13	44,000	Although large increases in demand for drafting services are expected, they will be partially offset by the widespread use of computer-aided design equipment, which increases the productivity of drafters. Slower than average employment growth is expected.
Engineering technicians	755,000	28	210,000	Well-qualified engineering technicians will experience good opportunities. Anticipated increases in spending on research and development and continued rapid growth in the number of technical products are expected to result in faster than average growth.
Library technicians	65,000	11	7,300	Employment is expected to grow more slowly than average, following the growth pattern of other library workers.
Paralegals	90,000	85	77,000	Much faster than average growth is expected as the use of paralegals to aid lawyers increases. Competition for jobs is expected to increase. Opportunities will be best for graduates of well regarded formal paralegal training programs and paralegals with previous experience.
Science technicians	246,000	24	58,000	Science technicians with good technical and communication skills should experience very good employment opportunities. Expansion in research, development, and the production of technical products will result in average overall growth. The employment of biological technicians is expected to grow faster than most other science technicians; job opportunities for chemical technicians also are expected to be good.
Tool programmers, numerical control	7,800	6	(3)	Despite increased use of numerically controlled machine tools, employment will grow more slowly than average due to expected large increases in productivity.
MARKETING AND SALES OCCUPATIONS				
Cashiers	2,633,000	26	685,000	Faster than average employment growth is expected due to the anticipated increase in retail sales and the popularity of discount and self-service retailing, which has led to the rise of centralized cashier stations. Due to the large size of this occupation and its much higher than average turnover, both part- and full-time job opportunities will be excellent.
Counter and rental clerks	215,000	34	74,000	Faster than average employment growth is expected due to the anticipated growth in rental and leasing services. Prospects for full- and part-time jobs with flexible hours are excellent.
Insurance agents and brokers	439,000	20	88,000	Employment growth will not keep pace with rising insurance sales due to increased productivity and changing business practices, but it will still be as fast as average. In this highly competitive business, opportunities will be best for ambitious people who enjoy selling and develop expertise in a wide range of insurance and financial services.
Manufacturers' and wholesale sales representatives	1,944,000	15	284,000	Average employment growth is expected as the economy expands and as demand for goods increases. Job prospects will be good for qualified persons.
Real estate agents, brokers, and appraisers	413,000	19	79,000	The large proportion of the population between the ages of 25 and 54 is expected to increase sales of residential and commercial properties, resulting in average employment growth. Because turnover is high, positions should continue to be relatively easy to obtain. Well-trained, ambitious people who enjoy selling have the best chance for success in this highly competitive field.
Retail sales workers	4,754,000	29	1,381,000	Employment is expected to grow faster than average due to anticipated growth in retail sales. Job prospects will be excellent for full-time, part-time, and temporary workers.
Securities and financial services sales representatives	191,000	40	76,000	Employment is expected to grow much faster than average as economic growth and rising personal incomes increase the funds available for investment and as banks and other financial institutions offer an increasing array of financial services. However, job competition will remain keen, particularly in large firms, due to the potential for high earnings. Many beginners leave securities sales jobs because they are unable to establish a sufficient clientele.
Services sales representatives	588,000	55	325,000	The continued rapid increase in the demand for services will result in much faster than average employment growth. Applicants with college training or a proven sales record have the best job prospects.
Travel agents	132,000	62	82,000	Much faster than average employment growth is projected due to the large increases expected in both vacation and business-related travel.
ADMINISTRATIVE SUPPORT OCCUPATIONS INCLUDING CLERICAL				
Adjusters, investigators, and collectors	1,088,000	24	264,000	Employment is expected to grow about as fast as average, in line with a growing population and a rising number of business transactions. Growth should be slightly faster for claim representatives and bill and account collectors than for insurance clerks, adjustment clerks, or welfare eligibility workers.

1 Nearly all estimates are from the BLS industry-occupation matrix.
3 Less than 500.

CLUSTER Subgroup Occupation	Est. Emplmt. 1990[1]	Percent Change Emplmt. 1990-2005[1]	Number Change Emplmt. 1990-2005[1]	Employment prospects
Stenographers and court reporters	132,000	-5	-7,100	Overall employment is expected to decline because of the widespread use of dictation machines and continuing developments in voice-activated transcription equipment. Demand should be strong for court reporters, however, due to the growing number of court cases and the use of court reporters to record business proceedings.
Teacher aides	808,000	34	278,000	Employment is expected to grow faster than average, reflecting rising enrollments and greater use of aides.
Telephone operators	325,000	-32	-104,000	Employment is expected to decline due to innovations, such as voice recognition technologies and automatic switching, that will reduce labor requirements.
Typists, word processors, and data entry keyers	1,448,000	-3	-46,000	Little or no change in employment is expected because of the widespread use of personal computers, further developments in electronic equipment, and the trend towards professionals and other office workers doing more of their own word processing. Job opportunities will be best for those with good keyboard skills and knowledge of computer software packages.
SERVICE OCCUPATIONS				
Protective Service Occupations				
Correction officers	230,000	61	142,000	As correctional facilities expand and additional officers are hired to supervise and counsel a growing number of inmates, employment is expected to increase much faster than average. Rapid growth in demand coupled with job openings resulting from turnover should mean favorable opportunities.
Firefighting occupations	280,000	24	68,000	Due to population growth and the increasing need for protection from fires, employment will grow about as fast as average. Keen competition is expected in most areas; the best opportunities are likely to be found in smaller communities with expanding populations.
Guards	883,000	34	298,000	Increasing concern about crime, vandalism, and terrorism will stimulate the need for guards, resulting in faster than average growth. Overall, job opportunities are expected to be plentiful. Opportunities will be best for those who work for contract security agencies. Some competition is expected for in-house guard jobs, which generally have higher salaries, more benefits, better job security, and greater potential for advancement.

CLUSTER Subgroup Occupation	Est. Emplmt. 1990[1]	Percent Change Emplmt. 1990-2005[1]	Number Change Emplmt. 1990-2005[1]	Employment prospects
Billing clerks	413,000	4	18,000	Little change in employment is expected as computers are increasingly used to manage account information. More individualized and complex billing applications will require workers with greater technical expertise.
Bookkeeping, accounting, and auditing clerks	2,276,000	-6	-133,000	Employment is expected to decline because of the automation of bookkeeping, accounting, and auditing functions. Large organizations may continue to consolidate and eliminate duplicate functions, further reducing demand for these workers.
Brokerage clerks and statement clerks	93,000	10	9,000	Slower than average employment growth is expected as computers and changes in business practices reduce demand for these workers.
File clerks	271,000	11	29,000	Employment is expected to grow more slowly than average as recordkeeping systems become more automated. Opportunities should be good for part-time and temporary work, and in the health, legal, and computer service industries.
Library assistants and bookmobile drivers	117,000	11	13,000	Slower than average employment growth is expected, reflecting the slow growth in funding that is anticipated for local governments and schools.
Order clerks	291,000	3	8,700	Little change in employment is expected. The growing number of orders being placed for goods and services will be offset by a greater use of sophisticated inventory control, automatic billing, and other advanced systems. Prospects will be best for outside order clerks who deal directly with the public.
Payroll and timekeeping clerks	171,000	3	4,700	Little change in employment is expected as office automation facilitates calculation and recording of information. These tasks are increasingly being assigned to other workers in smaller offices.
Personnel clerks	129,000	21	27,000	Average employment growth is expected. Despite increasing workloads, rising productivity through automation will moderate demand for personnel clerks. Many job openings will arise as workers transfer to other occupations or leave the work force.
Secretaries	3,576,000	15	540,000	Average employment growth is expected as the labor force grows and more workers are employed in offices. Productivity increases brought about by office automation will be offset somewhat by the trend to have secretaries assume responsibilities traditionally reserved for managers and professionals. Job prospects should be good.

1 Nearly all estimates are from the BLS industry-occupation matrix.

CHAPTER FIVE: Making Career Decisions and Getting a Good Job—in Less Time[1]

> This chapter was written by J. Michael Farr, a nationally known authority in the job search area. He is president of JIST Works, Inc., and has more than 15 years experience operating effective job-search programs. In addition, he has trained more than 9,000 instructors and trainers on job-search techniques. His results-oriented, job-search methods have been field-tested—and they do work! In fact, more schools and programs now use his books (over 600,000 copies sold) and techniques than any other job-search program. This chapter is based on one of his books, *The Very Quick Job Search*.

People change jobs or careers for many different reasons. Some change for more pay and responsibility or better benefits. Others willingly take a decrease in pay to work at something they love, or to work for a cause they believe in, while others opt for self-employment. Still others would prefer not to change occupations but find it necessary to do so for a variety of other reasons.

Regardless of your reason for making a change, the transition will take less time and get better results if you pay attention to the needs of the current job market. You'll find a lot of information about rapidly growing jobs and other major occupations throughout this book.

Changing Jobs and Careers Is Often Healthy

Most of us were told from an early age that each career move must be up, involving more money, responsibility, and prestige. Yet research indicates people change careers for many other reasons as well.

In a survey conducted by the Gallup Organization for the National Occupational Information Coordinating Committee, 44 percent of the working adults surveyed expected to be in a different job within three years. This is a very high turnover rate, yet only 41 percent had a definite plan to follow in mapping out their careers.

Logical, ordered careers are found more often with increasing levels of education. For example, while 25 percent of the high school dropouts took the only job available, this was true for only 8 percent of those with at least some college. But you should not assume this means that such occupational stability is healthy. Many adult developmental psychologists believe occupational change is not only normal but may even be necessary for sound adult growth and development. It is common, even normal, to reconsider occupational roles during your twenties, thirties, and forties, even in the absence of economic pressure to do so.

One viewpoint is that a healthy occupational change is one that allows some previously undeveloped aspect of the self to emerge. The change may be as natural as from clerk to supervisor; or as drastic as from professional musician to airline pilot. Although risk is always a factor when change is involved, reasonable risks are healthy and can raise self-esteem.

But Not Just Any Job Should Do—Or Any Job Search

Whether you are seeking similar work in another setting or changing careers, you need a workable plan to find the right job. The rest of this chapter gives you the information you need to help you find a good job quickly.

While the techniques in this chapter are presented briefly, they are based on my years of experience in helping people find good jobs (not just any job) and to find jobs in less time. The career decision-making section will help you consider the major issues you need to make a good decision about the job you want. The job-seeking skills that are presented are ones that have been proven to reduce the amount of time required to find a good job.

Of course, complete books have been written on job-seeking techniques and you may want to look into buying one or more of the better ones to obtain additional information. But, short as this chapter is, it DOES present you with the basic skills to find a good job in less time. The techniques work.

Six Steps for a Successful Job Search

You can't just read about getting a job. The best way to get a job is to go out there and get interviews! And the best way to get interviews is to make a job out of getting a job. That's what this chapter will help you do.

Here are the six basic steps of a quick and successful job search:

1. Know your skills.
2. Have a clear job objective.
3. Know where and how to look.
4. Spend at least 25 hours a week looking.
5. Get two interviews a day.
6. Follow up on all contacts.

Know Your Skills

One survey of employers found that 90 percent of the people they interviewed could not explain their skills. They could not answer the question, "Why should I hire you?"

Knowing what you are good at is important in interviewing. It also helps you decide what type of job you will enjoy and do well. Most people think of "skills" as job-related skills. Everyone has other types of skills that are also important for success on a job. The two most important types are self-management and transferable skills.

---

[1] Based on the career planning and job search book titled *The Very Quick Job Search* by J. Michael Farr, published by JIST Works, Inc. Used with permission.

Self-Management Skills

Write down three things about yourself that you think make you a good worker.

1. _____

_____

2. _____

_____

3. _____

_____

The things you wrote down may be the most important things for an employer to know about you! They have to do with your basic personality, your ability to manage yourself in a new environment. They are some of the most important things to bring up in an interview. Review the following list and put a checkmark beside any skills you have. After you are done with the list, circle five skills you feel are most important. The first group, Key Skills, are skills that employers find particularly important. If one or more of the Key Skills apply to you, mentioning them in an interview can help you greatly.

Key Skills

___ accept supervision	___ hard worker
___ get along with co-workers	___ honest
___ get things done on time	___ productive
___ good attendance	___ punctual

Other Skills

___ able to coordinate	___ friendly
___ ambitious	___ good-natured
___ assertive	___ helpful
___ capable	___ humble
___ cheerful	___ imaginative
___ competent	___ independent
___ complete assignments	___ industrious
___ conscientious	___ informal
___ creative	___ intelligent
___ dependable	___ intuitive
___ discreet	___ learn quickly
___ eager	___ loyal
___ efficient	___ mature
___ energetic	___ methodical
___ enthusiastic	___ modest
___ expressive	___ motivated
___ flexible	___ natural
___ formal	___ open-minded

___ optimistic	___ sincere
___ original	___ solve problems
___ patient	___ spontaneous
___ persistent	___ steady
___ physically strong	___ tactful
___ practice new skills	___ take pride in work
___ reliable	___ tenacious
___ resourceful	___ thrifty
___ responsible	___ trustworthy
___ self-confident	___ versatile
___ sense of humor	___ well-organized

Other similar skills you have:

_____

_____

_____

Note: Some people find it helpful to now complete the section called "Essential Job Search Data" which can be found later in this chapter. Those of you with work experience may find it helpful to use that section to list your skills and accomplishments from previous jobs and other life experiences. Then you will have a better idea of what skills you have that you may want to use on your next job.

Transferable Skills

These are skills you can transfer from one job or career to another. Some are more important in one job than another. *Your success requires you to find a job that requires the skills you have.*

In the following list, put a check beside the skills that you have. You may have used them in a previous job or in some non-work setting. When done, circle the five skills you feel are most important for you to use in your next job.

Key Skills

___ instructing others	___ negotiating
___ managing money, budget	___ organize/manage projects
___ managing people	___ public speaking
___ meeting deadlines	___ written communication
___ meeting the public	skills

Working with Things

___ assemble things	___ observe/inspect
___ build things	___ operate tools, machines
___ construct/repair/build	___ repair things
___ drive, operate vehicles	___ use complex equipment
___ good with hands	

Working with Data

___ analyze data	___ evaluate
___ audit records	___ investigate
___ budget	___ keep financial records
___ calculate/compute	___ locate information
___ check for accuracy	___ manage money
___ classify things	___ observe/inspect
___ compare	___ record facts
___ compile	___ research
___ count	___ synthesize
___ detail-oriented	___ take inventory

Working with People

___ administer	___ patient
___ advise	___ perceptive
___ care for	___ persuade
___ confront others	___ pleasant
___ counsel people	___ sensitive
___ demonstrate	___ sociable
___ diplomatic	___ supervise
___ help others	___ tactful
___ instruct	___ teaching
___ interview people	___ tolerant
___ kind	___ tough
___ listen	___ trusting
___ negotiate	___ understanding
___ outgoing	

Working with Words, Ideas

___ articulate	___ inventive
___ communicate verbally	___ library research
___ correspond with others	___ logical
___ create new ideas	___ public speaking
___ design	___ remember information
___ edit	___ write clearly
___ ingenious	

Leadership

___ arrange social functions	___ mediate problems
___ competitive	___ motivate people
___ decisive	___ negotiate agreements
___ delegate	___ planning
___ direct others	___ results-oriented
___ explain things to others	___ risk-taker
___ influence others	___ run meetings
___ initiate new tasks	___ self-confident

___ make decisions	___ self-motivate
___ manage or direct others	___ solve problems

Creative/Artistic

___ artistic	___ expressive
___ dance, body movement	___ perform, act
___ drawing, art	___ present artistic idea

Other similar skills you have:

_____

_____

_____

_____

_____

_____

Job Content Skills

These are the skills you need to do a particular job. A carpenter, for example, needs to know how to use various tools and be familiar with a variety of tasks related to that job. Use separate pieces of paper to list the special job content skills you have from previous jobs, hobbies, training or other life experiences. Use separate sheets for each group of related job content skills as needed.

Include any job-related skills you have gained, even if you don't intend to use these skills in the job you are likely to look for. Later, you can decide which of the skills you have best support the job you want. After you are finished with separate lists, list the job related skills you have below that you would like to use on your next job.

_____

_____

_____

_____

_____

Have a Clear Job Objective

Even if you don't have a specific job title, you *must* know the type of things you want to do and you are good at *before* you start your job search. This means defining *the* job rather than *a* job. If you already have a good idea of the type of job you want, answering the following questions will help you define it even more clearly.

Job Objective Questionaire

What skills do you have that you want to use? Select the top five skills from the previous lists that you enjoy using and want most to use in your next job.

1. _____

2. _____

3. _____

4. _____

5. _____

What type of special knowledge do you have that you might use in your next job? Perhaps you know how to fix radios, keep accounting records or cook food. Write down the things you know about from schooling, training, hobbies, family experiences, and other sources. Perhaps one or more of them could make you a very special applicant in the right setting.

_____

_____

_____

_____

_____

What type of people do you prefer to work with? Do you prefer to work by yourself, to be part of a group, or to supervise others?

_____

_____

_____

_____

What type of work environment do you prefer? Do you want to work inside, outside, in a quiet place, a busy place, a clean place, or have a window with a nice view?

_____

_____

_____

_____

_____

Where do you want your next job to be located—in what city or region? Near a bus line? Close to a child care center? If you are open to live or work anywhere, what would your ideal community be like?

_____

_____

_____

_____

_____

_____

How much money do you hope to make in your next job? Many people will take less money if the job is great in other ways—or to survive. Think about the minimum you would take as well as what you would eventually like to earn. Your next job will probably be somewhere between.

_____

_____

_____

_____

_____

How much responsibility are you willing to accept? Usually, the more money you want to make, the more responsibility you must accept. Do you want to work by yourself, be part of a group, or be in charge? If so, at what level?

_____

_____

_____

_____

_____

What things are important or have meaning to you that you would prefer to include as a basis of the work you do? For example, some people work to help others, some to clean up our environment, build things, make machines work, gain power or prestige, or care for animals or plants. Think about what is important to you and how you might include this in your next job.

_____

_____

_____

_____

_____

_____

Your Ideal Job

Use the points above and on previous page to help you define the ideal job for you. Think about each one and select the points that are most important to you. Write them on a separate piece of paper.

If you need help figuring out what type of job to look for, remember that most areas have free or low cost career counseling and testing services. Contact local government agencies and schools for referrals.

Avoid a job title that is too narrow, like "Secretary" or "COBOL Programmer." Better objectives might be "General Office/Office Manager" or "Programming/Systems Analyst." Most libraries have a copy of the ***Occupational Outlook Handbook*** which gives excellent information on over 250 of the most popular jobs. Reading it will help you keep your options open. Many interesting jobs will need a person with your skills, but have job titles that you may not have considered. When you are clear about what type of job you want, write it in the following spaces.

My Job Objective:

_____

_____

_____

_____

_____

_____

_____

_____

_____

Know Where and How to Look

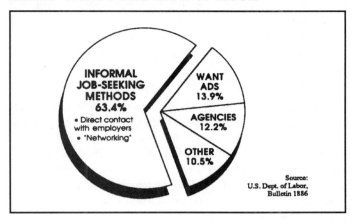

One survey found that 85 percent of all employers don't advertise at all. They hire people they already know, people who find out about the jobs through word of mouth, or people who simply happen to be at the right place at the right time. This is sometimes just luck, but this book will teach you ways to increase your "luck" in finding job openings.

The chart above shows that fewer than 15 percent of all job seekers get jobs from reading the want ads. Let's take a quick look at want ads and other traditional job search methods.

Traditional Job-Search Methods

Help Wanted Ads: Everyone who reads the paper knows about these job openings. So competition for these jobs is fierce. Still, some people do get jobs this way, so go ahead and apply. Just be sure to spend most of your time using more effective methods.

The State Employment Service: Often called the "Unemployment Office," they offer free job leads and other services in addition to the unemployment compensation checks for the unemployed. Each state has a network of these offices. Only about 5 percent of all job seekers get their jobs here. This service usually knows of only one-tenth (or fewer) of the available jobs in your area. Still, it is worth a weekly visit. If you ask for the same counselor, you might impress the person enough to remember you and refer you to the better openings.

Private Employment Agencies: One out of 20 job seekers gets a job using a private agency. This means that 95 percent don't. Private agencies charge a fee to either you (as high as 20 percent of your annual salary!) or the employer. Most of them call employers asking if they have any openings—something you could do yourself. Unless you have skills that are in high demand, you will probably do better on your own. And save money...

Sending Out Resumes: *One survey found that you would have to mail more than 500 unsolicited resumes to get one interview!* A much better approach is to contact by phone the person who might hire you to set up an interview directly, then send a resume. If you insist on sending out unsolicited resumes, do this on weekends—save your "prime time" for more effective job search techniques.

Filling Out Applications: Most applications are used to screen you out. Larger organizations may require them, but remember that your task is to get an interview, not fill out an application. If you do complete them, make them neat, error free, and do not include anything that could get you screened out. If necessary, leave a problem section blank. It can always be explained after you get an offer.

Personnel Departments: Hardly anyone gets hired by someone in a personnel department. Their job is to screen you and refer the "best" applicants to the person who would actually supervise you. You may need to cooperate with them, but it is often better to go directly to the person who is most likely to supervise you even if there is no job opening just now.

Remember that most organizations don't even have a personnel office—only the larger ones!

Informal Job Search Methods

Two-thirds of all people get their jobs using informal methods. These jobs are often not advertised and are part of the "hidden" job market. How do you find them?

There are two basic informal job search methods: networking with people you know, and making direct contacts with an employer. They are both based on the most important job search rule of all:

> ### Don't wait until the job is open!

Most jobs are filled by someone the employer meets before a job is formally "open." So the trick is to meet people who can hire you **before** a job is available! Instead of saying "Do you have any jobs open?" say "I realize you may not have any openings now, but I would still like to talk to you about the possibility of future openings."

Develop a Network of Contacts

One study found that 40 percent of all people found their jobs through a lead provided by a friend, a relative or an acquaintance. Developing new contacts is called "networking" and here's how it works:

Make lists of people you know. Develop a list of anyone you are friendly with, then make a separate list for all your relatives. These two lists alone often add up to 25 to 100 people or more. Then think of other groups of people with whom you have something in common, like people you used to work with; people who went to your school; people in your social or sports groups; members of your professional association; former employers, and members of your religious group. You may not know many of these people personally, but most **will** help you if you ask them.

Contact them in a systematic way. Each of these people is a contact for you. Obviously, some lists and some people on those lists will be more helpful than others, but almost any one of them could help you find a job lead.

Present yourself well. Start with your friends and relatives. Call them up and tell them you are looking for a job and need their help. Be as clear as possible about what you are looking for and what skills and qualifications you have. Look at the sample JIST Card and phone script later in this chapter for presentation ideas.

Ask them for leads. It is possible that they will know of a job opening just right for you. If so, get the details and get right on it! More likely, however, they will not, so here are three questions you should ask.

> ### Three Magic Networking Questions
>
> 1. *Do you know of any openings for a person with my skills?* If the answer is no, then ask:
> 2. *Do you know of someone else who might know of such an opening?* If they do, get that name and ask for another one. If they don't, then ask:
> 3. *Do you know of anyone who might know of someone else who might?* Another way to ask this is, "Do you know someone who knows lots of people?" If all else fails, this will usually get you a name.

Contact these referrals and ask them the same questions. For each original contact, you can extend your network of acquaintances by hundreds of people. Eventually, one of these people will hire you—or refer you to someone who will!

Contact Employers Directly

It takes more courage, but contacting an employer directly is a very effective job-search technique. Use the *Yellow Pages* to identify types of organizations that could use a person with your skills. Then call the organizations listed and ask to speak to the person who is most likely to hire you. There is a sample telephone script later in this chapter to give you ideas about what to say.

You can also just walk in and ask to speak to the person in charge. This is particularly effective in small businesses, but it works surprisingly well in larger ones, too. Remember, you want an interview even if there are no openings now. If your timing is inconvenient, ask for a better time to come back for an interview.

Where the Jobs Are

About two-thirds of all new jobs are now created by small businesses. While the largest corporations have reduced the number of employees, small businesses have been creating as many as 80 percent of the new jobs. There are many opportunities to obtain training and advance in smaller organizations, too. Many do not even have a personnel department, so non-traditional job search techniques are particularly effective with them.

JIST Cards

This is a job search tool that gets results. Typed, printed or even neatly written on a 3-by-5 inch card, a JIST Card contains the essential information most employers want to know. Look at the sample cards that follow:

THOMAS WELBORN   **Home:** (602) 253-9678
Leave Message: (602) 257-6643

OBJECTIVE: Electronics — installation, maintenance and sales

SKILLS: Four years work experience plus two years advanced training in electronics. A.S. degree in Electronics Engineering Technology. Managed a $300,000/yr. business while going to school full time, with grades in the top 25%. Familiar with all major electronic diagnostic and repair equipment. Hands-on experience with medical, consumer, communications, and industrial electronics equipment and applications. Good problem-solving and communication skills. Customer service oriented.

Willing to do what it takes to get the job done.

SANDY ZAREMBA

Home: (219) 232-7608   **Message**: (219) 234-7465
Position: General Office/Clerical

Over two years work experience plus one year of training in office practices. Type 75 wpm, trained in word processing operations, post general ledger, handle payables, receivables, and most accounting tasks. Responsible for daily deposits averaging $5,000. Good interpersonal skills. Can meet strict deadlines and handle pressure well.

Willing to work any hours.

Organized, honest, reliable, and hard working.

JIST Cards are an effective job-search tool! Give one to friends and network contacts. Attach it to a resume. Enclose one in your thank-you notes before or after an interview. Leave it with employers as a "business card." Use them in many creative ways. Even though they can be typed or even handwritten, it is best to have 100 or more printed so you can put lots of them in circulation. Thousands of job seekers have used them and they get results!

Telephone Contacts

Once you have your JIST Card, it is easy to create a telephone contact "script" based on it. Adapt the basic script to call people you know or your *Yellow Pages* leads. Just pick out *Yellow Page* index categories that might use a person with your skills. Then ask for the person who is most likely to supervise you and present your phone script.

While it doesn't work all the time, with practice, most people can get one or more interviews in an hour by making these "cold" calls. Here is a phone script based on another JIST card:

"Hello, my name is Pam Nykanen. I am interested in a position in hotel management. I have four years experience in sales, catering and accounting with a 300 room hotel. I also have an Associate Degree in Hotel Management plus one year with the Bradey Culinary Institute. During my employment, I helped double revenue from meetings and conferences and increase bar revenues by 46 percent. I have good problem-solving skills and am good with people. I am also well-organized, hard working, and detail-oriented. When can I come in for an interview?"

Spend at Least Twenty-Five Hours a Week Looking

Average job seekers spend about five hours weekly actually looking for work. They are also unemployed an average of three or more months! People who follow JIST's advice spend much more time on their job search each week. They also get jobs in less than half the average time. Time management is the key.

Decide how many hours per week you plan to look for a job. JIST suggests at least 25 hours per week if you are unem-

thing is to decide how many hours you can commit to your job search, and stay with it.

Decide on which days you will look for work. How many hours will you look each day? At what time will you begin and end your job search on each of these days? Look at the sample job search schedule that follows to see how one person planned her time. Create your own schedule on a sheet of paper or, better yet, buy a weekly or monthly planner at a department store or stationery store.

Schedule how to spend your time each day. This is **very** important since most job seekers find it hard to stay productive each day. You already know which job search methods are most effective and you should plan on spending more of your time using these methods. The sample daily schedule that follows has been very effective for people who have used it, and will give you ideas for your own schedule.

Sample Daily Schedule

7:00 - 8:00 a.m	Get up, shower, dress, eat breakfast.
8:00 - 8:15	Organize work space; review schedule for interviews or follow ups; update schedule.
8:15 - 9:00	Review old leads for follow up; develop new leads (want ads, *Yellow Pages*, networking lists, etc.).
9:00 - 10:00	Make phone calls, set up interviews.
10:00 - 10:15	Take a break!
10:15 - 11:00	Make more calls.
11:00 - 12:00 p.m.	Make follow up calls as needed.
12:00 - 1:00	Lunch break.
1:00 - 5:00	Go on interviews; cold contacts in the field; research or interviews at the library.

Get Two Interviews a Day

The average job seeker gets about five interviews a month—fewer than two interviews a week. Yet many job seekers using JIST techniques find it easy to get two interviews a day! To do this, you must redefine what an interview is.

An interview is face-to-face contact with anyone who has the authority to hire or supervise a person with your skills. They may or may not have a job opening at the time you interview with them.

With this definition, it is *much* easier to get interviews. You can now interview with all kinds of potential employers, not just those who have a job opening. Many job seekers use the *Yellow Pages* to get two interviews with just an hour of calls by using the telephone contact script discussed earlier! Others simply drop in on potential employers and ask for an unscheduled interview—and they get them. Not always, of course, but often enough.

Getting two interviews a day equals 10 a week—over 40 a month. That's 800 percent more interviews than the average job seeker gets. Who do you think will get a job offer quicker?

Answering Interview Questions

Here's a list of 10 questions asked most often during interviews:

1. Why don't you tell me about yourself?
2. Why should I hire you?
3. What are your major strengths?
4. What are your major weaknesses?
5. What sort of pay do you expect to receive?
6. How does your previous experience relate to the jobs we have here?
7. What are your plans for the future?
8. What will your former employer (or references) say about you?
9. Why are you looking for this type of position and why here?
10. Why don't you tell me about your personal situation?

We don't have the space here to give thorough answers to all of these questions. There are potentially hundreds more. While the employer may ask questions to weed some applicants out, you want to end up presenting your skills. Rather than giving you answers to questions you may not be asked, it is more important to learn an approach to answering almost any interview question.

The Three Step Answer Formula

1. **Understand what is really being asked.**

   Most questions are really trying to find out about your self-management skills. While they are rarely this blunt, the employer's *real* question is often:
   - Can I depend on you?
   - Are you easy to get along with?
   - Are you a good worker?
   - Do you have the experience and training to do the job if we hire you?

2. **Answer the question briefly.**

   Acknowledge the facts, but...
   - Present them as an advantage, not a disadvantage.

3. **Answer the real concern by presenting your related skills.**
   - Base your answer
   - on your key skills you identified earlier in this chapter.
   - Give examples to support your skills statements.

For example, an employer might say, "We were looking for someone with more experience in this field. Why should we consider you?" Here is one possible answer: "I'm sure there are people who have more experience, but I *do* have over six years of work experience including three years of advanced training and hands-on experience using the latest methods and techniques. Because my training is recent, I am open to new ideas and am used to working hard and learning quickly."

Whatever your situation, learn to use it to your advantage! Use " The Three Step Answer Formula" to practice your interview process. It works!

Dress and Grooming Rule

If you make a negative first impression, you won't get a second chance to make a good one. So do everything possible to make a good impression. A good rule for dressing for an interview is:

> **Dress like you think the boss will dress—**
> *only neater.*

Dress for success! If necessary, get help selecting an interview outfit from someone who dresses well. Pay close attention to your grooming, too. Written things like correspondence and resumes must be neat and error-free since they create an impression as well.

Follow Up on All Contacts

People who follow up with potential employers and with others in their network get jobs faster than those who do not. Here are three rules:

1. Send a thank-you note to every person who helps you in your job search.
2. Send the thank-you note within 24 hours after you speak with them.
3. Develop a system to follow up on "good" contacts.

Thank-You Notes

Thank-you notes can be handwritten or typed on nice paper and matching envelopes. Keep them simple, neat and error-free. Here's a sample:

2234 Riverwood Ave.
Philadelphia, PA 17963
April 16, 19XX

Ms. Helen A. Colcord
Henderson & Associates, Inc.
1801 Washington Blvd., Suite 1201
Philadelphia, PA 17963

Dear Ms. Colcord:

Thank you for sharing your time with me so generously today. I really appreciate seeing your state-of-the-art computer equipment.

Your advice has already proved helpful. I have an appointment to meet with Mr. Robert Hopper on Friday as you anticipated.

Please consider referring me to others if you think of someone else who might need a person with my skills.

Sincerely,
William Richardson

Job Lead Cards

Use a simple 3-by-5 inch card to keep essential information on each person in your network. Buy a 3-by-5 inch card file box and tabs for each day of the month. File the cards under the date you want to contact the person, and the rest is easy. I've found that staying in touch with a good contact every other week can pay off big. Here's a sample card to give you ideas to create your own:

Organization: _____

Contact Person: _____

Source of Lead: _____

Notes: _____

_____

_____

_____

Essential Job Search Data

Complete this section in pencil to allow changes. Take it with you to help in completing applications. It will also help in answering interview questions and writing resumes. In all sections, emphasize the skills and accomplishments that best support your ability to do the job you want! Use extra sheets as needed.

Key Accomplishments

List the three accomplishments which best prove your ability to do well in the kind of job you want.

1._____

_____

2._____

_____

3._____

_____

Education/Training

Name of high school(s)/years attended:

_____

_____

_____

_____

_____

Subjects related to job objective:

_____

_____

_____

_____

_____

_____

Extracurricular Activities/Hobbies/Leisure Activities:

_____

_____

_____

_____

_____

_____

_____

Accomplishments/Things You Did Well:

_____

_____

_____

_____

_____

_____

_____

Schools You Attended After High School, Years Attended, Degrees/Certificates Earned:

_____

_____

_____

_____

_____

Courses related to job objective:

_____

_____

_____

_____

_____

_____

Extracurricular Activities/Hobbies/Leisure Activities:

_____

_____

_____

_____

_____

_____

Accomplishments/Things You Did Well:

_____

_____

_____

_____

_____

_____

Military Training, On-the-Job, or Informal Training, Such as from a Hobby, Dates of Training, Type of Certificate Earned:

_____

_____

_____

_____

_____

_____

Specific things you can do as a result:

_____

_____

_____

_____

_____

_____

Work and Volunteer History

List your most recent job first, followed by each previous job. Include military experience and unpaid work here, too. Use additional sheets to cover *all* your significant jobs or unpaid experiences.

Whenever possible, provide numbers to support what you did: number of people served over one or more years, number of transactions processed, percent of sales increase, total inventory value you were responsible for, payroll of the staff you supervised, total budget you were responsible for, etc. As much as possible, mention results using numbers, too. These can be very impressive when mentioned in an interview or resume!

Job #1

Name of Organization: _____

_____

_____

_____

Address:_____

_____

_____

_____

Phone Number: _____

_____

Dates Employed: _____

Job Title(s): _____

_____

_____

Supervisor's Name: _____

_____

Details of any raises or promotions:

_____

_____

_____

_____

_____

_____

_____

Machinery or equipment you handled:

_____

_____

_____

_____

_____

_____

_____

Special skills this job required:

_____

_____

_____

_____

_____

_____

_____

List what you accomplished or did well:

_____

_____

_____

_____

_____

_____

_____

Job #2

Name of Organization: _____

_____

_____

_____

Address: _____

_____

_____

_____

Phone Number:_____

_____

Dates Employed: _____

Job Title(s): _____

_____

_____

Supervisor's Name: _____

_____

Details of any raises or promotions:

_____

_____

_____

_____

_____

_____

Machinery or equipment you handled:

_____

_____

_____

_____

_____

_____

_____

Special skills this job required:

_____

_____

_____

_____

_____

_____

_____

List what you accomplished or did well:

_____

_____

_____

_____

_____

_____

_____

Machinery or equipment you handled:

_____

_____

_____

_____

_____

_____

_____

Job #3

Name of Organization: _____

_____

_____

Address:_____

_____

_____

Phone Number: _____

_____

Dates Employed: _____

Job Title(s): _____

_____

_____

Supervisor's Name: _____

_____

Details of any raises or promotions:

_____

_____

_____

_____

_____

_____

Special skills this job required:

_____

_____

_____

_____

_____

_____

_____

List what you accomplished or did well:

_____

_____

_____

_____

_____

_____

References

Contact your references and let them know what type of job you want and why you are qualified. Be sure to review what they will say about you! Since some employers will not give out references by phone or in person, have previous employers write a letter of reference for you in advance. If you have a bad reference from a previous employer, negotiate what they will say about you or get written references from other people you worked with there. When creating your list of references, be sure to include your reference's name and job title, where he or she works, a business address and phone number, how that person knows you, and what your reference will say about you.

Writing Your Resume

You have already learned that sending out resumes and waiting is *not* an effective job-seeking technique. However, many employers *will* ask you for them, and they are a useful tool in your job search. Here are some basic tips to create a superior resume:

Write it yourself. It's OK to look at other resumes for ideas, but write yours yourself. It will force you to organize your thoughts and background.

Make it error free. One spelling or grammar error will create a negative impression. Get someone else to review your final draft for any errors. Then review it again!

Make it look good. Poor copy quality, cheap paper, bad type quality or anything else that creates a poor physical appearance will turn off employers to the best resume content. Get professional help with typing and printing if necessary. Most print shops can do it all for you.

Be brief, be relevant. Many good resumes fit on one page—few justify more than two. Include only the most important points. Use short sentences and action words. If it doesn't relate to and support the job objective, cut it!

Be honest. Don't overstate your qualifications. If you end up getting a job you can't handle, it will **not** be to your advantage. Most employers will see right through it and not hire you.

Be positive. Emphasize your accomplishments and results. This is no place to be too humble or to display your faults.

Be specific. Rather than "I am good with people," say "I supervised four people in the warehouse and increased productivity by 30 percent." Use numbers whenever possible, such as the number of people served, percent of increase, or dollar increase.

You should also know that everyone feels they are a resume expert. Whatever you do, someone will tell you it is wrong. For this reason, it is important to understand that a resume is a job-search tool. You should never delay or slow down your job search because your resume is not "good enough." The best approach is to create a simple and acceptable resume as soon as possible, then use it! As time permits, make a better one if you feel you need to.

Simple Chronological Resume

This is the resume format most people use. It is a simple resume that presents previous experience in chronological order: the most recent experience is listed first followed by each previous job. Look at the following resumes of Judith Jones on pages 153 and 154. Both are chronological resumes, but notice that the second resume includes some improvements over her first. The improved resume is clearly better, but both would be acceptable to most employers. Here are some tips for completing your basic resume:

Name. Use your formal name rather than a nickname if it sounds more professional.

Address. Be complete. Include zip code and avoid abbreviations. If you may move, use the address of a friend or relative or be certain to include a forwarding address.

Telephone Number. If your home number is often left unanswered during the day, include an alternate number where a message can be left. A reliable friend or relative will usually agree to this, but you could get an answering machine. Employers are most likely to try to reach you by phone, so having a reliable way to be reached is very important.

Job Objective. This is optional for a very basic resume but is still important to include. Notice that Judy is keeping her options open with her objective. Saying "Secretary" or "Clerical" might limit her to lower paying jobs, or even prevent her from being considered for jobs she might take.

Education and Training. Include any formal training you've had plus any training that supports the job you seek. If you did not finish a formal degree or program, list what you did complete. Include any special accomplishments.

Previous Experience. The standard approach is to list employer, job title, dates employed, and responsibilities. But there are better ways of presenting your experience. Look over the "Improved Chronological Resume" for ideas. The improved version emphasizes results, accomplishments and performance.

Personal Data. Neither of the sample resumes have the standard height, weight, or marital status included on so many resumes. That information is simply not relevant! If you do include some personal information, put it at the bottom and keep it related to the job you want.

References. There is no need to list references. If employers want them, they will ask. If your references are particularly good, it's OK to say so.

Improved Chronological Resume

Once you have a simple, error-free and eye-pleasing resume, get on with your job search. There is no reason to delay! But you may want to create a better one in your spare time (evenings and/or weekends). If you do, here are some tips:

Job Objective: Job objectives often limit the type of jobs for which you will be considered. Instead, think of the type of work you want to do and can do well and describe it in more general terms. Instead of "Restaurant Manager," for example, say "Managing a small to mid-sized business" if that is what you are qualified to do.

Education and Training: New graduates should emphasize their recent training and education more than those with five years or so of recent and related work experience. Think about any special accomplishments while in school and include these if they relate to the job. Did you work full-time while in school? Did you do particularly well in work-related classes, get an award, participate in sports?

Skills and Accomplishments: Employers are interested in what you accomplished and did well. Include those things that relate to doing well in the job you are after now. Even "small" things count. Perhaps your attendance was perfect, you met a tight deadline, did the work of others during vacations, etc. Be specific and include numbers—even if you have to estimate them.

Judith J. Jones   (317) 653-9217 (home)
115 South Hawthorne Avenue   (317) 653-7608 (leave message)
Chicago, Illinois 46204

JOB OBJECTIVE

Desire a position in the office management, secretarial or clerical area. Prefer a position requiring responsibility and a variety of tasks.

EDUCATION AND TRAINING

Acme Business College, Indianapolis, Indiana — Graduate of a one-year
    business/secretarial program, 1993.
John Adams High School, South Bend, Indiana — Diploma, business education.
U.S. Army — Financial procedures, accounting functions.
Other: Continuing Education classes and workshops in business communication, scheduling
    systems, and customer relations.

EXPERIENCE

1992-1993 — Returned to school to complete and update my business skills. Learned word
    processing, spread sheet, and other new office techniques.
1989-1992 — Claims Processor, Blue Spear Insurance Co., Indianapolis, Indiana. Handled
    customer medical claims, used a CRT, filed, miscellaneous clerical duties.
1987-1989 — Sales Clerk, Judy's Boutique, Indianapolis, Indiana. Responsible for counter
    sales, display design, and selected tasks.
1985-1987 — E4, U.S. Army. Assigned to various stations as a specialist in finance
    operations. Promoted prior to honorable discharge.
Previous jobs — Held part-time and summer jobs throughout high school.

PERSONAL

I am reliable, hard working, and good with people.

Judith J. Jones   (317) 653-9217 (home)
115 South Hawthorne Avenue   (317) 653-7608 (message)
Chicago, Illinois 46204

POSITION DESIRED

Seeking position requiring excellent management and secretarial skills in office environment. Position could require a variety of tasks including typing, word processing, accounting/bookkeeping functions, and customer contact.

EDUCATION AND TRAINING

Acme Business College, Indianapolis, Indiana. Completed one-year program in Professional Secretarial and Office Management. Grades in top 30% of my class. Courses: word processing, accounting theory and systems, time management, basic supervision & others.

John Adams High School, South Bend, Indiana. Graduated with emphasis on business and secretarial courses. Won shorthand contest.

Other: Continuing education at my own expense (Business Communications, Customer Relations, Computer Applications, other courses).

EXPERIENCE

1992-1993 — Returned to Business School to update skills. Advanced coursework in accounting and office management. Learned to operate word processing equipment including Wang, IBM, DEC. Gained operating knowledge of computers.

1989-1992 — Claims Processor, Blue Spear Insurance Company, Indianapolis, Indiana. Handled 50 complex medical insurance claims per day — 18% above department average. Received two merit raises for performance.

1987-1989 — Assistant Manager, Judy's Boutique, Indianapolis, Indiana. Managed sales, financial records, inventory, purchasing, correspondence and related tasks during owner's absence. Supervised four employees. Sales increased 15% during my tenure.

1985-1987 — Finance Specialist (E4), U.S. Army. Responsible for the systematic processing of 500 invoices per day from commercial vendors. Trained and supervised eight others. Devised internal system allowing 15% increase in invoices processed with a decrease in personnel.

Previous — Various part-time and summer jobs through high school. Learned to deal with customers, meet deadlines and other skills.

SPECIAL SKILLS AND ABILITIES

80 words per minute on electric typewriter, more on word processor, can operate most office equipment. Good math skills. Accept supervision, able to supervise others. Excellent attendance record.

PERSONAL

I have excellent references, learn quickly, and am willing to relocate.

Job Titles: Many job titles don't accurately reflect the job you did. For example, your job title may have been "cashier" but you also opened the store, trained new staff, and covered for the boss on vacations. Perhaps "Head Cashier and Assistant Manager" would be more accurate. Check with your previous employer if not sure.

Promotions: If you were promoted or got good evaluations, say so. A promotion to a more responsible job can be handled as a separate job if this makes sense.

Problem Areas: Employers look for any sign of instability or lack of reliability. It is very expensive to hire and train someone who won't stay or who won't work out. Gaps in employment, jobs held for short periods of time or a lack of direction in the jobs you've held are all things that employers are concerned about. If you have any legitimate explanation, use it. For example:

"1987—Continued my education at..."

"1988—Traveled extensively throughout the U.S."

"1988 to present—Self-employed barn painter and widget maker"

"1989—Had first child, took year off before returning to work"

Use entire years or even seasons of years to avoid displaying a shorter gap you can't explain easily: "Spring 1992—Fall 1993" will not show you as unemployed from January to March, 1993, for example.

Remember that a resume can get you screened out, but it is up to you to get the interview and the job. So, cut out *anything* that is negative in your resume!

Skills and Combination Resumes

There are no firm rules on how you should do your resume. Different formats make sense for different people.

Besides the chronological format, the functional or "skills" resume is often used. This resume emphasizes your most important *skills,* supported by specific examples of how you have used them. This approach allows you to use any part of your life history to support your ability to do the job you want.

While the skills resume can be very effective, it does require more work to create. And some employers don't like them because they can hide a job seeker's faults better than a chronological resume (such as job gaps, lack of formal education or no related work experience).

Still, a skills resume may make sense for you. Look over the sample resumes provided on the following pages for ideas. Notice that one resume includes elements of a skills *and* a chronological resume. These are called "combination" resumes—an approach that makes sense if your previous job history or education and training is positive.

The Quick Job Search Review

Go at your job search as if it were a job itself. Get organized and spend at least 25 hours per week actively looking. Follow up on all the leads you generate and send thank-you notes. If you want to get a good job quickly, you must get lots of interviews!

Pay attention to all the details, then be yourself in the interview. Remember that employers are people, too. They will hire someone they feel will do the job well, who will be reliable, and who will fit easily into their work environment. When you want the job, tell the employer why they should hire you. Tell them you want the job and why. It's that simple.

I wish you well in your job search and your life.

ALAN ATWOOD
3231 East Harbor Road
Grand Rapids, Michigan 41103
Home: (303) 447-2111   Message (303) 547-8201

Objective: A responsible position in retail sales

Areas of Accomplishment:

Customer Service
- Communicate well with all age groups.
- Able to interpret customer concerns to help them find the items they want.
- Received 6 Employee of the Month awards in 3 years.

Merchandise Display
- Developed display skills via in-house training and experience.
- Received Outstanding Trainee Award for Christmas Toy Display.
- Dress mannequins, arrange table displays, and organize sale merchandise.

Stock Control and Marketing
- Maintained and marked stock during department manager's 6 week illness.
- Developed more efficient record-keeping procedures.

Additional Skills
- Operate cash register, IBM compatible hardware, calculators, and electronic typewriters.
- Punctual, honest, reliable, and a hardworking self-starter.

Experience: Harper's Department Store
Grand Rapids, Michigan
19XX to Present

Education: Central High School
Grand Rapids, Michigan
3.6/4.0 grade point average
Honor Graduate in Distributive Education
Two years retail sales training in Distributive
Education. Also courses in Business Writing,
Accounting, Typing, and Word Processing.

LILI LI LU
1536 Sierra Way • Piedmont, California 97435 • Telephone 736-436-3874

OBJECTIVE
Program Development, Coordination & Administration
Especially in a people-oriented organization where there is a need to assure broad cooperation through the use of sound planning and strong administration and persuasive skills to achieve community goals.

MAJOR AREAS OF EXPERTISE AND ABILITY
Budgeting & Management for Sound Program Development
With partner, established new association devoted to maximum personal development and self-realization for each of its members. Over a period of time, administered budget totaling $285,000. Jointly planned growth of group and related expenditures, investments, programs, and development of property holdings to realize current and long-term goals. As a result, holdings increased 25 fold over the period, reserves invested increased 1200%, and all major goals for members have been achieved.

Purchasing to Assure Smooth Flow of Needed Supplies and Services
Made most purchasing decisions to assure maximum production from available funds. Maintained continuous stock inventory to meet on-going needs, selected suppliers, assured proper disbursements to achieve a strong continuing line of credit while minimizing financing costs.

Transportation Management
Determined transportation needs of group. Assured maximum utilization of limited motor pool. Arranged four major moves of all facilities, furnishings, and equipment to new locations — two across country.

Other Functions Performed
Crisis management, proposal preparation, political analysis, nutrition, recreation planning and administration, stock market operations, taxes, community organization, social affairs administration (including VIP entertaining), landscaping (two awards for excellence), contract negotiations, teaching and more.

SOME SPECIFIC RESULTS
Above experience gained in 20 years devoted to family development and household management in partnership with my husband, Harvey Wangchung Lu, who is equally responsible for results produced. **Primary achievements:** Son Lee, 19, honor student at Harvard majoring in physics, state forensics champion. Daughter Su, 18, leading candidate for U.S. Olympic team in gymnastics, entering pre-law studies at the U of C, Berkeley. **Secondary achievements:** President of Piedmont High School PTA two years. Organized successful citizen protest to stop incursion of Oakland commercialism on Piedmont area. Appointed by Robert F. Kennedy as coordinator of his campaign in Oakland.

PERSONAL DATA AND OTHER FACTS
Bachelor of Arts (Asian History), Cody College, Cody, California. Highly active in community affairs. Have learned that there is a spark of genius in almost everyone, which, when nurtured, can flare into dramatic achievement.

*This resume is based on one found in *Who's Hiring Who* by Richard Lathrop and published by Ten Speed Press.

Thomas Welborn

637 Wickham Road   Home: (602) 253-9678
Phoenix, AZ 85009   Leave Message: (602) 257-6643

JOB OBJECTIVE

Position in the electronics industry requiring skills in the design, sale, installation, maintenance, and repair of audio, video, and other advanced electronics. Prefer tasks needing creative problem-solving skills and customer contact.

EDUCATION

ITT TECHNICAL INSTITUTE

Phoenix, AZ
A.S. Degree,
Electronics Engineering
Technology
1992-1993

Completed a comprehensive, two-year curriculum including over 2,000 hours of class and advanced laboratory. Theoretical, practical and hands-on knowledge of audio and RF amplifiers, AM/FM transmitter-receiver circuits, OP amplifiers, microwave and radar communications, digital circuits, and much more. Excellent attendance while working part-time to pay tuition. Graduating in top 25%.

PLAINS JR. COLLEGE

Phoenix, AZ
1991-1992

Courses included digital electronics, programming, business, and computer applications. Worked full-time and maintained a B+ average.

DESERT VIEW H.S.

1989 graduate

College prep. courses including advanced math, business, marketing, merchandising, computer orientation, and Basic programming. Very active in varsity sports. National Jr. Honor Society for two years.

SKILLS

PROBLEM-SOLVING: Familiar with the underlying theory of most electronic systems and am particularly strong in isolating problems by using logic and persistence. I enjoy the challenge of solving complex problems and will work long hours, if necessary, to do this on a deadline.

INTERPERSONAL: Have supervised five staff and trained many more. Comfortable with one-to-one and small group communications. Can explain technical issues simply to customers of varying levels of sophistication. Had over 10,000 customer contacts in one job with no complaints and several written commendations.

TECHNICAL: Background in a variety of technical areas including medical equipment, consumer electronics, computers, automated cash registers, photocopiers, standard office and computer equipment and peripherals. Have designed special application combinational and sequential logic circuits using TTL logic. Constructed Z-80 microprocessor and wrote several machine language programs for this system. Can diagnose and repair problems in digital and analog circuits.

ORGANIZATIONAL: Have set up and run my own small business and worked in another responsible job while going to school full-time. Earned enough money to live independently and pay all school expenses during this time. I can work independently and have learned to use my time efficiently.

EXPERIENCE

BANDLER'S INN: 1991-present. Waiter, promoted to night manager. Complete responsibility for all operations of a shift grossing over $300,000 in sales per year. Supervised five full-time and three part-time staff. Business increased during my employment by 35% and profits by 42%, much of it due to word-of-mouth advertising of satisfied customers. Worked nights and weekends while attending school full time.

FRANKLIN HOSPITAL: 1989-91. Electronic Service Technicians' Assistant. Worked in Medical, Physics, and Electronics Departments. Assisted technicians in routine service and maintenance of a variety of hospital equipment. Part time while going to school.

TOM'S YARD SERVICE: 1986-1988. Set up a small business while in school. Worked part-time and summers doing yard work. Made enough money to buy a car and save for tuition.

APPENDIX A: Employment Projections Through the Year 2005 For the 500 Largest Occupations[1]

This appendix contains a listing providing additional information for over 500 of the largest occupations. Three alternative scenarios were projected by the U.S. Department of Labor for the year 2005: moderate, low-growth, and high-growth. We will deal primarily with the moderate projections.

The moderate growth rates among the occupations listed range from an increase of 92 percent to a decline of 60 percent, a much greater range than for the major occupational groups of jobs. The table in this appendix presents current and projected employment data on each of the occupations. These occupations fall into three basic categories, which are explained below.

Fastest Growing Occupations

Nearly half of the 20 fastest growing occupations are in health services, reflecting the very rapid growth of the health services industries as a whole. The health-related occupation projected to grow most rapidly between 1990 and 2005 is medical assistant, with a projected growth rate of 76 percent. Home health aides will also be in great demand to serve the needs of the growing aged and ill population who live at home. Other health occupations with rapid projected growth include: radiologic technicians and technologists, medical record technicians, medical secretaries, physical therapists, surgical technologists, physical and corrective therapy assistants and aides, and occupational therapists.

Computer technology is also creating rapid growth in computer-related occupations such as data processing equipment repair and operations research analysis.

Paralegals are expected to benefit from the rapid growth of the legal services industry as well as increasing use of paralegals within the profession. This is projected to be the second fastest growing occupation through 2005.

Securities and financial services sales representatives, travel agents, and social welfare service aides will also enjoy a growing demand for their services in the job market.

Occupations with the Largest Job Growth

In addition to rapidly growing occupations, occupations having the largest numerical increases are important in identifying careers that will provide favorable job opportunities.

Retail trade, health services, and educational services currently have high employment levels and are projected to continue to grow. Retail trade includes the occupation with the largest expected job growth—retail salespersons. Within retail trade, the rapidly growing food and beverage establishments industry has two of the top 20 occupations with the largest growth: chefs, cooks, and other kitchen workers; and food and beverage service workers. Cashiers will also see an increase in job opportunities.

Health services has the profession with one of the highest expected increases—registered nurses. Nursing aides and licensed practical nurses are also included among the top growth occupations.

Many secondary school teachers, preschool workers, and teacher aids will also be needed. Other occupations with a wide range of skills and earnings are expected to have large job gains, but are not easily identifiable with an industry group. Demand for general managers and top executives is projected to grow because of the increasing complexity of industrial and commercial organizations. More general office clerks will be needed for record keeping needs and other office procedures that are not easily automated.

Declining Occupations and Worker Displacement

This analysis deals only with the potential job losses implied by the 1990-2005 employment projections. It does not take into consideration workers who may lose jobs because of business failures. Workers in declining occupations should be heartened to know that not all whose jobs are eliminated become displaced. Their employers may place them in similar occupations or provide training for other jobs.

The outlook for reemployment in the same occupation is dim for assemblers and textile machine operators whose jobs are eliminated. Most such jobs are specialized in declining manufacturing industries.

Workers employed in declining industries whose jobs entail skills which are transferable to other types of organizations will find similar work more easily. For example, many secretaries employed in declining industries will lose their jobs. However, employment for secretarial workers is projected to increase significantly in the growing industries, producing an increase of 540,000 secretarial jobs.

Other occupations with projected large job losses in the declining industries, but which will have even greater job gains in growing industries include: hand freight, stock, and material movers; blue-collar worker supervisors; bookkeeping, accounting and auditing clerks; general office clerks, and general managers and top executives.

Increased use of technology will reduce overall demand for precision inspectors, testers, and graders, as well as for electrical and electronic assemblers, welders and cutters, and typists and word processors.

1 The narrative and charts in this section are based on information from "Occupational Projections and Training Data," Bulletin 2401, and "Outlook 1990-2005," Bulletin 2401, both by the U.S. Department of Labor.

More Education and Training Equals More Opportunities

In general, employment is projected to increase faster in occupational groups requiring more education than in those requiring less. The fastest growing occupational groups (executive, administrative, and managerial; professional specialty; and technicians and related support occupations) have the highest proportion of workers who completed at least four years of college.

There are some exceptions to this pattern. Service workers, a major group having relatively few workers with a college degree and a high proportion with less than a high school education, are projected to grow faster than average. And only average growth is projected for college and university professionals, at a rate of 19 percent, because college enrollments are not expected to increase between 1990 and 2005.

The overall occupational structure is expected to remain stable over the 1990-2005 period. This implies that workers with a broad spectrum of educational requirements will continue to be needed. Jobs will be available for the less educated as well as for those with college degrees. But workers in all occupations with four-year college degrees earn more on average than workers without such degrees.

Must You Have a College Degree to Get a Good Job?

Don't assume that good jobs will be available in the future only for people with college degrees and only in those fields that are projected to grow faster than average. Many individual jobs within various occupational groups do not require a four-year college degree and have above-average earnings. Many such occupations are expected to offer good employment prospects through 2005 due to projected growth rates that are at least average and to have many job openings to replace workers who leave the labor force or transfer to other occupations.

Several of these occupations are found in the construction trades, including bricklayers and stonemasons; electricians; plumbers and pipefitters, and structural and reinforcing iron workers. Favorable employment opportunities exist for other skilled workers such as mechanics, installers, and repairers; and heating, air conditioning and refrigeration technicians.

Although nearly half of all workers in marketing and sales occupations have some college training, most of these jobs do not require a four-year college degree. Among those that are expected to have very good employment prospects through 2005, and that currently have above-average earnings, are insurance agents and brokers, travel agents, and real estate sales agents.

Occupations in other fields that are expected to be equally promising include: paralegals; airplane pilots and flight engineers; flight attendants; reservation and transportation ticket agents and travel clerks; dental assistants, and engineering, science, and data processing managers.

Workers with the highest levels of education, however, will continue to have a competitive advantage over workers with less education, as well as more job options.

Table 6. Occupational employment and job openings data, 1990-2005, and worker characteristics, 1990

(Numbers in thousands)

1990 Matrix occupation	Total employment		Employment change, 1990-2005		Annual average job openings, 1990-2005		Worker characteristics, percent of workers				
	1990	2005	Number	Percent	Growth plus total replacement needs	Growth plus net replacement needs	Self-employ-ed	Part time	Fe-male	Black	Hisp-anic
Total, all occupations	122,573	147,191	24,618	20.1	24,162	4,385	8.3	16.9	45.4	10.1	7.5
Executive, administrative, and managerial occupations	12,451	15,866	3,414	27.4	1,395	433	12.8	6.2	40.0	5.7	3.9
Managerial and administrative occupations	8,838	11,174	2,336	26.4	901	305	15.0	–	–	–	–
Administrative services managers	221	273	52	23.4	22	7	0.0	–	–	–	–
Communication, transportation, and utilities operations managers	143	189	45	31.7	16	5	0.0	–	–	–	–
Construction managers	183	243	60	32.9	20	7	1.1	–	–	–	–
Education administrators	348	434	85	24.5	36	14	8.9	8.6	54.1	9.5	3.8
Engineering, mathematical, and natural science managers	315	423	108	34.2	35	12	0.0	–	–	–	–
Financial managers	701	894	193	27.5	67	24	1.0	2.6	44.1	4.1	2.9
Food service and lodging managers	595	793	198	33.2	65	23	41.5	–	–	–	–
Funeral directors and morticians	35	41	6	17.2	3	1	34.2	5.6	12.1	11.1	1.8
General managers and top executives	3,086	3,684	598	19.4	294	90	0.0	–	–	–	–
Government chief executives and legislators	71	74	3	4.4	4	2	0.0	–	–	–	–
Industrial production managers	210	251	41	19.6	20	6	0.0	–	–	–	–
Marketing, advertising, and public relations managers	427	630	203	47.4	59	23	3.0	2.6	31.1	2.9	3.1
Personnel, training, and labor relations managers	178	235	57	31.8	19	8	0.6	1.8	55.1	6.7	3.2
Property and real estate managers	225	302	76	33.8	30	8	39.5	14.1	45.2	6.5	5.1
Purchasing managers	248	298	49	19.9	15	8	0.0	2.1	31.9	4.8	3.5
All other managers and administrators	1,850	2,412	562	30.4	196	67	50.1	–	–	–	–
Management support occupations	3,613	4,691	1,079	29.9	494	128	7.5	–	–	–	–
Accountants and auditors	985	1,325	340	34.5	144	38	10.4	6.3	50.8	7.4	3.8
Budget analysts	64	78	14	22.2	9	2	0.0	–	–	–	–
Claims examiners, property and casualty insurance	30	40	9	30.6	4	1	0.0	–	–	–	–
Construction and building inspectors	60	71	11	18.9	4	2	1.7	3.7	5.1	7.3	4.1
Cost estimators	173	215	42	24.3	24	5	0.0	–	–	–	–
Credit analysts	36	46	10	27.4	5	1	0.0	–	–	–	–
Employment interviewers and personnel specialists[1]	361	468	107	29.5	44	14	3.1	6.8	60.8	11.9	4.2
Employment interviewers, private or public employment service	83	102	19	23.4	9	3	0.0	–	–	–	–
Inspectors and compliance officers, except construction	156	202	46	29.8	14	6	1.9	–	–	–	–
Loan officers and counselors	172	219	47	27.6	24	6	0.0	–	–	–	–
Management analysts	151	230	79	52.3	32	7	44.9	19.2	34.0	6.5	2.0
Personnel, training, and labor relations specialists	278	366	87	31.4	34	11	4.0	–	–	–	–
Purchasing agents, except wholesale, retail, and farm products	218	266	47	21.7	25	7	2.7	2.8	43.6	4.9	4.9
Tax examiners, collectors, and revenue agents	62	70	8	12.9	5	2	0.0	–	–	–	–
Underwriters	105	130	25	24.2	14	4	0.0	5.1	67.6	8.1	5.2
Wholesale and retail buyers, except farm products	194	235	41	21.0	30	7	13.4	11.1	50.7	3.8	4.3
All other management support workers	846	1,097	251	29.7	116	29	6.3	–	–	–	–
Professional specialty occupations	15,800	20,907	5,107	32.3	1,904	626	9.2	15.1	51.2	6.7	3.4
Engineers	1,519	1,919	400	26.3	100	61	2.4	–	–	–	–
Aeronautical and astronautical engineers	73	88	15	20.5	4	3	1.4	1.1	7.3	4.8	2.4
Chemical engineers	48	54	6	11.6	2	2	4.1	0.6	10.9	1.7	2.2
Civil engineers, including traffic engineers	198	257	59	30.0	18	8	3.5	2.6	5.0	4.0	3.2
Electrical and electronics engineers	426	571	145	34.1	26	19	1.4	1.6	8.7	3.8	3.3
Industrial engineers, except safety engineers	135	160	26	18.9	4	5	1.5	1.3	11.9	4.4	3.2
Mechanical engineers	233	289	56	23.9	14	9	2.1	1.6	5.4	3.5	1.9
Metallurgists and metallurgical, ceramic, and materials engineers	18	22	4	21.3	1	1	0.0	5.1	6.5	0.0	0.5
Mining engineers, including mine safety engineers	4	4	0	4.2	0	0	0.0	3.2	2.4	0.7	0.0
Nuclear engineers	18	18	0	-0.3	1	0	0.0	0.5	5.1	5.9	1.3
Petroleum engineers	17	18	0	1.2	1	0	5.7	2.0	13.3	2.0	0.7
All other engineers	347	436	89	25.8	28	14	3.5	–	–	–	–
Architects and surveyors	236	284	48	20.2	29	7	19.1	–	–	–	–
Architects[1]	128	160	32	25.3	15	4	30.5	9.2	18.4	0.9	3.5
Architects, except landscape and marine	108	134	26	24.2	13	4	33.3	–	–	–	–
Landscape architects	20	26	6	31.3	3	1	15.1	–	–	–	–
Surveyors	108	123	15	14.2	14	2	5.6	5.7	5.7	3.5	2.7
Life scientists	174	230	56	32.3	15	9	4.0	–	–	–	–
Agricultural and food scientists	25	32	7	26.6	2	1	12.0	14.3	20.5	0.2	4.4
Biological scientists	62	83	21	33.9	5	3	1.6	5.6	40.9	2.7	3.1
Foresters and conservation scientists	29	32	4	12.5	2	1	3.5	1.4	11.2	1.0	3.6
Medical scientists	19	31	12	66.0	2	1	10.6	–	–	–	–

See footnotes at end of table.

Table 6. Occupational employment and job openings data, 1990-2005, and worker characteristics, 1990 — Continued

(Numbers in thousands)

1990 Matrix occupation	Total employment		Employment change, 1990-2005		Annual average job openings, 1990-2005		Worker characteristics, percent of workers				
	1990	2005	Number	Percent	Growth plus total replacement needs	Growth plus net replacement needs	Self-employed	Part time	Female	Black	Hispanic
All other life scientists	39	51	12	31.8	3	2	0.0	–	–	–	–
Computer, mathematical, and operations research analysts	571	987	416	72.8	79	33	8.1	–	–	–	–
Actuaries	13	18	4	33.6	1	0	0.0	0.8	34.3	5.8	0.7
Systems analysts and computer scientists	463	829	366	78.9	67	28	9.1	4.6	34.5	7.0	3.3
Statisticians	16	18	2	11.7	1	0	6.3	14.1	49.9	4.1	2.3
Mathematicians and all other mathematical scientists	22	24	2	9.5	2	0	0.0	–	–	–	–
Operations research analysts	57	100	42	73.2	7	4	5.2	3.5	41.5	5.2	4.2
Physical scientists	200	241	41	20.5	15	9	5.5	–	–	–	–
Chemists	83	96	13	15.6	6	3	1.2	2.3	27.0	4.6	5.9
Geologists, geophysicists, and oceanographers	48	58	11	22.3	4	2	14.7	2.4	14.3	0.6	0.4
Meteorologists	5	7	2	29.5	0	0	5.0	17.5	0.0	0.0
Physicists and astronomers	20	21	1	5.1	1	1	10.0	7.5	7.3	1.1	3.6
All other physical scientists	44	59	15	33.9	4	2	2.3	–	–	–	–
Social scientists	224	320	96	42.8	29	10	29.0	–	–	–	–
Economists	37	45	8	21.4	8	2	29.4	9.5	43.8	4.0	3.3
Psychologists	125	204	79	63.6	13	6	40.9	20.7	58.4	6.6	3.6
Urban and regional planners	23	28	4	18.8	3	1	0.0	6.6	33.6	6.4	1.0
All other social scientists	38	43	4	10.8	4	1	7.8	–	–	–	–
Social, recreational, and religious workers	1,049	1,376	327	31.2	143	34	4.5	–	–	–	–
Clergy	209	228	19	9.1	13	5	15.8	8.2	9.6	6.9	2.1
Directors, religious activities and education	62	69	7	11.7	7	1	4.8	–	–	–	–
Human services workers	145	249	103	71.2	25	8	0.0	–	–	–	–
Recreation workers	194	241	47	24.3	42	6	0.5	20.8	70.9	14.7	6.1
Social workers, and human services workers[1]	583	837	254	43.5	81	23	1.7	10.1	68.2	21.8	6.1
Social workers	438	588	150	34.3	56	14	2.3	–	–	–	–
Lawyers and judicial workers	633	850	217	34.3	44	27	31.3	–	–	–	–
Judges, magistrates, and other judicial workers	46	57	11	23.6	3	2	0.0	6.1	25.4	11.2	0.3
Lawyers	587	793	206	35.1	41	26	33.8	5.9	20.6	3.2	2.8
Teachers, librarians, and counselors	5,687	7,280	1,593	28.0	762	209	2.3	–	–	–	–
Teachers, elementary	1,362	1,675	313	23.0	164	48	0.0	11.2	85.2	9.7	3.2
Teachers, preschool and kindergarten	425	598	173	40.9	73	14	1.6	–	–	–	–
Teachers, special education	332	467	134	40.5	34	12	0.0	10.2	84.8	11.8	2.2
Teachers, secondary school	1,280	1,717	437	34.2	159	58	0.0	10.5	53.1	7.1	3.3
College and university faculty	712	846	134	18.9	107	32	0.0	–	–	–	–
Other teachers and instructors	757	963	206	27.2	108	18	14.3	–	–	–	–
Farm and home management advisors	18	19	1	4.3	2	0	0.0	–	–	–	–
Instructors and coaches, sports and physical training	221	274	53	24.0	31	5	0.0	–	–	–	–
Adult and vocational education teachers	517	669	152	29.4	75	13	20.9	–	–	–	–
Instructors, adult (nonvocational) education	219	289	70	32.1	32	6	49.3	–	–	–	–
Teachers and instructors, vocational education and training	298	380	82	27.5	43	7	0.0	–	–	–	–
All other teachers and instructors	511	636	125	24.4	74	15	3.1	–	–	–	–
Librarians, archivists, curators, and related workers	166	187	21	12.4	19	5	0.6	–	–	–	–
Curators, archivists, museum technicians, and restorers	17	21	4	21.3	2	1	5.8	–	–	–	–
Librarians, professional	149	165	17	11.4	17	4	0.0	29.2	83.3	5.5	3.3
Counselors	144	192	49	34.0	23	6	1.4	11.5	61.9	16.3	4.1
Health diagnosing occupations	855	1,101	247	28.9	47	37	31.7	–	–	–	–
Dentists	174	196	21	12.3	7	6	52.7	13.2	9.5	4.9	3.5
Optometrists	37	45	8	20.3	2	1	32.1	13.4	11.8	1.3	1.1
Physicians	580	776	196	33.8	34	27	24.0	7.4	19.3	3.0	4.5
Podiatrists	16	23	7	46.4	1	1	50.7	17.7	11.9	1.2	0.0
Veterinarians and veterinary inspectors	47	62	14	30.8	3	2	42.5	4.8	23.9	0.3	0.0
Health assessment and treating occupations	2,305	3,304	999	43.4	231	106	3.0	–	–	–	–
Dietitians and nutritionists	45	56	11	24.4	3	2	6.7	–	–	–	–
Pharmacists	169	204	35	20.9	6	6	8.9	14.3	37.2	4.1	4.1
Physician assistants	53	72	18	33.9	6	2	1.9	–	–	–	–
Registered nurses	1,727	2,494	767	44.4	172	78	1.0	25.1	94.5	7.4	2.5
Therapists	311	479	168	53.9	44	18	10.6	–	–	–	–
Occupational therapists	36	56	20	55.2	5	2	5.5	21.3	94.9	1.2	3.5
Physical therapists	88	155	67	76.0	14	6	18.1	26.7	75.0	4.1	2.7
Recreational therapists	32	45	13	39.3	4	2	12.4	–	–	–	–
Respiratory therapists	60	91	31	52.1	8	3	0.0	16.2	60.1	11.7	2.8
Speech-language pathologists and audiologists	68	91	23	33.9	8	3	11.7	24.4	88.1	2.8	3.3
All other therapists	26	40	13	51.4	4	1	11.4	–	–	–	–
Writers, artists, and entertainers	1,542	1,915	373	24.2	258	54	33.5	–	–	–	–
Artists and commercial artists	230	303	73	31.7	41	10	62.2	24.7	51.2	2.8	4.5
Athletes, coaches, umpires, and referees	32	43	11	34.3	6	1	34.1	–	–	–	–

See footnotes at end of table.

Table 6. Occupational employment and job openings data, 1990-2005, and worker characteristics, 1990 — Continued

(Numbers in thousands)

1990 Matrix occupation	Total employment		Employment change, 1990-2005		Annual average job openings, 1990-2005		Worker characteristics, percent of workers				
	1990	2005	Number	Percent	Growth plus total replacement needs	Growth plus net replacement needs	Self-employed	Part time	Female	Black	Hispanic
Dancers and choreographers	9	12	3	38.1	2	0	11.6	51.1	78.8	21.7	5.3
Designers	339	428	89	26.3	55	11	33.6	–	–	–	–
Designers, except interior designers	270	335	65	24.2	43	8	31.9	–	–	–	–
Interior designers	69	93	24	34.5	12	3	40.3	–	–	–	–
Musicians	252	276	24	9.4	42	7	29.7	51.1	31.9	9.6	4.5
Photographers and camera operators	120	148	28	23.4	19	5	40.8	20.1	27.8	2.9	5.5
Camera operators, television, motion picture, video	13	17	5	36.9	2	1	7.9	–	–	–	–
Photographers	107	131	23	21.8	17	4	44.7	–	–	–	–
Producers, directors, actors, and entertainers	95	134	39	40.9	18	4	22.2	14.1	36.5	5.9	1.9
Public relations specialists and publicity writers	109	130	21	19.3	21	5	11.0	11.4	58.7	7.7	2.8
Radio and TV announcers and newscasters	57	68	11	20.1	9	2	5.3	33.3	18.5	6.9	2.7
Writers[1]	299	373	74	24.6	45	10	29.4	17.7	52.8	3.2	2.3
Reporters and correspondents	67	81	14	20.5	9	2	14.9	–	–	–	–
Writers and editors, including technical writers	232	292	60	25.8	36	8	33.6	–	–	–	–
All other professional workers	808	1,102	294	36.5	153	30	0.0	–	–	–	–
Technicians and related support occupations	4,204	5,754	1,550	36.9	593	183	2.6	12.4	64.7	9.2	5.8
Health technicians and technologists	1,833	2,595	763	41.6	263	80	2.3	–	–	–	–
Clinical lab technologists and technicians	258	321	63	24.5	25	9	1.2	17.6	76.3	15.1	4.1
Dental hygienists	97	137	40	40.9	13	4	0.0	49.9	99.1	2.5	3.0
EEG technologists	7	11	4	57.0	1	0	0.0	–	–	–	–
EKG technicians	16	15	-1	-5.1	2	0	0.0	–	–	–	–
Emergency medical technicians	89	116	26	29.6	14	3	0.0	–	–	–	–
Licensed practical nurses	644	913	269	41.9	80	29	0.8	23.2	96.3	17.6	3.8
Medical records technicians	52	80	28	54.3	8	3	1.9	11.7	94.0	15.4	8.1
Nuclear medicine and radiologic technicians and technologists[1]	159	268	109	68.4	26	10	0.7	18.7	76.4	12.8	4.8
Nuclear medicine technologists	10	16	6	53.2	2	1	0.0	–	–	–	–
Opticians, dispensing and measuring	64	88	24	37.5	13	3	3.1	14.3	57.5	5.3	6.9
Radiologic technologists and technicians	149	252	103	69.5	25	9	0.7	–	–	–	–
Surgical technologists	38	59	21	55.2	7	2	0.0	–	–	–	–
All other health professionals, paraprofessionals, and technicians	409	588	179	43.8	73	16	7.1	–	–	–	–
Engineering and science technicians and technologists	1,327	1,640	312	23.5	180	52	1.8	–	–	–	–
Engineering technicians	755	965	210	27.8	98	28	1.3	–	–	–	–
Electrical and electronic technicians/technologists	363	488	125	34.4	44	13	1.4	2.9	15.4	8.2	5.8
All other engineering technicians and technologists	392	477	85	21.7	54	15	1.3	7.6	30.0	7.9	3.6
Drafters	326	370	44	13.4	55	14	3.1	7.0	18.9	6.4	5.1
Science and mathematics technicians	246	305	58	23.6	27	10	1.6	10.3	31.8	7.5	7.2
Technicians, except health and engineering and science	1,044	1,519	475	45.5	151	52	4.0	–	–	–	–
Aircraft pilots and flight engineers	90	120	31	34.4	6	5	3.3	17.9	5.1	0.6	3.3
Air traffic controllers	32	34	2	7.1	1	1	0.0	2.4	33.1	4.0	0.6
Broadcast technicians	33	34	1	3.6	4	1	9.2	9.5	26.2	11.6	2.2
Computer programmers	565	882	317	56.1	89	34	2.7	6.2	36.0	5.8	2.5
Legal assistants and technicians, except clerical	220	329	109	49.5	35	9	4.5	9.7	78.8	6.1	3.7
Paralegals	90	167	77	85.2	19	6	2.2	–	–	–	–
Title examiners and searchers	29	33	4	13.5	4	0	23.8	–	–	–	–
All other legal assistants, including law clerks	100	129	28	27.9	11	3	1.0	–	–	–	–
Programmers, numerical, tool, and process control	8	8	0	5.5	1	0	0.0	2.6	6.6	2.4	0.2
Technical assistants, library	65	72	7	11.3	10	1	0.0	–	–	–	–
All other technicians	33	40	7	22.6	5	1	33.6	–	–	–	–
Marketing and sales occupations	14,088	17,489	3,401	24.1	3,681	585	13.0	24.7	49.2	6.4	5.3
Cashiers	2,633	3,318	685	26.0	1,004	129	1.0	51.3	81.4	13.5	8.4
Counter and rental clerks	215	289	74	34.3	81	8	7.9	39.4	69.4	9.1	5.7
Insurance sales workers	439	527	88	20.1	44	17	31.7	8.0	32.7	5.2	3.5
Real estate agents, brokers, and appraisers	413	492	79	19.2	72	12	61.8	15.5	51.1	3.0	3.6
Brokers, real estate	69	83	14	20.0	12	2	65.2	–	–	–	–
Real estate appraisers	44	54	11	24.5	8	1	25.2	–	–	–	–
Sales agents, real estate	300	355	55	18.2	52	8	66.3	–	–	–	–
Salespersons, retail	3,619	4,506	887	24.5	1,087	169	5.2	40.1	59.1	6.6	6.2
Securities and financial services sales workers	191	267	76	39.5	31	7	24.6	5.9	23.4	3.6	3.2
Stock clerks, sales floor	1,242	1,451	209	16.8	452	48	0.0	–	–	–	–
Travel agents	132	214	82	62.3	62	9	19.7	–	–	–	–
All other sales and related workers	5,204	6,426	1,222	23.5	849	186	21.8	–	–	–	–

See footnotes at end of table.

Table 6. Occupational employment and job openings data, 1990-2005, and worker characteristics, 1990 — Continued

(Numbers in thousands)

1990 Matrix occupation	Total employment		Employment change, 1990-2005		Annual average job openings, 1990-2005		Worker characteristics, percent of workers				
	1990	2005	Number	Percent	Growth plus total replacement needs	Growth plus net replacement needs	Self-employed	Part time	Female	Black	Hispanic
Administrative support occupations, including clerical	21,951	24,835	2,884	13.1	4,306	650	1.5	19.3	79.8	11.4	6.5
Adjusters, investigators, and collectors	1,058	1,313	255	24.1	192	28	1.2	–	–	–	–
Adjustment clerks, credit authorizers and checkers, loan and credit clerks, and loan interviewers[1]	560	688	128	22.9	102	14	0.0	10.7	76.6	13.1	6.7
Adjustment clerks	320	390	70	21.9	58	8	0.0	–	–	–	–
Bill and account collectors	183	244	60	32.9	47	6	2.7	13.9	67.5	13.1	6.7
Insurance claims and policy processing occupations	423	521	98	23.0	65	10	0.9	–	–	–	–
Insurance adjusters, examiners, and investigators	147	189	42	28.4	21	4	2.7	–	–	–	–
Insurance claims clerks	104	128	24	22.9	14	3	0.0	–	–	–	–
Insurance policy processing clerks	172	204	32	18.5	30	3	0.0	–	–	–	–
Welfare eligibility workers and interviewers	93	111	18	19.2	16	4	0.0	11.1	90.1	14.7	4.0
All other adjusters and investigators	38	47	9	22.9	6	1	10.5	–	–	–	–
Communications equipment operators	345	236	-108	-31.5	40	9	0.6	–	–	–	–
Telephone operators	325	221	-104	-32.0	38	8	0.3	15.6	89.0	19.7	7.2
Central office operators	53	22	-31	-59.2	5	1	0.0	–	–	–	–
Directory assistance operators	26	11	-16	-59.4	3	1	0.0	–	–	–	–
Switchboard operators	246	189	-57	-23.2	30	6	0.4	–	–	–	–
All other communications equipment operators	20	15	-5	-23.1	3	1	5.1	–	–	–	–
Computer operators and peripheral equipment operators	320	361	42	13.0	56	6	1.6	–	–	–	–
Computer operators, except peripheral equipment	282	320	38	13.4	49	5	1.8	11.5	65.7	13.1	6.9
Peripheral EDP equipment operators	37	41	4	9.8	6	1	0.0	8.6	68.4	39.9	4.7
Financial records processing occupations	2,860	2,750	-110	-3.8	463	67	5.2	–	–	–	–
Billing, cost, and rate clerks	318	332	14	4.5	68	10	0.6	13.9	88.6	8.6	6.1
Billing, posting, and calculating machine operators	95	99	4	3.9	25	3	1.1	20.3	86.0	12.0	8.2
Bookkeeping, accounting, and auditing clerks	2,276	2,143	-133	-5.8	346	48	6.3	25.9	92.2	5.2	5.0
Payroll and timekeeping clerks	171	176	5	2.7	23	6	0.6	12.8	91.0	11.5	3.6
Information clerks	1,418	2,003	584	41.2	451	62	1.4	–	–	–	–
Hotel desk clerks	118	158	40	34.3	39	5	0.9	22.0	70.6	9.5	7.2
Interviewing clerks, except personnel and social welfare	144	200	56	39.1	45	7	1.4	25.6	81.2	11.5	7.9
New accounts clerks, banking	106	121	14	13.5	28	4	0.0	–	–	–	–
Receptionists and information clerks	900	1,322	422	46.9	318	40	1.8	30.4	97.0	8.1	6.7
Reservation and transportation ticket agents and travel clerks	150	202	52	34.4	21	6	0.7	15.5	60.2	12.2	8.7
Mail clerks and messengers	280	306	26	9.4	66	8	2.9	–	–	–	–
Mail clerks, except mail machine operators and postal service	137	146	9	6.7	37	5	1.5	22.1	47.0	23.8	7.7
Messengers	143	160	17	12.0	29	4	4.2	33.1	28.2	17.9	7.9
Postal clerks and mail carriers	439	519	80	18.3	22	14	0.0	–	–	–	–
Postal mail carriers	305	380	74	24.4	12	11	0.0	6.6	24.9	14.4	6.1
Postal service clerks	134	140	6	4.5	10	3	0.0	8.1	45.2	25.1	4.7
Material recording, scheduling, dispatching, and distributing occupations	2,513	2,754	241	9.6	495	65	0.4	–	–	–	–
Dispatchers	209	269	60	28.7	30	8	2.4	7.0	54.8	9.2	4.4
Dispatchers, except police, fire, and ambulance	138	181	43	31.4	20	6	2.9	–	–	–	–
Dispatchers, police, fire, and ambulance	71	87	17	23.6	10	3	1.4	–	–	–	–
Meter readers, utilities	50	37	-12	-24.8	8	1	0.0	2.7	15.2	9.9	3.4
Order fillers, wholesale and retail sales	197	211	14	7.3	35	6	0.0	–	–	–	–
Procurement and stock clerks[1]	808	837	29	3.6	161	19	0.4	15.7	43.2	13.3	8.0
Procurement clerks	56	51	-4	-7.6	10	1	0.0	–	–	–	–
Production, planning, and expediting clerks	237	239	1	0.6	37	6	0.4	11.9	56.0	8.8	4.7
Stock clerks, stockroom, warehouse, or yard	752	786	34	4.5	151	18	0.4	–	–	–	–
Traffic, shipping, and receiving clerks	762	860	97	12.8	167	16	0.1	10.0	26.8	15.3	11.7
Weighers, measurers, checkers, and samplers, recordkeeping	37	38	1	3.6	9	1	2.7	15.7	45.3	14.8	7.5
All other material recording, scheduling, and distribution workers	214	263	50	23.1	48	8	0.0	–	–	–	–
Records processing occupations, except financial	949	1,045	96	10.1	239	33	0.5	–	–	–	–
Advertising clerks	18	21	3	15.5	3	1	0.0	17.2	90.1	25.0	0.6
Brokerage clerks	60	68	8	13.2	15	2	1.7	–	–	–	–
Correspondence clerks	30	37	7	22.2	6	1	0.0	11.1	85.9	6.3	3.1
File clerks	271	300	29	10.6	99	11	0.4	34.9	83.8	14.0	9.0
Library assistants and bookmobile drivers	117	130	13	11.0	33	5	0.0	63.0	76.2	9.1	5.0
Order clerks and customer service representatives, utilities[1]	401	420	19	4.8	69	11	0.5	12.2	77.9	15.1	6.5
Order clerks, materials, merchandise, and service	291	300	9	3.0	49	8	0.7	–	–	–	–
Personnel clerks, except payroll and timekeeping	129	155	27	20.7	25	5	0.0	8.5	88.6	21.7	7.3
Statement clerks	33	34	1	3.3	8	1	3.0	–	–	–	–
Secretaries, stenographers, and typists	4,680	5,110	429	9.2	796	138	1.9	–	–	–	–

See footnotes at end of table.

Table 6. Occupational employment and job openings data, 1990-2005, and worker characteristics, 1990 — Continued

(Numbers in thousands)

1990 Matrix occupation	Total employment		Employment change, 1990-2005		Annual average job openings, 1990-2005		Worker characteristics, percent of workers				
	1990	2005	Number	Percent	Growth plus total replacement needs	Growth plus net replacement needs	Self-employed	Part time	Female	Black	Hispanic
Secretaries	3,576	4,116	540	15.1	566	116	1.4	16.8	99.0	7.6	5.2
Legal secretaries	281	413	133	47.4	57	15	0.0	–	–	–	–
Medical secretaries	232	390	158	68.3	53	16	0.0	–	–	–	–
Secretaries, except legal and medical	3,064	3,312	248	8.1	456	85	1.6	–	–	–	–
Stenographers	132	125	-7	-5.4	25	3	12.1	17.0	83.7	7.6	2.8
Typists and word processors	972	869	-103	-10.6	205	19	2.5	25.2	95.5	15.1	7.3
Other clerical and administrative support workers	7,090	8,439	1,349	19.0	1,487	220	0.6	–	–	–	–
Bank tellers	517	492	-25	-4.8	114	19	0.0	27.6	90.4	9.9	7.0
Clerical supervisors and managers	1,218	1,481	263	21.6	128	47	0.1	3.0	58.3	11.8	6.0
Court clerks	47	58	11	23.7	9	1	0.0	–	–	–	–
Credit authorizers, credit checkers, and loan and credit clerks	240	298	58	24.2	44	6	0.0	–	–	–	–
Credit authorizers	21	26	5	24.5	4	0	0.0	–	–	–	–
Credit checkers	48	60	12	24.5	9	1	0.0	–	–	–	–
Loan and credit clerks	151	187	37	24.5	28	3	0.0	–	–	–	–
Loan interviewers	20	25	4	21.1	4	1	0.0	–	–	–	–
Customer service representatives, utilities	109	120	11	9.6	20	3	0.0	–	–	–	–
Data entry keyers, except composing	456	510	54	11.7	126	11	0.7	17.4	87.2	19.5	8.0
Data entry keyers, composing	19	23	4	20.3	6	1	0.0	–	–	–	–
Duplicating, mail, and other office machine operators	169	191	22	12.8	30	7	0.6	23.2	61.3	17.1	5.1
General office clerks	2,737	3,407	670	24.5	708	85	0.5	27.0	81.8	13.1	7.0
Municipal clerks	22	27	5	23.1	4	0	0.0	–	–	–	–
Proofreaders and copy markers	29	28	-2	-5.3	6	1	3.4	32.3	81.6	9.4	7.3
Real estate clerks	29	34	5	17.4	7	1	0.0	–	–	–	–
Statistical clerks	85	54	-31	-36.1	5	2	2.4	15.4	72.3	12.9	6.7
Teacher aides and educational assistants	808	1,086	278	34.4	189	32	0.0	48.4	94.5	14.1	11.8
All other clerical and administrative support workers	604	629	25	4.2	93	5	2.8	–	–	–	–
Service occupations	19,204	24,806	5,602	29.2	6,271	882	6.4	33.1	64.9	17.0	11.5
Cleaning and building service occupations, except private household	3,435	4,068	633	18.4	887	108	7.0	–	–	–	–
Housekeepers, institutional	142	177	35	24.5	17	6	2.1	–	–	–	–
Janitors and cleaners, including maids and housekeeping cleaners	3,007	3,562	555	18.5	797	94	7.4	30.3	45.2	22.6	17.2
Pest controllers and assistants	51	55	4	8.5	12	1	13.8	4.8	4.7	6.1	3.1
All other cleaning and building service workers	235	274	39	16.8	60	7	3.0	–	–	–	–
Food preparation and service occupations	7,705	10,031	2,325	30.2	3,372	432	1.0	–	–	–	–
Chefs, cooks, and other kitchen workers	3,069	4,104	1,035	33.7	1,397	168	1.7	–	–	–	–
Cooks, except short order	1,170	1,594	424	36.3	414	53	4.0	35.7	47.7	18.3	14.6
Bakers, bread and pastry	140	192	52	36.8	50	6	4.3	–	–	–	–
Cooks, institution or cafeteria	415	530	115	27.8	140	16	0.0	–	–	–	–
Cooks, restaurant	615	872	257	41.8	225	30	6.7	–	–	–	–
Cooks, short order and fast food	743	989	246	33.0	379	50	0.0	54.9	32.7	25.5	10.5
Food preparation workers	1,156	1,521	365	31.6	604	66	0.3	52.5	70.7	12.8	12.5
Food and beverage service occupations	4,400	5,623	1,223	27.8	1,883	252	0.6	–	–	–	–
Bartenders	400	422	21	5.3	119	14	3.2	33.7	55.6	3.6	6.7
Dining room and cafeteria attendants and bar helpers	461	619	158	34.3	183	30	0.4	56.2	39.1	16.0	21.4
Food counter, fountain, and related workers	1,607	2,158	550	34.2	864	104	0.1	70.9	72.7	11.5	7.3
Hosts and hostesses, restaurant, lounge, or coffee shop	184	229	44	24.0	53	5	2.2	–	–	–	–
Waiters and waitresses	1,747	2,196	449	25.7	664	99	0.4	51.4	80.8	4.7	7.6
All other food preparation and service workers	236	304	67	28.6	92	12	0.4	–	–	–	–
Health service occupations	1,972	2,832	860	43.6	499	84	1.7	–	–	–	–
Ambulance drivers and attendants, except EMT's	12	15	2	20.4	3	0	0.0	–	–	–	–
Dental assistants	176	236	60	33.8	38	8	0.0	37.0	98.7	5.6	7.4
Medical assistants	165	287	122	73.9	51	10	0.0	–	–	–	–
Nursing aides and psychiatric aides	1,374	1,960	587	42.7	348	58	2.5	–	–	–	–
Nursing aides, orderlies, and attendants	1,274	1,826	552	43.4	324	55	2.7	24.6	90.8	30.7	6.5
Psychiatric aides	100	134	34	34.2	24	4	0.0	–	–	–	–
Occupational therapy assistants and aides	10	15	5	56.9	3	0	0.0	–	–	–	–
Pharmacy assistants	83	101	18	22.1	19	2	0.0	–	–	–	–
Physical and corrective therapy assistants and aides	45	74	29	64.0	13	2	0.0	–	–	–	–
All other health service workers	107	144	37	34.6	26	3	0.0	–	–	–	–
Personal service occupations	2,192	3,164	972	44.3	659	97	37.6	–	–	–	–
Amusement and recreation attendants	184	228	44	24.1	75	8	1.6	44.4	40.2	9.1	5.7
Baggage porters and bellhops	31	42	10	32.8	10	1	0.0	16.2	9.7	27.7	19.7
Barbers	77	76	-1	-1.2	5	1	76.8	17.2	18.7	17.4	9.9

See footnotes at end of table.

Table 6. Occupational employment and job openings data, 1990-2005, and worker characteristics, 1990 — Continued

(Numbers in thousands)

1990 Matrix occupation	Total employment		Employment change, 1990-2005		Annual average job openings, 1990-2005		Worker characteristics, percent of workers				
	1990	2005	Number	Percent	Growth plus total replacement needs	Growth plus net replacement needs	Self-employed	Part time	Female	Black	Hispanic
Child care workers	725	1,078	353	48.8	336	31	64.3	38.5	97.0	12.1	6.4
Cosmetologists and related workers	636	793	157	24.7	104	17	46.6	—	—	—	—
Hairdressers, hairstylists, and cosmetologists	597	742	145	24.2	97	16	48.1	33.9	89.8	9.2	7.1
Manicurists	25	35	10	37.8	5	1	35.5	—	—	—	—
Shampooers	14	17	3	21.3	2	0	0.0	—	—	—	—
Flight attendants	101	159	59	58.5	12	6	0.0	35.2	83.2	11.2	6.0
Homemaker-home health aides	391	733	343	87.7	100	30	0.0	—	—	—	—
Home health aides	287	550	263	91.7	75	22	0.0	—	—	—	—
Social welfare service aides	103	183	79	76.7	25	7	0.0	—	—	—	—
Ushers, lobby attendants, and ticket takers	48	55	6	13.3	18	2	0.0	72.8	37.3	11.6	18.0
Private household workers	782	555	-227	-29.0	216	17	0.2	—	—	—	—
Child care workers, private household	314	190	-124	-39.5	132	11	0.3	53.9	97.9	9.8	13.3
Cleaners and servants, private household	411	310	-101	-24.5	73	5	0.2	61.6	95.5	35.5	23.7
Cooks, private household	12	10	-2	-16.2	2	0	51.8	86.6	22.8	7.4	
Housekeepers and butlers	45	45	0	0.6	9	1	0.0	43.0	97.4	30.7	30.3
Protective service occupations	2,266	2,995	729	32.2	425	111	0.3	—	—	—	—
Firefighting occupations	280	348	68	24.5	14	14	0.0	—	—	—	—
Fire fighters	210	262	51	24.5	13	11	0.0	1.4	1.2	11.5	4.5
Fire fighting and prevention supervisors	58	72	14	24.5	1	3	0.0	—	0.3	8.8	4.4
Fire inspection occupations	12	15	3	24.2	1	1	0.0	11.2	18.6	4.5	2.6
Law enforcement occupations	886	1,187	302	34.1	68	45	0.0	—	—	—	—
Correction officers	230	372	142	61.4	36	12	0.0	0.9	17.7	22.8	4.7
Police and detectives	655	815	160	24.4	32	33	0.0	—	—	—	—
Police and detective supervisors	93	113	20	21.5	2	5	0.0	0.1	8.6	12.9	2.4
Police detectives and patrol officers[1]	453	578	125	27.5	23	24	0.0	1.1	12.1	13.5	5.5
Police detectives and investigators	69	83	14	19.7	3	3	0.0	—	—	—	—
Police patrol officers	384	495	111	28.9	20	21	0.0	—	—	—	—
Sheriffs and deputy sheriffs	72	81	9	12.0	4	3	0.0	—	—	—	—
Other law enforcement occupations	37	43	7	18.5	4	1	0.0	—	—	—	—
Other protective service workers	1,101	1,460	359	32.6	343	52	0.7	—	—	—	—
Detectives, except public	47	66	19	40.5	14	2	4.3	—	—	—	—
Guards	883	1,181	298	33.7	256	39	0.6	17.1	14.8	21.2	7.8
Crossing guards	54	57	2	4.5	15	2	0.0	85.5	73.3	17.0	5.7
All other protective service workers	116	157	40	34.4	59	9	0.0	—	—	—	—
All other service workers	852	1,161	309	36.2	212	34	4.2	—	—	—	—
Agriculture, forestry, fishing, and related occupations	3,506	3,665	158	4.5	769	89	39.4	19.8	—	—	—
Animal caretakers, except farm	106	145	40	37.6	28	5	21.8	34.9	63.8	3.9	8.1
Farm occupations	901	828	-73	-8.1	213	25	3.9	—	—	—	—
Farm workers	837	745	-92	-11.0	194	22	4.1	22.1	21.0	8.2	26.9
Nursery workers	64	83	19	30.2	19	3	1.6	20.1	49.7	3.8	29.4
Farm operators and managers	73	88	15	20.5	4	3	1.4	1.1	7.3	4.8	2.4
Farmers	1,074	850	-224	-20.9	81	9	100.0	15.4	15.5	0.8	1.4
Farm managers	149	173	24	15.9	16	4	0.0	8.3	17.6	1.4	4.1
Fishers, hunters, and trappers	61	69	8	12.7	4	2	63.5	—	—	—	—
Captains and other officers, fishing vessels	8	10	1	18.0	1	0	37.1	14.1	5.9	6.1	21.9
Fishers, hunters, and trappers	53	60	6	11.9	3	2	67.5	12.8	4.5	7.1	3.4
Forestry and logging occupations	148	150	1	1.0	32	4	23.6	—	—	—	—
Forest and conservation workers	40	43	3	8.1	9	1	7.5	18.2	23.4	5.2	22.3
Timber cutting and logging occupations	108	106	-2	-1.6	23	3	29.6	—	—	—	—
Fallers, log handling equipment, and all other timber cutters[1]	79	76	-3	-3.4	18	2	36.7	11.7	1.7	11.4	1.4
Fallers and buckers	36	35	-1	-3.0	8	1	52.4	—	—	—	—
Logging tractor operators	29	30	1	3.1	5	1	10.3	—	—	—	—
Log handling equipment operators	16	17	1	4.2	4	1	18.4	—	—	—	—
All other timber cutting and related logging workers	27	24	-2	-8.5	6	1	26.4	—	—	—	—
Gardeners and groundskeepers, except farm	874	1,222	348	39.8	345	33	19.0	26.8	5.7	11.7	20.1
Supervisors, farming, forestry, and agricultural related occupations	65	72	7	10.3	8	2	12.3	3.2	7.2	3.5	16.9
All other agricultural, forestry, fishing, and related workers	129	156	27	21.4	43	5	0.0	—	—	—	—
Precision production, craft, and repair occupations	14,124	15,909	1,785	12.6	1,793	457	11.9	5.8	8.5	7.8	8.5
Blue-collar worker supervisors	1,792	1,912	120	6.7	145	54	7.3	1.6	14.7	7.1	7.5
Construction trades	3,763	4,557	794	21.1	597	127	24.9	—	—	—	—
Bricklayers and stone masons	152	183	31	20.3	30	5	24.4	7.6	0.2	14.4	10.7

See footnotes at end of table.

Table 6. Occupational employment and job openings data, 1990-2005, and worker characteristics, 1990 — Continued

(Numbers in thousands)

1990 Matrix occupation	Total employment		Employment change, 1990-2005		Annual average job openings, 1990-2005		Worker characteristics, percent of workers				
	1990	2005	Number	Percent	Growth plus total replacement needs	Growth plus net replacement needs	Self-employed	Part time	Female	Black	Hispanic
Carpenters	1,057	1,209	152	14.4	186	29	35.3	7.5	1.3	4.8	8.7
Carpet installers	73	88	15	21.2	8	3	61.8	12.0	2.1	4.2	11.2
Ceiling tile installers and acoustical carpenters	20	22	2	11.5	3	0	0.0	–	–	–	–
Concrete and terrazzo finishers	113	128	15	13.1	3	5	5.3	7.1	0.6	23.1	23.7
Drywall installers and finishers	143	175	33	22.9	35	5	21.7	7.7	1.0	5.1	15.5
Electricians	548	706	158	28.8	48	23	10.6	2.9	1.7	6.2	5.2
Glaziers	42	51	9	22.1	7	1	7.1	1.9	0.4	3.6	7.7
Hard tile setters	28	35	7	23.5	1	1	38.7	11.1	2.0	4.9	14.3
Highway maintenance workers	151	188	37	24.5	18	4	0.0	–	–	–	–
Insulation workers	70	87	17	24.5	25	4	5.7	3.2	1.5	10.9	19.4
Painters and paperhangers, construction and maintenance	453	564	111	24.5	77	16	47.2	17.0	6.9	9.1	12.8
Paving, surfacing, and tamping equipment operators	73	95	22	29.7	13	3	1.4	–	–	–	–
Pipelayers and pipelaying fitters	55	72	17	30.6	7	2	0.0	–	–	–	–
Plasterers	28	32	4	13.3	4	1	24.8	10.4	0.1	15.1	25.0
Plumbers, pipefitters, and steamfitters	379	459	80	21.0	55	14	17.2	5.1	0.9	6.6	6.5
Roofers	138	169	31	22.7	45	4	34.1	12.5	0.3	8.5	13.6
Structural and reinforcing metal workers	80	95	16	19.7	13	3	2.5	3.2	0.2	3.7	8.0
All other construction trades workers	160	198	38	24.0	18	5	20.1	–	–	–	–
Extractive and related workers, including blasters	237	247	9	3.9	45	5	2.5	–	–	–	–
Oil and gas extraction occupations	80	78	-2	-2.0	15	1	2.5	–	–	–	–
Roustabouts	38	36	-1	-3.6	7	1	0.0	–	–	–	–
All other oil and gas extraction occupations	42	42	0	-0.6	8	1	4.7	–	–	–	–
Mining, quarrying, and tunneling occupations	24	20	-5	-18.8	4	0	4.1	–	–	–	–
All other extraction and related workers	133	148	15	11.7	26	3	2.3	–	–	–	–
Mechanics, installers, and repairers	4,900	5,669	769	15.7	593	164	8.3	–	–	–	–
Communications equipment mechanics, installers, and repairers	125	77	-48	-38.5	14	2	0.0	–	–	–	–
Central office and PBX installers and repairers; frame wirers; station installers and repairers, telephone [1]	138	72	-67	-48.2	10	3	2.2	1.4	11.3	9.7	3.8
Central office and PBX installers and repairers	80	46	-34	-42.5	8	1	0.0	–	–	–	–
Frame wirers, central office	11	5	-7	-59.7	1	0	0.0	–	–	–	–
Radio mechanics	13	13	0	-1.4	2	0	0.0	–	–	–	–
Signal or track switch maintainers	4	2	-2	-40.0	0	0	0.0	–	–	–	–
All other communications equipment mechanics, installers, and repairers	16	11	-5	-33.3	2	0	0.0	–	–	–	–
Electrical and electronic equipment mechanics, installers, and repairers	530	540	10	1.8	40	16	7.2	–	–	–	–
Data processing equipment repairers	84	134	50	60.0	11	4	6.0	4.5	11.4	10.6	5.6
Electrical powerline installers and repairers	99	108	9	8.7	6	4	1.0	0.5	1.7	8.2	4.2
Electronic home entertainment equipment repairers	41	46	5	12.6	6	1	32.1	–	–	–	–
Electronics repairers, commercial and industrial equipment	75	88	13	17.4	12	2	16.0	–	–	–	–
Station installers and repairers, telephone	47	21	-26	-55.0	0	1	6.4	–	–	–	–
Telephone and cable TV line installers and repairers	133	92	-40	-30.4	0	3	0.1	6.9	8.6	8.1
All other electrical and electronic equipment mechanics, installers, and repairers	52	51	-1	-2.3	4	1	7.7	–	–	–	–
Machinery and related mechanics, installers, and repairers	1,675	1,980	305	18.2	221	49	3.3	–	–	–	–
Industrial machinery mechanics	474	520	46	9.7	39	13	3.2	2.7	3.0	8.3	6.1
Maintenance repairers, general utility	1,128	1,379	251	22.2	171	33	3.6	–	–	–	–
Millwrights	73	82	9	12.3	10	3	0.0	0.7	2.8	4.6	2.3
Vehicle and mobile equipment mechanics and repairers	1,568	1,892	324	20.7	215	65	15.3	–	–	–	–
Aircraft mechanics and engine specialists	122	151	29	24.1	8	5	0.8	–	–	–	–
Aircraft engine specialists	17	21	4	22.1	1	1	6.0	2.7	2.8	9.8	8.4
Aircraft mechanics	105	131	26	24.4	7	4	0.0	1.5	7.8	9.0	4.8
Automotive body and related repairers	219	267	48	22.1	31	9	20.6	5.4	0.7	7.1	11.1
Automotive mechanics	757	923	166	21.9	123	33	20.1	6.6	0.8	8.7	9.4
Bus and truck mechanics and diesel engine specialists	268	326	58	21.7	24	11	5.2	2.4	0.4	6.6	6.0
Farm equipment mechanics	48	52	4	9.4	7	2	14.6	4.5	1.1	1.5	9.3
Mobile heavy equipment mechanics	104	117	13	12.7	15	4	5.8	–	–	–	–
Motorcycle, boat, and small engine mechanics	50	55	5	9.8	6	2	29.9	7.7	0.2	4.5	5.3
Motorcycle repairers	12	13	1	11.4	2	0	34.7	–	–	–	–
Small engine specialists	39	42	4	9.3	5	1	28.5	–	–	–	–
Other mechanics, installers, and repairers	1,002	1,180	177	17.7	103	32	7.3	–	–	–	–
Bicycle repairers	15	17	2	11.0	1	0	38.8	–	–	–	–
Camera, musical instrument, and watch repairers [1]	23	22	-1	-3.9	0	1	47.7	15.6	13.2	2.6	10.0
Camera and photographic equipment repairers	7	9	1	16.5	0	0	54.4	–	–	–	–
Coin and vending machine servicers and repairers	26	26	0	-1.0	2	0	0.0	–	–	–	–

See footnotes at end of table.

Table 6. Occupational employment and job openings data, 1990-2005, and worker characteristics, 1990 — Continued

(Numbers in thousands)

1990 Matrix occupation	Total employment		Employment change, 1990-2005		Annual average job openings, 1990-2005		Worker characteristics, percent of workers				
	1990	2005	Number	Percent	Growth plus total replacement needs	Growth plus net replacement needs	Self-employed	Part time	Female	Black	Hispanic
Electric meter installers and repairers	14	16	2	18.2	0	0	0.0	2.1	7.4	12.7	3.5
Electromedical and biomedical equipment repairers	8	12	4	50.5	1	0	0.0	–	–	–	–
Elevator installers and repairers	19	22	3	16.7	1	1	0.0	2.1	1.1	6.3	6.8
Heat, air-conditioning, and refrigeration mechanics and installers	219	266	46	21.1	18	6	15.5	4.6	0.5	6.4	4.9
Home appliance and power tool repairers	71	70	-1	-1.0	5	2	12.8	5.7	1.5	9.3	6.8
Musical instrument repairers and tuners	9	9	0	2.3	0	0	46.0	–	–	–	–
Office machine and cash register servicers	73	82	9	13.0	2	2	2.7	5.1	5.4	6.7	5.6
Precision instrument repairers	50	54	4	7.8	1	1	6.0	–	–	–	–
Riggers	14	14	0	-0.3	2	0	0.0	–	–	–	–
Tire repairers and changers	81	95	14	17.4	35	4	0.0	–	–	–	–
Watchmakers	7	5	-2	-32.9	0	0	42.7	–	–	–	–
All other mechanics, installers, and repairers	390	484	94	24.1	36	13	2.1	–	–	–	–
Production occupations, precision	3,134	3,208	74	2.4	401	96	6.5	–	–	–	–
Assemblers, precision	352	236	-116	-33.0	36	9	0.6	–	–	–	–
Aircraft assemblers, precision	32	34	2	5.7	3	1	0.0	–	–	–	–
Electrical and electronic equipment assemblers, precision	171	90	-81	-47.5	20	4	1.2	3.3	66.7	10.5	14.8
Electromechanical equipment assemblers, precision	49	31	-18	-36.5	6	1	0.0	–	–	–	–
Fitters, structural metal, precision	15	13	-2	-14.3	1	0	0.0	1.2	18.4	13.3	14.6
Machine builders and other precision machine assemblers	50	42	-8	-16.6	4	1	0.0	–	–	–	–
All other precision assemblers	34	26	-8	-23.8	3	1	0.0	–	–	–	–
Food workers, precision	301	286	-15	-4.9	47	8	4.3	–	–	–	–
Bakers, manufacturing	34	32	-1	-3.8	6	1	11.9	–	–	–	–
Butchers and meatcutters	234	220	-14	-5.9	36	6	2.6	9.6	22.1	13.9	21.8
All other precision food and tobacco workers	34	34	0	1.0	5	1	8.9	20.0	65.5	8.8	10.4
Inspectors, testers, and graders, precision	668	659	-9	-1.4	78	16	0.6	–	–	–	–
Metal workers, precision	936	1,021	85	9.0	98	30	4.3	–	–	–	–
Boilermakers	22	23	1	3.1	4	1	4.5	1.7	1.4	11.4	5.7
Jewelers and silversmiths	40	48	8	19.9	4	2	44.8	–	–	–	–
Machinists	386	427	41	10.5	33	12	2.3	1.6	3.9	6.1	7.9
Sheet metal workers and duct installers	233	263	30	12.9	43	9	1.7	3.2	4.6	5.5	7.3
Shipfitters	13	12	0	-3.8	1	0	0.0	–	–	–	–
Tool and die makers	141	145	4	2.8	5	4	1.4	1.3	1.6	5.1	2.3
All other precision metal workers	101	103	2	1.9	8	3	6.0	–	–	–	–
Printing workers, precision	161	195	33	20.7	26	6	4.3	–	–	–	–
Bookbinders	7	8	1	13.2	1	0	14.0	12.0	51.2	11.1	11.7
Compositors and typesetters; precision, and machine operators[1]	40	46	6	13.7	6	1	12.4	12.4	68.0	4.8	8.8
Compositors and typesetters, precision	14	14	0	-2.5	2	0	34.8	–	–	–	–
Job printers	15	18	3	22.6	2	1	0.0	–	–	–	–
Lithography and photoengraving workers; precision, and machine operators[1]	119	146	28	23.5	20	5	0.0	6.0	25.5	1.7	6.1
Pasteup workers	30	34	4	13.2	6	1	0.0	–	–	–	–
Electronic pagination systems workers	12	16	4	33.4	2	1	0.0	–	–	–	–
Photoengravers	8	9	1	12.8	1	0	0.0	–	–	–	–
Camera operators	17	20	4	21.3	2	1	0.0	–	–	–	–
Strippers	32	43	11	34.4	5	2	0.0	–	–	–	–
Platemakers	14	17	3	23.5	2	1	0.0	–	–	–	–
All other printing workers, precision	12	15	3	23.3	2	0	8.1	–	–	–	–
Textile, apparel, and furnishings workers, precision	272	302	29	10.7	32	9	33.0	–	–	–	–
Custom tailors and sewers	116	137	21	18.5	14	5	52.7	–	–	–	–
Patternmakers and layout workers, fabric and apparel	16	15	-1	-3.9	2	0	0.0	–	80.1	0.0	5.0
Shoe and leather workers and repairers, precision	27	22	-5	-18.9	3	1	25.7	15.8	14.7	10.8	12.7
Upholsterers	64	70	6	9.6	6	2	31.3	13.2	25.1	8.3	12.6
All other precision textile, apparel, and furnishings workers	50	57	7	14.9	8	1	4.0	–	–	–	–
Woodworkers, precision	213	240	27	12.8	44	9	13.2	8.6	13.7	3.5	8.4
Cabinetmakers and bench carpenters	107	122	14	13.5	22	5	18.6	–	–	–	–
Furniture finishers	34	38	4	12.4	7	1	23.7	–	–	–	–
Wood machinists	46	51	5	11.6	9	2	0.0	–	–	–	–
All other precision woodworkers	25	29	3	12.8	5	1	0.0	–	–	–	–
Other precision workers	231	270	39	17.1	40	9	9.1	–	–	–	–
Dental lab technicians, precision	57	59	3	4.4	9	2	19.4	18.1	36.4	7.6	7.2
Optical goods workers, precision	19	25	6	28.9	4	1	0.0	–	–	–	–
Photographic process workers, precision	18	21	3	15.7	4	1	27.8	–	–	–	–
All other precision workers	137	165	28	20.8	24	6	3.7	–	–	–	–
Plant and system occupations	297	317	19	6.5	13	10	0.7	–	–	–	–

See footnotes at end of table.

Table 6. Occupational employment and job openings data, 1990-2005, and worker characteristics, 1990 — Continued

(Numbers in thousands)

1990 Matrix occupation	Total employment		Employment change, 1990-2005		Annual average job openings, 1990-2005		Worker characteristics, percent of workers				
	1990	2005	Number	Percent	Growth plus total replacement needs	Growth plus net replacement needs	Self-employed	Part time	Female	Black	Hispanic
Chemical plant and system operators	35	30	-5	-14.5	1	1	0.0	–	–	–	–
Electric power generating plant operators, distributors, and dispatchers	44	48	4	8.8	2	1	0.0	–	–	–	–
Power distributors and dispatchers	18	19	1	5.9	1	0	0.0	–	–	–	–
Power generating and reactor plant operators	26	29	3	10.7	1	1	0.0	–	–	–	–
Gas and petroleum plant and system occupations	31	27	-3	-11.3	1	1	3.2	–	–	–	–
Stationary engineers and boiler operators, low pressure[1]	57	57	1	1.0	2	2	1.7	1.5	3.6	11.8	3.8
Stationary engineers	35	36	0	1.3	1	1	2.8	–	–	–	–
Water and liquid waste treatment plant and system operators	78	101	23	29.4	3	4	0.0	1.0	2.2	9.7	3.3
All other plant and system operators	74	75	1	0.7	3	2	0.0	–	–	–	–
Operators, fabricators, and laborers	**17,245**	**17,961**	**716**	**4.1**	**3,449**	**479**	**3.2**	**6.3**	**25.5**	**15.0**	**12.2**
Machine setters, setup operators, operators, and tenders	4,905	4,579	-326	-6.6	739	132	1.9	–	–	–	–
Numerical control machine tool operators and tenders, metal and plastic	70	87	16	23.0	11	3	0.0	–	35.0	3.6	3.7
Combination machine tool setters, setup operators, operators, and tenders	93	113	21	22.6	15	4	1.1	–	–	–	–
Machine tool cutters and form setters, operators, and tenders, metal and plastic	765	585	-179	-23.4	72	18	0.5	–	–	–	–
Drilling and boring machine tool setters and setup operators, metal and plastic	52	39	-13	-25.6	6	1	0.0	1.1	27.3	9.4	5.1
Grinding machine setters and setup operators, metal and plastic	72	54	-18	-25.1	10	1	4.1	2.5	17.2	9.1	11.7
Lathe and turning machine tool setters and setup operators, metal and plastic	80	61	-20	-24.4	9	2	0.0	0.6	9.1	3.5	7.7
Machine forming operators and tenders, metal and plastic	174	131	-43	-24.5	12	6	0.0	–	–	–	–
Machine tool cutting operators and tenders, metal and plastic	145	104	-42	-28.6	9	2	0.7	3.6	8.5	5.5	12.2
Punching machine setters and setup operators, metal and plastic	52	42	-10	-18.5	5	1	0.0	3.0	29.2	13.2	13.6
All other machine tool cutting and forming etc.	189	155	-34	-18.2	20	5	0.0	–	–	–	–
Metal fabricating machine setters, operators, and related workers	140	149	9	6.4	18	4	0.0	–	–	–	–
Metal fabricators, structural metal products	34	37	4	10.5	5	1	0.0	–	–	–	–
Solders and brazers, machine operators, setters, and hand workers[1]	39	34	-5	-12.0	6	1	0.0	3.2	43.3	7.6	26.6
Soldering and brazing machine operators and tenders	11	11	0	-1.3	2	0	0.0	–	–	–	–
Welders and cutters, machine operators, setters, and hand workers[1]	427	445	18	4.3	51	12	6.1	2.0	67.3	8.8	12.2
Welding machine setters, operators, and tenders	95	101	6	5.8	12	3	0.0	–	–	–	–
Metal and plastic processing machine setters, operators, and related workers	393	396	3	0.9	45	15	0.0	–	–	–	–
Electric and nonelectric plating machine operators and tenders[1]	50	44	-7	-13.1	7	2	0.0	2.3	7.7	7.2	25.9
Electrolytic plating machine operators and tenders, setters, and setup operators, metal and plastic	43	38	-6	-12.8	6	2	0.0	–	–	–	–
Foundry mold assembly and shakeout workers	10	7	-3	-26.2	1	0	0.0	–	–	–	–
Furnace and heat equipment operators[1]	54	53	0	-0.8	7	2	0.0	2.7	9.6	9.6	1.9
Furnace operators and tenders	22	21	0	-2.3	2	0	0.0	–	–	–	–
Heaters, metal and plastic	5	5	0	1.5	1	0	0.0	–	–	–	–
Heating equipment setters and setup operators, metal and plastic	7	7	0	-0.3	1	0	0.0	–	–	–	–
Heat treating machine operators and tenders, metal and plastic	21	21	0	0.2	3	1	0.0	–	–	–	–
Metal molding machine operators and tenders, setters, and setup operators	38	31	-7	-18.1	3	1	0.0	1.4	29.5	13.5	10.3
Nonelectrolytic plating machine operators and tenders, setters, and setup operators, metal and plastic	7	6	-1	-14.7	1	0	0.0	–	–	–	–
Plastic molding machine operators and tenders, setters, and setup operators	143	173	31	21.4	15	7	0.0	–	–	–	–
All other metal and plastic machine setters, operators, and related workers	99	88	-11	-11.0	14	3	0.0	–	–	–	–
Printing, binding, and related workers	393	466	72	18.3	49	13	3.1	–	–	–	–
Bindery machine operators and setup operators	71	79	8	11.2	10	2	0.0	–	–	–	–
Printing press operators	224	268	44	19.5	25	7	5.4	4.5	14.4	7.5	10.4
Letterpress operators	16	14	-2	-10.0	1	0	0.0	–	–	–	–
Offset lithographic press operators	91	122	31	33.9	11	4	6.6	–	–	–	–

See footnotes at end of table.

Table 1. Specific Industry assumptions for 2005 projections

Industry	Assumptions
Agricultural services	Increased demand for landscaping and lawn and garden services is expected to continue during the projection period.
Coal mining	Production assumptions based on Department of Energy forecasts.
Crude petroleum, natural gas, and gas liquids	Higher prices, efficiency in the use of energy, and advances in the production and transmission of electricity will keep petroleum demand at moderate levels. Foreign sources are projected to supply an increasing portion of demand; domestic production is projected to decline. These assumptions are based on Department of Energy forecasts.
Nonmetallic minerals, except fuels	Growth in the construction industries will translate into growth for the products of this industry.
New nonfarm housing	Single and multifamily housing construction will slow from rates of early 1980's because of the expected slowdown in new household formation.
New industrial buildings	Moderate growth is projected for new factory construction. Modernization of existing facilities will slow from the growth of the 1980's.
New commercial buildings	Office and other commercial buildings are expected to recover from recent oversupply, but future growth will be slower than during the building boom of 1984-86.
New educational buildings	After years of decline, new school construction will continue to swing upward at a modest pace, reflecting growth in the school-age population.
New hospitals and institutions	Increases expected in both hospital and nursing home construction.
New nonfarm buildings, n.e.c.	Growing inmate populations and emphasis on longer incarceration periods will cause continued growth in construction of correctional facilities.
New electric utility facilities	Expenditures will move upward following the 1979-90 cutbacks
New water supply and sewer facilities	Increased demand for sewage treatment plants and waste disposal facilities was assumed.
New roads	Replacement of aging bridges and highways will lead to continued growth of road construction.
Logging	Growth in the paper products industries as well as increases in residential construction will lead to increased demand for logging, although at a slower pace than in the past.
Sawmills and planing mills	Growth in construction will lead to moderate growth in this industry.
Millwork and structural wood members, n.e.c.	Structure of industry does not permit extensive automation. Demand for this industry's products depends mainly on new residential construction and the repair/remodeling sector.
Household furniture	The prospective of demand for household furniture is positive since the older and higher income baby boom groups tend to favor higher quality goods.
Partitions and fixtures	Growth will moderate due to a slowdown in office and shopping center construction along with capital spending.
Office and miscellaneous furniture and fixtures	Increase in demand due to investment. Demand for new office furniture will be strong. No significant technological advances in production processes expected for this sector.
Glass and glass products	Continued percentage decline in use of glass for packaging foods and beverages is expected.
Cement, concrete, gypsum, and plaster products	Little technological change expected.
Blast furnaces and basic steel products	Only slight growth projected for this industry. Imports will continue to hold approximately 15 percent of the market. Mini-mills will take a larger share of U.S. steel business. Imports will be mainly of semifinished steel, to be processed in U.S. finishing mills.
Primary nonferrous metals	Continuing increases in the efficiency of domestic mills and stabilization of world prices will result in stable growth.
Metal cans and shipping containers	Continued relative decline in use of metal cans as a packaging material for many foods and beverages due to use of plastics and increase in microwave and frozen foods.
Fabricated structural metal products	Growth of construction will lead to growth of this industry.
Screw-machine products, bolts, rivets, etc.	This industry will continue to grow due to increasing demand for capital equipment.
Stampings, except automotive	Growth expected in intermediate demand for computer casings. Technological advances and diffusion are likely to come slowly since much of this industry consists of small job shops.
Metal services, n.e.c.	Productivity growth limited by the large number of small firms in the industry and product diversity.
Small arms and small arms ammunition	Decreased defense purchases cause output declines.

Table 1. Specific industry assumptions for 2005 projections—Continued

Industry	Assumptions
Ammunition and ordnance, except small arms	Decreased defense purchases cause output declines.
Miscellaneous fabricated metal products	Output growth generated by construction activity.
Engines and turbines	Imports are expected to increase their market share slightly while exports will recover due to expanding markets abroad.
Farm and garden machinery	Demand expected to increase as a result of capital spending by the real estate and farming sectors.
Construction machinery	Increased purchases due to investment. Demand should be strong because of maintenance of the nation's infrastructure.
Mining and oil field machinery	Due to the amount of exploration abroad all of this industry's output is caused by exports.
Materials handling machinery and equipment	Increased factory automation, leading to increased investment expenditures, will stimulate this sector. Exports are expected to increase due to lower exchange rate.
Special industry machinery	The food, paper, printing, and rubber industries buy investment goods from this industry. Imports made strong inroads in this industry's markets, while sales to foreign markets will grow at a healthy rate.
Computer equipment	Technological advances in the personal computer market are expected to continue to make systems more capable and easier to use. All industries are projected to have very strong investment demand for computer equipment. Computer-aided design, flexible manufacturing systems, and computer-integrated manufacturing will affect all areas of manufacturing. Both exports and imports are expected to have strong gains; a favorable net balance of trade for the United States is expected for this industry.
Electrical industrial apparatus	Most of the demand for the products of this industry are from mature markets—mainly appliances and industrial machinery and equipment. As a result, there is little potential for rapid growth.
Household appliances	Appliances will have more microprocessors replacing electromechanical controls. Productivity improvements are likely; there are many hand assemblers, and many products can be standardized. The industry could use robots and other automation methods. Imports will grow as a share, but will not dominate. The prospect of demand for household appliances is more positive because of demographic trends: the older and higher income baby boom groups tend to favor higher quality goods with advanced features.
Household audio and video equipment	The consumer electronics market is projected to continue the trend of very high levels of demand. Consumers will upgrade their existing systems by purchasing such items as super VCR's, wider screen TV sets, and compact disc players. It is assumed that much of the production and assembly of this equipment will be done overseas; the domestic industry will be concentrated on management and research and development. Growth in high-priced stereo equipment in motor vehicles will also help to fuel growth of this industry.
Telephone and telegraph apparatus	The communications sector will buy investment goods from this industry. Growth will continue to be very healthy because of technological advances while in the future portable phones will become an essential rather than a luxury item. In the future, cellular phones will be considered an essential item, not a luxury.
Broadcasting and communications equipment	Increases in civilian requirements will offset decreases in defense demand. Increased more than sophistication of other machinery and equipment requires higher purchases of communications equipment as an input. Future growth will be attributable to the private sector. There will be more private purchases of satellites, fiber optic systems, and equipment related to telecommunications. Impact of High Definition TV will be felt by 2005.
Semiconductors and related devices	More equipment and instruments will have electronic components. There are some limits to growth as this industry matures and imports rise, but domestic production will still expand rapidly. Increased demand will be driven by growth chiefly in the computers and telecommunication sectors.
Motor vehicles and car bodies	The growth of the driving age population is slowing but the aging of the population will result in a tendency toward larger, higher-valued cars.
Aircraft	Defense demand is expected to decline; the slack will be taken up by exports and investment purchases.
Aircraft and missile engines	Defense demand is expected to decline. Exports are expected to show strong growth.
Aircraft and missile parts and equipment	Defense demand is expected to decline. Exports are expected to show strong growth.
Guided missiles and space vehicles	Defense spending assumed to decline. Exports are expected to show strong growth.
Ship building and repairing	Defense spending assumed to be much lower than in the 1980's.
Boat building and repairing	Defense spending assumed to be much lower than in the 1980's.
Measuring and controlling devices; watches	Demand will be dependent on investment, especially by public utilities, and by exports. More instruments and equipment will incorporate automatic sensors. Continued growth of imported watches will lead to a decline in the domestic industry.

Table 1. Specific Industry assumptions for 2005 projections—Continued

Industry	Assumptions
Ophthalmic goods	Personal consumption expenditures will grow due to the aging of the population which requires more vision care.
Medical instruments and supplies	Increased demand because of high investment by health services. Consumer demand is also expected to show a strong growth because of the expanding elderly population.
X-ray and other electromedical apparatus	The health industries buy investment goods from this sector; demand is assumed to be especially strong because of rapid growth in health services and advances in biotechnology.
Photographic equipment and supplies	Increased demand due to the capital needs of the trade and service sectors due to consumer expenditures and advances in technology will lead to continued purchases of new equipment and as inputs into the medical sectors.
Jewelry, silverware, and plated ware	Continued growth of imported goods will lead to slow growth for the domestic industry.
Toys and sporting goods	Output will continue to grow despite the growth of imports.
Meat products	Slow growth of meat products due to slower population growth and less meat consumption. Poultry will increasingly replace pork and beef for health reasons. Productivity will continue to increase, but at a much slower rate because mechanization and assembly line speed are reaching limits.
Dairy products	Slow growth is expected. Health concerns expected to lead movement to low-fat products.
Preserved fruits and vegetables	Demand will be very strong for dried or frozen specialties but weak for canned goods.
Grain mill products and fats and oils	Health concerns will boost demand for grain products.
Sugar and confectionery products	Health concerns will lead to a relative decrease in the use of sugar as an ingredient in prepared foods.
Alcoholic beverages	Consumers are expected to continue to drink less alcoholic beverages per capita.
Soft drinks and flavorings	The slower growth of the teenage population will limit demand for soft drinks. Some increase expected as consumers substitute soft drinks for alcoholic beverages.
Tobacco manufactures	Health concerns and antismoking campaigns will cause domestic sales of tobacco to decline. Export growth is expected to remain strong, but will not fully offset the domestic decline.
Weaving, finishing, yarn, and thread mills	Already heavily mechanized, but automated production technologies will become more widespread.
Knitting mills	Industry already heavily automated; domestic producers very competitive with importers.
Apparel	Consumer demand will grow somewhat faster than population due to rising income levels, but more of it will be met by imports. Domestic production will increase moderately.
Pulp, paper, and paperboard mills	Continued growth of paper products and printing and publishing industries will lead to growth. Industry will continue to have strong productivity growth.
Miscellaneous publishing	Production will be high due to the growth of catalogs, directories, newsletters, technical manuals, and other types of miscellaneous publishing.
Commercial printing and business forms	Firms will continue their purchases of commercial printing and business forms; desk-top publishing will not have a dramatic impact.
Industrial chemicals	Disposal of toxic wastes will be a troublesome problem for the industry.
Plastics materials and synthetics	Output grows as plastics and composites continue to substitute for metals.
Drugs	Strong long-term growth is projected due to a strong demand for established drugs, a vast array of new products, and an expanding elderly population. Biotechnology advances are expected to contribute to the number of products available. Strong export growth is assumed.
Agricultural chemicals	Continued decline in the relative input of agricultural chemicals, as consumers and growers alike become increasingly wary of the environmental and health problems associated with some of these products. Growth due mainly to growth of exports.
Petroleum refining	Industries will continue energy conservation measures in an attempt to control costs. Vehicles will become more energy efficient. The use of coal for electric generation will increase. Production projections based on assumptions of Department of Energy.
Miscellaneous plastic products, nec	Substitution of plastic products for metal and glass will continue to spur growth.
Footwear except rubber and plastic	Output will decline as imports continue to increase.
Luggage, handbags, and leather products, n.e.c.	Output will decline as imports continue to increase.
Water transportation	Continued relative decline in shipping as means of transporting goods to market.

Table 1. Specific industry assumptions for 2005 projections—Continued

Industry	Assumptions
Air transportation	Demand for air travel will continue to grow rapidly despite safety concerns and already congested airports. Significant increase in consumer demand reflects growth in discretionary income and the impact of airline deregulation on the fare structure.
Passenger transportation arrangement	Rapid growth in business and personal travel, as well as a more complex fare system, will cause increased use of travel agents.
Communications, except broadcasting	Telephone services are expected to show rapid growth with new applications and extensions of current technology. Productivity growth will be high.
Radio and television broadcasting, cable TV	The increasing popularity of cable TV is expected to continue as the industry makes an effort to develop better programs. There are limits to growth in this sector as cable TV approaches market saturation. Advertising revenues will continue to spur growth of this sector. Employment will expand in sales and service.
Electric utilities including combined services	The shift away from oil and natural gas in home heating and towards electricity is expected to continue. Demand for electric utilities is expected to grow more rapidly than demand for other energy sources. Conservation of energy will continue.
Gas utilities including combined services	Continued energy conservation measures will decrease relative use of natural gas by all industries. This assumption is based on estimates by the Department of Energy.
Water and sanitation including combined services	This industry is expected to grow due to general growth of the economy and to increasing demand for refuse and waste disposal.
Retail trade, except eating and drinking places	Retailers will have difficulty finding part-time workers; past declines in the workweek will taper. Grocery stores will be faced with increasing pressure to raise productivity, but at the same time they will offer more labor-intensive services (salad bars, prepared foods, delicatessens, etc.), and more grocery stores will extend hours. Teleshopping is not assumed to have a major impact on retailers through 2005.
Eating and drinking places	Demand for fast-food growth will slow as the population ages. The increasing popularity of microwave ovens and the availability of prepared meals from grocery and specialty stores also explain the slowdown in food-away-from-home sales. Full-service restaurants are expected to grow, as is contracting for food service operations by hospitals, schools, and other institutions.
Security and commodity brokers	Personal spending on brokerage charges and investment counseling has undergone tremendous growth recently. Growth is expected to continue, although the projected growth rate is not expected to match that of recent years. Consumers will increase their demand for financial planning advice. Other growth will come from expanding pension funds, college endowments, and retirement programs such as IRA and Keogh; under deregulation, brokerage firms can offer more financial and credit services.
Insurance services	Increasing demand is assumed for specialized insurance, such as accident and health or fire and casualty, which is not easily standardized. Work force may have to increase because of the demand for new commercial coverage such as product liability, prepaid legal, or pollution liability. Competition from noninsurance firms, such as banks and department stores, and from foreign companies may take away some of the insurance industry's business. However, this should be partially offset by expansion of insurance firms into other financial services.
Hotels and other lodging places	Personal expenditures are expected to outstrip business expenditures as more discretionary income and more senior citizens lead to increased vacation expenditures.
Personal services, n.e.c.	An expanding array of new personal services such as diet workshops and buyers' clubs assumed; demand expected to be high due to two-earner families.
Services to buildings	Businesses will increase their expenditures on these services as building managers continue to contract out for many of these services, especially those performed on an irregular basis. Higher government purchases of contract cleaning services assumed.
Personnel supply services	Businesses will increase their expenditures, especially for temporary help services. They will continue their use of employment agencies in an attempt to find the best qualified jobseekers. The market for temporaries will expand even further beyond office clerical workers to include more nursing, engineering, and industrial workers. More contracts for facilities management on the part of government assumed.
Computer and data processing services	Business expenditures will increase as firms attempt to find the right software to fill their needs, and as specialized software is designed and developed. Strong government demand assumed.
Detective, guard, and security services	Business and government will continue to increase their expenditures for these services. However, as the industry matures, guard services are not expected to grow as rapidly as in the past. Some additional growth will come from the sale and operation of security systems.
Business services, n.e.c.	Business expenditures on miscellaneous services are expected to increase as the number of services expands.
Electrical repair shops	Growth in consumer demand is expected to continue.

Table 1. Specific industry assumptions for 2005 projections—Continued

Industry	Assumptions
Video tape rental	The vigorous expansion in the 1980's will come to an end due to market saturation.
Producers, orchestras, and entertainers	Output will be stimulated by rising personal incomes and the increased programming required for cable television.
Offices of health practitioners	More health services will be performed in offices and group practice centers rather than in hospitals.
Nursing and personal care facilities	Fueling the demand for nursing homes and skilled-care nursing facilities will be strong growth in the elderly population, especially those over age 85.
Hospitals, private	Some growth will occur as the demand for health care grows, as health care technology becomes more complex, and as hospitals expand their own outpatient facilities. Partially offsetting this growth will be cost-containment pressures and new technologies that permit more procedures to be performed in doctors' offices and other outpatient facilities.
Health services, n.e.c.	Greater reliance on outpatient and home health care, more contracting out of medical laboratory work, and general growth of demand for health services will result in more outpatient visits and increased demand for home care services.
Legal services	Increased litigation and the trend toward more specialized services and regional expansion of law firms will boost output.
Colleges and universities	Spending will increase moderately due to higher enrollments, particularly among older students and minorities.
Libraries, vocational and other schools	Vocational programs will grow due to increased efforts to train entrants to the workforce.
Individual and miscellaneous social services	Demand and employment are projected to grow rapidly (although slower than during 1979-90), especially for counseling, senior services, and fundraising activities. Growth will be driven by insurance reimbursement for counseling services; lack of jail space, which will force other types of rehabilitative efforts; and mandatory counseling for drivers convicted of driving while intoxicated.
Child daycare services	Growth will occur as the number of children under age 5 increases, as more mothers enter the work force, and as care shifts from home-based babysitting to the commercial sector.
Residential care	This sector will be affected by the shift away from hospital care. Strong growth is expected for drug and alcohol rehabilitation centers and elderly residential care.
Engineering and architectural services	As buildings become more complex, and zoning and building codes more demanding, the construction industry will increase its purchases of these services. Other industries, especially in manufacturing, will also increase their purchases of engineering services.
Management and public relations	Businesses will increase expenditures as they continue to contract out for specialized services, Government agencies are assumed to contract out for more managerial and consulting services.
Accounting, auditing, and services, n.e.c.	The growing complexity of tax laws, accounting procedures, and reporting requirements will cause continued expenditures by business for these services.
Private households	Demand for housekeeping and babysitting will grow, but will be met more by contract firms than by private individuals.

n.e.c = not elsewhere classified.

APPENDIX C: Earnings, Education Required, Employment Rates and Other Details for Over 200 Jobs[1]

There are a number of tables in this appendix and they can be used in a variety of useful ways. The first series of tables (Tables 1 through 5) present several hundred of the most important jobs and provide details on the number of persons working in each job by their level of education. This is followed by Table 8, which lists jobs based on the level of education typically required. This would be a useful table for determining, for example, jobs that are related to the level of education you now have or hope to achieve.

Tables 1 through 5

These tables present data on over 200 of the most popular occupations and include information on employment growth projections, median earnings, unemployment rates, percent working part-time, and types of training required for entry.

This information may help you evaluate the employment outlook for various occupations, and compare that information with data for other occupations. Perhaps you are interested in an occupation with a growth rate of 28 percent. You can better evaluate whether that growth is fast or slow when you compare that occupation with the others listed in the tables.

The technique used by these tables to compare occupations was to rank them according to where they fell in the entire range of values for each variable, such as unemployment rate or numerical change in employment. The larger the value for the variable, the higher the ranking; the higher the ranking, the greater the magnitude implied.

The 20 percent of occupations with the greatest projected percentage increase in employment between 1990 and 2005 would be ranked in the top range and described as having a "VH" (Very High) growth rate. It would of course be desirable to see a "VL" (Very Low) or "L" (Low) ranking for unemployment rate.

It is important to note that an adjective describing a variable may differ between tables because the rankings are based on different groups of occupations. For example, in Table 1, the 1990 employment of a professional occupation may be ranked "H" (High), based on rankings of data for all occupations. Yet in Table 2, which ranks data only for occupations requiring a four-year college degree, the designation could be "A" (Average). Also, in some occupations, more than one type of training may qualify employees for a job. For example, Table 1 indicates that registered nurses can be trained in four-year college degree programs or through post-secondary school training, but less than a bachelor's degree. So you will find information about registered nurses in Tables 2 and 3.

Information on all occupations for which statistics are compared in this chapter appears in Table 1. The jobs cover only those occupations with 40,000 or more employed in that occupation. This table is an appropriate starting point if you are beginning an investigation of occupational information or seeking comparisons of job characteristics.

Type of training—college degree, vocational, etc.—significant for each occupation is also indicated in Table 1. While in some professions the training indicated is a requirement, in others it may only be preferred.

Tables 2 through 5, respectively, present information about occupations in which a four-year college degree is a significant employment factor; post-secondary school training but less than a bachelor's degree is desired; formal employer training; or high school vocational training. Each category is discussed below.

Understanding the Information Provided in the Various Columns of the Accompanying Charts

Each of the charts that follow provides information in various columns. Here are some brief comments to help you understand and interpret this information.

Keys to Understanding the Code Letters in the Accompanying Charts

To save space, various letter codes are used in the various columns. The boxed information that follows provides basic definitions of the code meanings.

What The Letter Codes Mean	
VH =	Very high—within the top 20 percent of occupations measured
H =	High—within next 20 percent
A =	Average—within middle 20 percent
L =	Low—within next 20 percent
VL =	Very low—within lowest 20 percent
CD =	4-year college degree programs, bachelor's degree
PS =	Post-secondary school training, but less than a bachelor's degree
E =	Formal employer-provided training
HS =	High school vocational education training

What the Columns Refer To

Here are some brief descriptions for each of the columns used in the accompanying chart and what they mean.

Employment: This column represents the projected growth rate of the occupations in the base year of 1990 as well as through

---

1 Data used in this appendix is based on information obtained from "Occupational Projections and Training Data," Bulletin 2401, U.S. Department of Labor.

the year 2005. Large occupations generally have more openings than small ones because replacement needs are the major source of job openings in most occupations.

Employment Change: There are two columns under this column category. The "Number" column refers to the projected numerical change in job gains or losses. The "Percentage" column refers to the projected rate of change. Note that in larger occupations, a modest percentage increase can result in many more job openings than in a small occupation that is growing rapidly.

Annual Average Job Openings: This column has two columns beneath it. The one listing "Total replacement needs" provides the broadest measure of opportunities and identifies the total number of employees needed to enter that occupation annually. The one listing "Net replacement needs" estimates the number of new entrants needed for an occupation annually and measures minimum training needs.

Median Earnings of Full-Time Workers: This information can be used to determine relative earnings among occupations.

Unemployment Rate: Some occupations are more susceptible to the factors that result in unemployment—seasonality, fluctuations in economic conditions, and business failures. A high unemployment rate indicates that individuals are more likely to become unemployed than those in an occupation with a low rate.

Part-Time Workers: Presents the relative proportion of workers who work fewer than 35 hours per week. If you want part-time work, this may provide useful information for you.

Significant Sources of Formal Training: For most occupations, training can be obtained in a variety of ways and most individuals acquire skills from more than one source. The accompanying charts indicate the most common source or sources of training for those employed in that occupation.

Some Additional Information on Training Options

There are many ways to get the training you need for most occupations. The most common methods are covered below.

Occupations That Generally Require Completion of a Four-Year College Degree Program

Occupations requiring at least a bachelor's degree are concentrated in the professional specialty group: physicians and surgeons, dentists, lawyers, and teachers. While a four-year degree may be an advantage for personnel managers, computer programmers and securities and financial services sales workers, it is not always required.

The data indicates an increase in the conferment of bachelor's, master's, and doctoral degrees from a decade ago. The number of associate degrees conferred, however, has remained unchanged and the number of first professional degrees has declined slightly.

Many graduates do not pursue careers in their field of study. However, most new graduates with occupationally-oriented degrees, such as those in medicine, law, or engineering tend to enter related occupations. Liberal arts graduates are more likely to enter occupations which are not related to their college major.

Occupations for Which Post-Secondary School Training, but Less Than a Bachelor's Degree, Is Significant

Occupations in this group are very diverse and are found in almost all major occupational clusters. Workers in these occupations need specific formal training, but not to the extent generally required in most professional specialties.

Schools such as those which train hairstylists or dog groomers provide training for a specific occupation only, while others offer a variety of occupationally oriented training programs. Still others provide a general education curriculum or training.

Community and junior colleges constitute only about 10 percent of the institutions offering post-secondary vocational education training, but 70 percent of enrollments. Many programs are designed to provide a general background in arts and sciences. Interested students can then transfer to a four-year college. Students who wish to specialize in a particular field may enroll in vocational or occupational curriculums, such as dental hygiene or data processing. Most programs in junior and community colleges last two years and lead to an associate degree. Some programs last less than two years, and students are awarded certificates or other forms of recognition upon completion.

Occupations for Which Formal Employer Training Is Significant

Employees in precision production, craft, and repair occupations most frequently acquire their skills through employer training programs. (See Table 4.) Office machine and cash register repairers, electricians, plumbers and pipefitters, and tool and die makers often qualify for their jobs through formal company training. Many are trained in apprenticeship programs. Insurance, securities and financial services sales workers; police detectives and patrol officers; and correction officers and jailers often acquire their skills through formal employer training programs.

Formal employer training programs range from scheduled training conducted by designated instructors to periodic classroom instruction offered during or outside working hours, in combination with on-the-job training. These courses normally are designed to meet specific company needs. Some companies use college or university courses for classroom instruction. Employees are usually partially or fully reimbursed for job-related courses taken outside working hours.

The Armed Forces

The various Armed Forces are a major employer of youth, providing training in many specialized occupational skills such as computer repair, medical care, and aircraft engine maintenance and repair.

Some military occupations are specific only to the needs of the Armed Forces while others provide many, but not all, of the skills needed for a civilian job. For example, additional training may be needed before an electrician's mate can become an electronics technician.

Occupations for Which High School Vocational Education Training Is Useful

Many employees in administrative support occupations, including clerical, such as secretaries, typists and rate clerks, obtained training to qualify for their jobs in high school vocational programs. (See Table 5.) Other occupations in which such training is valuable include drafting, automobile repair, and typesetting. High school vocational training frequently provides specific skills that are readily transferable to the workplace. It can also serve as the foundation for development of advanced skills or simply as career exploration.

Table 8

This table presents data on the number of completions of educational programs by the type of program and field of study for the 1989-1990 academic year. The data is based on a survey of institutions of higher education conducted by the National Center for Education Statistics (NCES) and follows the Classification of Instructional Program (CIP) system to identify the field of study.

Table 1. Rankings of all occupations by selected characteristics[1]

Occupation as defined by National Industry-Occupation Matrix	Employment, 1990	Employment change, 1988-2000		Annual average job openings, 1990-2005		Median earnings of full-time workers	Unemployment rate	Part-time workers	Significant sources of formal training[2]
		Number	Percent	Growth plus total replacement needs	Growth plus net replacement needs				
MANAGERIAL AND MANAGEMENT-RELATED OCCUPATIONS									
Education administrators	H	H	H	H	H	VH	VL	A	CD
Financial managers	VH	VH	H	H	VH	VH	L	VL	CD PS E
Funeral directors and morticians	L	L	A	VL	L	-	VL	L	CD PS E
Marketing, advertising, and public relations managers	H	VH	VH	H	VH	VH	L	VL	CD E
Personnel, training, and labor relations managers	H	H	VH	A	H	VH	L	VL	CD PS E
Property and real estate managers	H	H	VH	H	H	A	L	A	PS
Purchasing managers	H	H	A	A	H	VH	VL	VL	CD PS E
Accountants and auditors	VH	VH	VH	VH	VH	H	L	L	CD
Construction and building inspectors	L	A	A	L	L	-	L	L	E
Employment interviewers and personnel specialists[3]	H	VH	H	H	H	VH	L	L	CD E
Management analysts	A	H	VH	H	H	VH	L	H	CD E
Purchasing agents, except wholesale, retail, and farm products	H	H	A	A	H	H	A	VL	CD PS
Underwriters	A	A	H	A	A	-	VL	L	CD E
Wholesale and retail buyers, except farm products	H	H	A	H	H	H	L	A	CD E
PROFESSIONAL SPECIALTY OCCUPATIONS									
Aeronautical and astronautical engineers	L	A	A	L	A	VH	VL	VL	CD
Chemical engineers	L	L	L	VL	L	VH	VL	VL	CD E
Civil engineers, including traffic engineers	H	H	H	A	H	VH	L	VL	CD E
Electrical and electronics engineers	H	VH	VH	A	VH	VH	VL	VL	CD E
Industrial engineers, except safety engineers	A	A	A	L	A	VH	L	VL	CD E
Mechanical engineers	H	H	H	A	H	VH	VL	VL	CD E
Architects[3]	A	H	H	A	A	VH	VL	A	CD E
Surveyors	A	A	A	A	L	-	A	L	
Biological scientists	L	A	VH	L	A	VH	L	L	CD
Systems analysts and computer scientists	H	VH	VH	H	VH	VH	VL	L	CD E
Operations research analysts	L	H	VH	A	A	VH	L	L	CD E
Chemists	A	A	A	L	A	VH	VL	VL	CD
Geologists, geophysicists, and oceanographers	L	A	H	L	L	-	A	VL	CD
Economists	L	A	A	L	L	VH	A	A	CD
Psychologists	A	H	VH	A	A	H	VL	H	CD
Clergy	H	A	L	A	A	A	VL	A	CD
Recreation workers	H	H	H	H	A	VL	H	H	CD
Social workers and human services workers[3]	VH	VH	VH	VH	VH	H	L	A	CD
Lawyers	VH	VH	VH	H	VH	VH	VL	L	CD
Teachers, elementary	VH	VH	H	VH	VH	H	VL	A	CD
Teachers, special education	H	VH	VH	H	H	H	VL	A	CD
Teachers, secondary school	VH	VH	VH	VH	VH	VH	VL	A	CD
Librarians, professional	A	A	L	A	A	H	VL	VH	CD
Counselors	A	H	VH	A	A	VH	VL	A	CD
Dentists	H	A	A	L	A	-	VL	A	CD
Physicians	VH	VH	VH	H	VH	VH	VL	L	CD
Veterinarians and veterinary inspectors	L	A	H	VL	L	-	VL	L	CD
Pharmacists	A	H	A	L	A	VH	VL	H	CD
Registered nurses	VH	VH	VH	VH	VH	VH	VL	H	CD PS
Physical therapists	A	H	VH	A	A	-	VL	VH	CD
Respiratory therapists	L	H	VH	L	A	-	VL	H	CD PS
Speech-language pathologists and audiologists	L	A	VH	L	A	-	VL	H	CD
Artists and commercial artists	H	H	VH	H	H	A	L	H	CD PS
Musicians	H	A	L	H	H	-	A	VH	CD
Photographers and camera operators	A	H	H	A	A	A	L	H	CD PS E
Producers, directors, actors, and entertainers	A	H	VH	A	A	-	VH	A	CD PS
Public relations specialists and publicity writers	A	A	A	A	A	VH	L	A	CD E
Radio and TV announcers and newscasters	L	A	A	L	L	-	A	VH	PS
Writers[3]	H	H	H	H	H	L	L	H	CD
TECHNICIAN OCCUPATIONS									
Clinical lab technologists and technicians	H	H	H	A	H	A	L	H	CD PS E

NOTE: Rankings are based on all detailed occupations in the National Industry-Occupation Matrix and those in the Current Population Survey with 40,000 or more employees. Codes for describing the variables are: VH = "Very high," H = "High," A = "Average," L = "Low," and VL = "Very low." A dash indicates data are not available.

See footnotes at end of table.

Table 1. Rankings of all occupations by selected characteristics[1]——Continued

Occupation as defined by National Industry-Occupation Matrix	Employment, 1990	Employment change, 1988-2000		Annual average job openings, 1990-2005		Median earnings of full-time workers	Unemployment rate	Part-time workers	Significant sources of formal training[2]
		Number	Percent	Growth plus total replacement needs	Growth plus net replacement needs				
Dental hygienists	A	H	VH	A	A	-	VL	VH	CD PS
Licensed practical nurses	VH	VH	VH	VH	VH	L	L	H	PS
Medical records technicians	L	H	VH	L	A	-	L	A	PS
Nuclear medicine and radiologic technicians and technologists[3]	A	VH	VH	A	H	H	VL	H	PS
Opticians, dispensing and measuring	L	A	VH	A	A	-	A	H	E
Electrical and electronic technicians and technologists	H	VH	VH	H	H	H	L	VL	CD PS E HS
All other engineering technicians and technologists	H	H	A	H	H	H	A	A	
Drafters	H	H	A	H	H	H	A	L	CD PS E HS
Science and mathematics technicians	H	H	H	H	H	VL	A	A	CD
Aircraft pilots and flight engineers	A	H	VH	L	A	VH	A	H	CD
Computer programmers	VH	VH	VH	VH	VH	VH	L	L	CD PS E
Legal assistants and technicians, except clerical	H	VH	VH	H	H	H	L	A	CD PS

MARKETING AND SALES OCCUPATIONS

Occupation	Employment, 1990	Number	Percent	Growth plus total replacement needs	Growth plus net replacement needs	Median earnings	Unemployment rate	Part-time workers	Significant sources
Cashiers	VH	VH	H	VH	VH	VL	VH	VH	
Counter and rental clerks	H	H	VH	VH	H	VL	H	VH	
Insurance sales workers	H	H	A	H	VH	H	VL	A	CD E
Real estate agents, brokers, and appraisers	H	H	A	H	H	H	VL	H	CD PS E
Salespersons, retail	VH	VH	H	VH	VH	VL	H	VH	
Securities and financial services sales workers	H	H	VH	H	H	VH	L	L	CD E

ADMINISTRATIVE SUPPORT OCCUPATIONS

Occupation	Employment, 1990	Number	Percent	Growth plus total replacement needs	Growth plus net replacement needs	Median earnings	Unemployment rate	Part-time workers	Significant sources
Adjustment clerks, credit authorizers and checkers, loan and credit clerks, and loan interviewers[3]	VH	VH	H	VH	H	A	A	A	
Bill and account collectors	H	H	VH	H	A	L	A	A	
Welfare eligibility workers and interviewers	A	A	A	A	A	A	A	A	PS E
Telephone operators	H	VL	VL	H	H	L	H	H	E
Computer operators, except peripheral equipment	H	H	A	H	A	A	A	A	PS
Billing, cost, and rate clerks	H	A	L	H	H	L	A	A	HS
Billing, posting, and calculating machine operators	A	L	L	A	A	-	A	H	
Bookkeeping, accounting, and auditing clerks	VH	VL	VL	VH	VH	L	A	H	PS HS
Payroll and timekeeping clerks	A	L	L	A	A	L	L	A	HS
Hotel desk clerks	A	H	VH	H	A	VL	VH	H	
Interviewing clerks, except personnel and social welfare	A	H	VH	H	H	L	H	H	HS
Receptionists and information clerks	VH	VH	VH	VH	VH	VL	H	VH	HS
Reservation and transportation ticket agents and travel clerks	A	H	VH	A	A	A	L	H	E
Mail clerks, except mail machine operators and postal service	A	A	L	H	A	L	H	H	
Messengers	A	A	L	H	A	L	H	VH	
Postal mail carriers	H	H	H	A	H	H	VL	L	
Postal service clerks	A	L	L	A	A	H	A	A	E
Dispatchers	H	H	H	H	H	A	A	L	E
Meter readers, utilities	L	VL	VL	L	L	-	VL	VL	
Procurement and stock clerks[3]	VH	H	L	VH	VH	L	H	H	
Production, planning, and expediting clerks	H	L	L	H	A	A	A	A	
Traffic, shipping, and receiving clerks	VH	H	A	VH	H	L	H	A	
Weighers, measurers, checkers, and samplers, recordkeeping	L	L	L	L	L	-	H	H	
File clerks	H	H	L	VH	H	VL	H	VH	HS
Library assistants and bookmobile drivers	A	A	L	H	A	VL	A	VH	
Order clerks and customer service representatives, utilities[3]	H	A	L	H	H	A	L	A	HS
Personnel clerks, except payroll and timekeeping	A	A	A	A	A	L	L	A	CD
Secretaries	VH	VH	A	VH	VH	L	A	H	PS HS
Stenographers	A	VL	VL	A	A	-	VL	H	CD PS
Typists and word processors	VH	VL	VL	VH	VH	L	H	H	HS
Bank tellers	H	VL	VL	VH	VH	VL	A	VH	E
Clerical supervisors and managers	VH	VH	A	VH	VH	H	VL	VL	E
Data entry keyers, except composing	H	H	L	H	H	L	H	H	PS HS
Duplicating, mail, and other office machine operators	A	A	A	H	H	-	H	H	
General office clerks	VH	VH	H	VH	VH	L	A	VH	HS
Statistical clerks	A	VL	VL	L	L	A	L	H	CD PS
Teacher aides and educational assistants	VH	VH	VH	VH	VH	VL	A	VH	

NOTE: Rankings are based on all detailed occupations in the National Industry-Occupation Matrix and those in the Current Population Survey with 40,000 or more employees. Codes for describing the variables are: VH = "Very high," H = "High," A = "Average," L = "Low," and VL = "Very low." A dash indicates data are not available.

See footnotes at end of table.

Table 1. Rankings of all occupations by selected characteristics[1]——Continued

Occupation as defined by National Industry-Occupation Matrix	Employment, 1990	Employment change, 1988-2000		Annual average job openings, 1990-2005		Median earnings of full-time workers	Unemployment rate	Part-time workers	Significant sources of formal training[2]
		Number	Percent	Growth plus total replacement needs	Growth plus net replacement needs				
SERVICE OCCUPATIONS									
Janitors and cleaners, including maids and housekeeping cleaners	VH	VH	A	VH	VH	VL	VH	VH	
Pest controllers and assistants	L	L	L	A	L	-	H	L	
Cooks, except short order	VH	VH	VH	VH	VH	VL	VH	VH	
Cooks, short order and fast food	VH	VH	VH	VH	VH	-	VH	VH	
Food preparation workers	VH	VH	VH	VH	VH	VL	VH	VH	
Bartenders	H	A	L	VH	H	VL	VH	VH	
Dining room and cafeteria attendants and bar helpers	H	VH	VH	VH	VH	VL	VH	VH	
Food counter, fountain, and related workers	VH	VH	VH	VH	VH	VL	VH	VH	
Waiters and waitresses	VH	VH	H	VH	VH	VL	VH	VH	
Dental assistants	H	H	VH	H	H	VL	A	VH	PS
Nursing aides, orderlies, and attendants	VH	VH	VH	VH	VH	VL	H	H	PS E
Amusement and recreation attendants	H	H	H	H	H	VL	VH	VH	
Barbers	A	VL	VL	L	L	-	VL	H	PS
Child care workers	VH	VH	VH	VH	VH	VL	A	VH	
Hairdressers, hairstylists, and cosmetologists	VH	VH	H	VH	H	VL	L	VH	PS
Flight attendants	A	H	VH	A	A	-	L	VH	E
Child care workers, private household	H	VL	VL	VH	H	VL	H	VH	
Cleaners and servants, private household	H	VL	VL	H	A	VL	H	VH	
Housekeepers and butlers	L	L	L	L	L	-	VH	VH	
Fire fighters	H	H	H	A	H	H	L	VL	PS E
Fire fighting and prevention supervisors	L	A	H	VL	A	-	VL	-	
Correction officers	H	VH	VH	H	H	A	VL	VL	E
Police and detective supervisors	A	A	A	VL	A	VH	VL	VL	CD PS E
Police detectives and patrol officers[3]	H	VH	H	A	VH	VH	VL	VL	PS E
Guards	VH	VH	VH	VH	VH	L	H	H	
FARMING, FORESTRY, FISHING, AND RELATED OCCUPATIONS									
Animal caretakers, except farm	A	H	VH	H	A	-	A	VH	
Farm workers	VH	VL	VL	VH	VH	VL	VH	H	
Farmers	VH	VL	VL	VH	H	-	VL	H	
Farm managers	A	A	A	A	A	-	VL	A	
Fishers, hunters, and trappers	L	L	L	VL	L	-	VH	A	
Fallers, log handling equipment, and all other timber cutters[3]	A	VL	VL	A	L	-	VH	A	
Gardeners and groundskeepers, except farm	VH	VH	VH	VH	VH	VL	VH	VH	
Supervisors, farming, forestry, and agricultural related occupations	L	L	L	L	L	VL	A	VL	
PRECISION PRODUCTION, CRAFT, AND REPAIR OCCUPATIONS									
Blue-collar worker supervisors	VH	VH	L	VH	VH	H	L	VL	E
Bricklayers and stone masons	A	H	A	H	A	H	VH	L	PS E HS
Carpenters	VH	VH	A	VH	VH	A	VH	L	HS
Carpet installers	L	A	A	L	A	-	H	A	
Concrete and terrazzo finishers	A	A	A	VL	A	A	VH	L	
Drywall installers and finishers	A	H	H	H	A	A	VH	A	
Electricians	VH	VH	H	H	VH	H	H	VL	PS E HS
Glaziers	L	A	H	L	L	-	H	VL	
Hard tile setters	VL	L	H	VL	L	-	VH	A	PS E
Insulation workers	L	A	H	A	A	-	VH	VL	
Painters and paperhangers, construction and maintenance	H	VH	H	H	H	L	VH	H	
Plumbers, pipefitters, and steamfitters	H	H	A	H	H	H	H	L	E HS
Roofers	A	H	H	H	A	L	VH	A	
Structural and reinforcing metal workers	A	A	A	A	A	-	VH	VL	E
Central office and PBX installers and repairers; frame wirers; station installers and repairers, telephone[3]	A	VL	VL	A	A	VH	VL	VL	E
Data processing equipment repairers	A	H	VH	A	A	VH	L	L	CD PS E

NOTE: Rankings are based on all detailed occupations in the National Industry-Occupation Matrix and those in the Current Population Survey with 40,000 or more employees. Codes for describing the variables are: VH = "Very high," H = "High," A = "Average," L = "Low," and VL = "Very low." A dash indicates data are not available.

See footnotes at end of table.

Table 1. Rankings of all occupations by selected characteristics[1]——Continued

Occupation as defined by National Industry-Occupation Matrix	Employment, 1990	Employment change, 1988-2000		Annual average job openings, 1990-2005		Median earnings of full-time workers	Unemployment rate	Part-time workers	Significant sources of formal training[2]
		Number	Percent	Growth plus total replacement needs	Growth plus net replacement needs				
Electrical powerline installers and repairers	A	A	L	L	A	VH	L	VL	E
Telephone and cable TV line installers and repairers	A	VL	VL	VL	A	VH	L	VL	E
Industrial machinery mechanics	H	H	L	H	H	H	A	VL	E
Millwrights	L	A	A	A	A	H	H	VL	PS E HS
Aircraft engine specialists	VL	L	H	VL	L	VH	L	VL	PS E
Automotive body and related repairers	H	H	H	H	H	A	H	L	E HS
Automotive mechanics	VH	VH	A	VH	VH	A	A	L	PS E HS
Bus and truck mechanics and diesel engine specialists	H	H	A	A	H	A	A	VL	E HS
Motorcycle, boat, and small engine mechanics	L	L	L	L	L	-	H	A	PS E HS
Heat, air-conditioning, and refrigeration mechanics and installers	H	H	A	A	A	A	A	L	PS E
Home appliance and power tool repairers	L	VL	L	L	L	-	L	L	PS E HS
Office machine and cash register servicers	L	A	A	VL	L	A	L	L	PS E
Electrical and electronic equipment assemblers, precision	A	VL	VL	A	A	L	VH	VL	
Butchers and meatcutters	H	VL	VL	H	A	L	H	A	
All other precision food and tobacco workers	L	L	L	L	L	-	H	H	
Machinists	H	H	L	H	H	H	A	VL	PS E HS
Sheet metal workers and duct installers	H	H	A	H	H	L	H	VL	
Tool and die makers	A	L	L	L	A	VH	L	VL	PS E HS
Compositors and typesetters, precision, and machine operators[3]	L	L	A	L	L	-	L	A	PS E HS
Lithography and photoengraving workers, precision, and machine operators[3]	A	H	H	A	A	-	A	L	
Upholsterers	L	L	L	L	L	-	A	A	HS
Woodworkers, precision	H	A	A	H	H	-	H	A	
Dental lab technicians, precision	L	L	L	L	L	-	H	H	PS
Stationary engineers and boiler operators, low pressure[3]	L	L	L	VL	L	VH	L	VL	PS E
Water and liquid waste treatment plant and system operators	A	A	H	VL	A	-	VL	VL	PS E
OPERATOR, FABRICATOR, AND LABORER OCCUPATIONS									
Grinding machine setters and setup operators, metal and plastic	L	VL	VL	A	L	A	H	VL	
Machine tool cutting operators and tenders, metal and plastic	A	VL	VL	L	L	A	H	L	HS
Punching machine setters and setup operators, metal and plastic	L	VL	VL	L	L	A	VH	VL	
Welders and cutters, machine operators, setters, and hand workers[3]	H	A	L	H	H	A	VH	VL	PS E HS
Metal molding machine operators and tenders, setters and setup operators	L	VL	VL	VL	L	L	VH	VL	PS E
Printing press operators	H	H	A	A	H	A	A	L	E HS
Pressing machine operators and tenders, textile, garment, and related materials	A	A	A	A	A	VL	VH	H	
Sewing machine operators[3]	VH	VL	VL	VH	H	VL	VH	L	
Head sawyers and sawing machine operators and tenders, setters, and setup operators	L	A	L	A	A	L	H	L	
Woodworking machine operators and tenders, setters and setup operators	L	A	A	A	L	-	VH	A	
Crushing and mixing machine operators and tenders	A	A	L	H	A	VL	H	L	
Cutting and slicing machine setters, operators, and tenders	A	L	L	A	L	L	VH	L	
Furnace, kiln, or kettle operators and tenders	L	VL	VL	L	L	H	H	VL	
Laundry and drycleaning machine operators and tenders, except pressing	A	H	H	H	A	VL	H	H	
Packaging and filling machine operators and tenders	H	VL	VL	H	A	VL	VH	A	
Painting and coating machine operators	A	VL	L	A	A	L	VH	L	
Separating and still machine operators and tenders	VL	VL	VL	L	L	H	A	VL	
Electrical and electronic assemblers	H	VL	VL	H	A	L	VH	VL	
Bus drivers	VH	VH	VH	VH	VH	A	A	VH	E
Taxi drivers and chauffeurs	A	H	H	H	A	L	H	H	
Driver/sales workers	H	H	H	H	H	H	A	A	
Truck drivers light and heavy	VH	VH	H	VH	VH	A	A	A	
Locomotive engineers and other rail vehicle operators[3]	VL	VL	VL	VL	L	-	A	VL	
Crane and tower operators	L	L	L	L	L	H	H	VL	E
Excavation and loading machine operators	L	A	L	L	L	A	VH	L	
Grader, dozer, and scraper operators	A	A	L	A	A	A	VH	L	
Industrial and logging truck and tractor operators[3]	H	H	L	H	H	A	H	VL	
Operating engineers	A	H	H	A	A	H	VH	VL	E

NOTE: Rankings are based on all detailed occupations in the National Industry-Occupation Matrix and those in the Current Population Survey with 40,000 or more employees. Codes for describing the variables are: VH = "Very high," H = "High," A = "Average," L = "Low," and VL = "Very low." A dash indicates data are not available.

See footnotes at end of table.

Table 1. Rankings of all occupations by selected characteristics'——Continued

Occupation as defined by National Industry-Occupation Matrix	Employ-ment, 1990	Employment change, 1988-2000		Annual average job openings, 1990-2005		Median earnings of full-time workers	Unem-ploy-ment rate	Part-time workers	Significant sources of formal training[2]
		Number	Percent	Growth plus total replace-ment needs	Growth plus net replace-ment needs				
Freight, stock, and material movers, hand	VH	VH	L	VH	VH	L	VH	H	
Hand packers and packagers	VH	H	L	VH	VH	VL	VH	H	
Helpers, construction trades	VH	H	A	VH	VH	VL	VH	A	
Machine feeders and offbearers	H	VL	VL	H	H	L	VH	A	
Parking lot attendants	L	A	H	A	L	-	VH	VH	
Refuse collectors	A	L	L	A	A	-	VH	A	
Service station attendants; tire repairers and changers[3]	H	VL	L	VH	H	VL	VH	VH	
Vehicle washers and equipment cleaners	H	H	H	VH	H	VL	VH	H	

Table 2. Rankings of occupations generally requiring a 4-year college degree, by selected characteristics[1]

Occupation as defined by National Industry-Occupation Matrix	Employment, 1990	Employment change, 1988-2000		Annual average job openings, 1990-2005		Median earnings of full-time workers	Unemployment rate	Part-time workers	Significant sources of formal training[2]
		Number	Percent	Growth plus total replacement needs	Growth plus net replacement needs				
MANAGERIAL AND MANAGEMENT-RELATED OCCUPATIONS									
Education administrators	H	H	H	H	H	VH	VL	A	CD
Financial managers	VH	VH	H	H	VH	VH	L	VL	CD PS E
Funeral directors and morticians	L	L	A	VL	L	-	VL	L	CD PS E
Marketing, advertising, and public relations managers	H	VH	VH	H	VH	VH	L	VL	CD E
Personnel, training, and labor relations managers	H	H	VH	A	H	VH	L	VL	CD PS E
Purchasing managers	H	H	A	A	H	VH	VL	VL	CD PS E
Accountants and auditors	VH	VH	VH	VH	VH	H	L	L	CD
Employment interviewers and personnel specialists[3]	H	VH	H	H	H	VH	L	L	CD E
Management analysts	A	H	VH	H	H	VH	L	H	CD E
Purchasing agents, except wholesale, retail, and farm products	H	H	A	A	H	H	A	VL	CD PS
Underwriters	A	A	H	A	A	-	VL	L	CD E
Wholesale and retail buyers, except farm products	H	H	A	H	H	H	L	A	CD E
PROFESSIONAL SPECIALTY OCCUPATIONS									
Aeronautical and astronautical engineers	L	A	A	L	A	VH	VL	VL	CD
Chemical engineers	L	L	L	VL	L	VH	VL	VL	CD E
Civil engineers, including traffic engineers	H	H	H	A	H	VH	L	VL	CD E
Electrical and electronics engineers	H	VH	VH	A	VH	VH	VL	VL	CD E
Industrial engineers, except safety engineers	A	A	A	L	A	VH	L	VL	CD E
Mechanical engineers	H	H	H	A	H	VH	VL	VL	CD E
Architects[3]	A	H	H	A	A	VH	VL	A	CD E
Biological scientists	L	A	VH	L	A	VH	L	L	CD
Systems analysts and computer scientists	H	VH	VH	H	VH	VH	VL	L	CD E
Operations research analysts	L	H	VH	L	A	VH	L	L	CD E
Chemists	A	A	A	L	A	VH	VL	VL	CD
Geologists, geophysicists, and oceanographers	L	A	H	L	L	-	A	VL	CD
Economists	L	A	A	L	L	VH	A	A	CD
Psychologists	A	H	VH	A	A	H	VL	H	CD
Clergy	H	A	L	A	A	A	VL	A	CD
Recreation workers	H	H	H	H	A	VL	H	H	CD
Social workers and human services workers[3]	VH	VH	VH	VH	VH	H	L	A	CD
Lawyers	VH	VH	VH	H	VH	VH	VL	L	CD
Teachers, elementary	VH	VH	H	VH	VH	H	VL	A	CD
Teachers, special education	H	VH	VH	H	H	H	VL	A	CD
Teachers, secondary school	VH	VH	VH	VH	VH	VH	VL	A	CD
Librarians, professional	A	A	L	A	A	H	VL	VH	CD
Counselors	A	H	VH	A	A	VH	VL	A	CD
Dentists	H	A	A	L	A	-	VL	A	CD
Physicians	VH	VH	VH	H	VH	VH	VL	L	CD
Veterinarians and veterinary inspectors	L	A	H	VL	L	-	VL	L	CD
Pharmacists	A	H	A	L	A	VH	VL	H	CD
Registered nurses	VH	VH	VH	VH	VH	VH	VL	H	CD PS
Physical therapists	A	H	VH	A	A	-	VL	VH	CD PS
Respiratory therapists	L	H	VH	L	A	-	VL	H	CD PS
Speech-language pathologists and audiologists	L	A	VH	L	A	-	VL	H	CD
Artists and commercial artists	H	H	VH	H	H	A	L	H	CD PS
Musicians	H	A	L	H	H	-	A	VH	CD
Photographers and camera operators	A	H	H	A	A	A	L	H	CD PS E
Producers, directors, actors, and entertainers	A	H	VH	A	A	-	VH	A	CD PS
Public relations specialists and publicity writers	A	A	A	A	A	VH	L	A	CD E
Writers[3]	H	H	H	H	H	L	L	H	CD
TECHNICIAN OCCUPATIONS									
Clinical lab technologists and technicians	H	H	H	A	H	A	L	H	CD PS E
Dental hygienists	A	H	VH	A	A	-	VL	VH	CD PS
Electrical and electronic technicians and technologists	H	VH	VH	H	H	H	L	VL	CD PS E HS
Drafters	H	H	A	H	H	H	A	L	CD PS E HS
Science and mathematics technicians	H	H	H	H	H	VL	A	A	CD

NOTE: Rankings are based on all detailed occupations in the National Industry-Occupation Matrix and those in the Current Population Survey with 40,000 or more employees. Codes for describing the variables are: VH = "Very high," H = "High," A = "Average," L = "Low," and VL = "Very low." A dash indicates data are not available.

See footnotes at end of table.

Table 2. Rankings of occupations generally requiring a 4-year college degree, by selected characteristics[1]——Continued

Occupation as defined by National Industry-Occupation Matrix	Employ- ment, 1990	Employment change, 1988-2000		Annual average job openings, 1990-2005		Median earnings of full-time workers	Unem- ploy- ment rate	Part- time workers	Significant sources of formal training[2]
		Number	Percent	Growth plus total replace- ment needs	Growth plus net replace- ment needs				
Aircraft pilots and flight engineers	A	H	VH	L	A	VH	L	H	CD
Computer programmers	VH	VH	VH	VH	VH	VH	L	L	CD PS E
Legal assistants and technicians, except clerical	H	VH	VH	H	H	H	L	A	CD PS
MARKETING AND SALES OCCUPATIONS									
Insurance sales workers	H	H	A	H	VH	H	VL	A	CD E
Real estate agents, brokers, and appraisers	H	H	A	H	H	H	VL	H	CD PS E
Securities and financial services sales workers	H	H	VH	H	H	VH	L	L	CD E
ADMINISTRATIVE SUPPORT OCCUPATIONS									
Personnel clerks, except payroll and timekeeping	A	A	A	A	A	L	L	A	CD
Stenographers	A	VL	VL	A	A	L	VL	H	CD PS
Statistical clerks	A	VL	VL	L	L	A	L	H	CD PS
SERVICE OCCUPATIONS									
Police and detective supervisors	A	A	A	VL	A	VH	VL	VL	CD PS E
PRECISION PRODUCTION, CRAFT, AND REPAIR OCCUPATIONS									
Data processing equipment repairers	A	H	VH	A	A	VH	L	L	CD PS E

[1] Each characteristic, and its data source, is discussed in the "Data sources" section of chapter I.

[2] Codes for source of formal training are: HS = high school vocational training program, E = formal employer training, PS = postsecondary school training, but less than a bachelor's degree, CD = 4-year college degree program.

[3] This title does not appear in the National Industry-Occupation Matrix, but was formed by combining several matrix occupations in order to achieve Current Population Survey comparability.

NOTE: Rankings are based on all detailed occupations in the National Industry-Occupation Matrix and those in the Current Population Survey with 40,000 or more employees. Codes for describing the variables are: VH = "Very high," H = "High," A = "Average," L = "Low," and VL = "Very low."   A dash indicates data are not available.

Table 3. Rankings of occupations for which postsecondary school training, but less than a bachelor's degree, is significant, by selected characteristics[1]

Occupation as defined by National Industry-Occupation Matrix	Employment, 1990	Employment change, 1988-2000		Annual average job openings, 1990-2005		Median earnings of full-time workers	Unemployment rate	Part-time workers	Significant sources of formal training[2]
		Number	Percent	Growth plus total replacement needs	Growth plus net replacement needs				
MANAGERIAL AND MANAGEMENT-RELATED OCCUPATIONS									
Financial managers	VH	VH	H	H	VH	VH	L	VL	CD PS E
Funeral directors and morticians	L	L	A	VL	L	-	VL	L	CD PS E
Personnel, training, and labor relations managers	H	H	VH	A	H	VH	L	VL	CD PS E
Property and real estate managers	H	H	VH	H	H	A	L	A	PS
Purchasing managers	H	H	A	A	H	VH	VL	VL	CD PS E
Purchasing agents, except wholesale, retail, and farm products	H	H	A	A	H	H	A	VL	CD PS
PROFESSIONAL SPECIALTY OCCUPATIONS									
Registered nurses	VH	VH	VH	VH	VH	VH	VL	H	CD PS
Respiratory therapists	L	H	VH	L	A	-	VL	H	CD PS
Artists and commercial artists	H	H	VH	H	H	A	L	H	CD PS
Photographers and camera operators	A	H	H	A	A	A	L	H	CD PS E
Producers, directors, actors, and entertainers	A	H	VH	A	A	-	VH	A	CD PS
Radio and TV announcers and newscasters	L	A	A	L	L	-	A	VH	PS
TECHNICIAN OCCUPATIONS									
Clinical lab technologists and technicians	H	H	H	A	H	A	L	H	CD PS E
Dental hygienists	A	H	VH	A	A	-	VL	VH	CD PS
Licensed practical nurses	VH	VH	VH	VH	VH	L	L	H	PS
Medical records technicians	L	H	VH	L	A	-	L	A	PS
Nuclear medicine and radiologic technicians and technologists[3]	A	VH	VH	A	H	H	VL	H	PS
Electrical and electronic technicians and technologists	H	VH	VH	H	H	H	L	VL	CD PS E HS
Drafters	H	H	A	H	H	H	A	L	CD PS E HS
Computer programmers	VH	VH	VH	VH	VH	VH	L	L	CD PS E
Legal assistants and technicians, except clerical	H	VH	VH	H	H	H	L	A	CD PS
MARKETING AND SALES OCCUPATIONS									
Real estate agents, brokers, and appraisers	H	H	A	H	H	H	VL	H	CD PS E
ADMINISTRATIVE SUPPORT OCCUPATIONS									
Welfare eligibility workers and interviewers	A	A	A	A	A	A	A	A	PS E
Computer operators, except peripheral equipment	H	H	A	H	A	A	A	A	PS
Bookkeeping, accounting, and auditing clerks	VH	VL	VL	VH	VH	L	A	H	PS HS
Secretaries	VH	VH	A	VH	VH	L	A	H	PS HS
Stenographers	A	VL	VL	A	A	-	VL	H	CD PS
Data entry keyers, except composing	H	H	L	VH	H	L	H	H	PS HS
Statistical clerks	A	VL	VL	L	L	A	L	H	CD PS
SERVICE OCCUPATIONS									
Dental assistants	H	H	VH	H	H	VL	A	VH	PS
Nursing aides, orderlies, and attendants	VH	VH	VH	VH	VH	VL	H	H	PS E
Barbers	A	VL	VL	L	L	-	VL	H	PS
Hairdressers, hairstylists, and cosmetologists	VH	VH	H	VH	H	VL	L	VH	PS
Fire fighters	H	H	H	A	H	H	L	VL	PS E
Police and detective supervisors	A	A	A	VL	A	VH	VL	VL	CD PS E
Police detectives and patrol officers[3]	H	VH	H	A	VH	VH	VL	VL	PS E
PRECISION PRODUCTION, CRAFT, AND REPAIR OCCUPATIONS									
Bricklayers and stone masons	A	H	A	H	A	H	VH	L	PS E HS
Electricians	VH	VH	H	H	VH	H	H	VL	PS E HS
Hard tile setters	VL	L	H	VL	L	-	VH	A	PS E

NOTE: Rankings are based on all detailed occupations in the National Industry-Occupation Matrix and those in the Current Population Survey with 40,000 or more employees. Codes for describing the variables are: VH = "Very high," H = "High," A = "Average," L = "Low," and VL = "Very low." A dash indicates data are not available.

See footnotes at end of table.

Table 3. Rankings of occupations for which postsecondary school training, but less than a bachelor's degree, is significant, by selected characteristics[1]——Continued

Occupation as defined by National Industry-Occupation Matrix	Employment, 1990	Employment change, 1988-2000		Annual average job openings, 1990-2005		Median earnings of full-time workers	Unemployment rate	Part-time workers	Significant sources of formal training[2]
		Number	Percent	Growth plus total replacement needs	Growth plus net replacement needs				
Data processing equipment repairers	A	H	VH	A	A	VH	L	L	CD PS E
Millwrights	L	A	A	A	A	H	H	VL	PS E HS
Aircraft engine specialists	VL	L	H	VL	L	VH	L	VL	PS E
Automotive mechanics	VH	VH	A	VH	VH	A	A	L	PS E HS
Motorcycle, boat, and small engine mechanics	L	L	L	L	L	-	H	A	PS E HS
Heat, air-conditioning, and refrigeration mechanics and installers	H	H	A	A	A	A	A	L	PS E
Home appliance and power tool repairers	L	VL	L	L	L	-	L	L	PS E HS
Office machine and cash register servicers	L	A	A	VL	L	A	L	L	PS E
Machinists	H	H	L	H	H	H	A	VL	PS E HS
Tool and die makers	A	L	L	L	A	VH	L	VL	PS E HS
Compositors and typesetters, precision, and machine operators[3]	L	L	A	L	L	-	L	A	PS E HS
Dental lab technicians, precision	L	L	L	L	L	-	L	H	PS
Stationary engineers and boiler operators, low pressure[3]	L	L	L	VL	L	VH	L	VL	PS E
Water and liquid waste treatment plant and system operators	A	A	H	VL	A	-	VL	VL	PS E
OPERATOR, FABRICATOR, AND LABORER OCCUPATIONS .									
Welders and cutters, machine operators, setters, and hand workers[3]	H	A	L	H	H	A	VH	VL	PS E HS
Metal molding machine operators and tenders, setters and setup operators	L	VL	VL	VL	L	L	VH	VL	PS E

[1] Each characteristic, and its data source, is discussed in the "Data sources" section of chapter I.

[2] Codes for source of formal training are: HS = high school vocational training program, E = formal employer training, PS = postsecondary school training, but less than a bachelor's degree, CD = 4-year college degree program.

[3] This title does not appear in the National Industry-Occupation Matrix, but was formed by combining several matrix occupations in order to achieve Current Population Survey comparability.

NOTE: Rankings are based on all detailed occupations in the National Industry-Occupation Matrix and those in the Current Population Survey with 40,000 or more employees. Codes for describing the variables are: VH = "Very high," H = "High," A = "Average," L = "Low," and VL = "Very low." A dash indicates data are not available.

Table 4. Rankings of occupations for which formal employer training is significant, by selected characteristics[1]

Occupation as defined by National Industry-Occupation Matrix	Employment, 1990	Employment change, 1988-2000		Annual average job openings, 1990-2005		Median earnings of full-time workers	Unemployment rate	Part-time workers	Significant sources of formal training[2]
		Number	Percent	Growth plus total replacement needs	Growth plus net replacement needs				
MANAGERIAL AND MANAGEMENT-RELATED OCCUPATIONS									
Financial managers	VH	VH	H	H	VH	VH	L	VL	CD PS E
Funeral directors and morticians	L	L	A	VL	L	-	VL	L	CD PS E
Marketing, advertising, and public relations managers	H	VH	VH	H	VH	VH	L	VL	CD E
Personnel, training, and labor relations managers	H	H	VH	A	H	VH	L	VL	CD PS E
Purchasing managers	H	H	A	A	H	VH	VL	VL	CD PS E
Construction and building inspectors	L	A	A	L	L	-	L	L	E
Employment interviewers and personnel specialists[3]	H	VH	H	H	H	VH	L	L	CD E
Management analysts	A	H	VH	H	H	VH	L	H	CD E
Underwriters	A	A	H	A	A	-	VL	L	CD E
Wholesale and retail buyers, except farm products	H	H	A	H	H	H	L	A	CD E
PROFESSIONAL SPECIALTY OCCUPATIONS									
Chemical engineers	L	L	L	VL	L	VH	VL	VL	CD E
Civil engineers, including traffic engineers	H	H	H	A	H	VH	L	VL	CD E
Electrical and electronics engineers	H	VH	VH	A	VH	VH	VL	VL	CD E
Industrial engineers, except safety engineers	A	A	A	L	A	VH	L	VL	CD E
Mechanical engineers	H	H	H	A	H	VH	VL	VL	CD E
Architects[3]	A	H	H	A	A	VH	VL	A	CD E
Systems analysts and computer scientists	H	VH	VH	H	VH	VH	VL	L	CD E
Operations research analysts	L	H	VH	L	A	VH	L	L	CD E
Photographers and camera operators	A	H	H	A	A	A	L	H	CD PS E
Public relations specialists and publicity writers	A	A	A	A	A	VH	L	A	CD E
TECHNICIAN OCCUPATIONS									
Clinical lab technologists and technicians	H	H	H	A	H	A	L	H	CD PS E
Opticians, dispensing and measuring	L	A	VH	A	A	-	A	H	E
Electrical and electronic technicians and technologists	H	VH	VH	H	H	H	L	VL	CD PS E HS
Drafters	H	H	A	H	H	H	A	L	CD PS E HS
Computer programmers	VH	VH	VH	VH	VH	VH	L	L	CD PS E
MARKETING AND SALES OCCUPATIONS									
Insurance sales workers	H	H	A	H	VH	H	VL	A	CD E
Real estate agents, brokers, and appraisers	H	H	A	H	H	H	VL	H	CD PS E
Securities and financial services sales workers	H	H	VH	H	H	VH	L	L	CD E
ADMINISTRATIVE SUPPORT OCCUPATIONS									
Welfare eligibility workers and interviewers	A	A	A	A	A	A	A	A	PS E
Telephone operators	H	VL	VL	H	H	L	H	H	E
Reservation and transportation ticket agents and travel clerks	A	H	VH	A	A	A	L	H	E
Postal service clerks	A	L	L	A	A	H	A	A	E
Dispatchers	H	H	H	H	H	A	A	L	E
Bank tellers	H	VL	VL	VH	VH	VL	A	VH	E
Clerical supervisors and managers	VH	VH	A	VH	VH	H	VL	VL	E
SERVICE OCCUPATIONS									
Nursing aides, orderlies, and attendants	VH	VH	VH	VH	VH	VL	H	H	PS E
Flight attendants	A	H	VH	A	A	-	L	VH	E
Fire fighters	H	H	H	A	H	H	L	VL	PS E
Correction officers	H	VH	VH	H	H	A	VL	VL	E
Police and detective supervisors	A	A	A	VL	A	VH	VL	VL	CD PS E
Police detectives and patrol officers[3]	H	VH	H	A	VH	VH	VL	VL	PS E

NOTE: Rankings are based on all detailed occupations in the National Industry-Occupation Matrix and those in the Current Population Survey with 40,000 or more employees. Codes for describing the variables are: VH = "Very high," H = "High," A = "Average," L = "Low," and VL = "Very low." A dash indicates data are not available.

See footnotes at end of table.

Table 4. Rankings of occupations for which formal employer training is significant, by selected characteristics[1]——Continued

Occupation as defined by National Industry-Occupation Matrix	Employ-ment, 1990	Employment change, 1988-2000		Annual average job openings, 1990-2005		Median earnings of full-time workers	Unemploy-ment rate	Part-time workers	Significant sources of formal training[2]
		Number	Percent	Growth plus total replace-ment needs	Growth plus net replace-ment needs				
PRECISION PRODUCTION, CRAFT, AND REPAIR OCCUPATIONS									
Blue-collar worker supervisors	VH	VH	L	VH	VH	H	L	VL	E
Bricklayers and stone masons	A	H	A	H	A	H	VH	L	PS E HS
Electricians	VH	VH	H	H	VH	H	H	VL	PS E HS
Hard tile setters	VL	L	H	VL	L	-	VH	A	PS E
Plumbers, pipefitters, and steamfitters	H	H	A	H	H	H	H	L	E HS
Structural and reinforcing metal workers	A	A	A	A	A	-	VH	VL	E
Central office and PBX installers and repairers; frame wirers; station installers and repairers, telephone[3]	A	VL	VL	A	A	VH	VL	VL	E
Data processing equipment repairers	A	H	VH	A	A	VH	L	L	CD PS E
Electrical powerline installers and repairers	A	A	L	L	A	VH	L	VL	E
Telephone and cable TV line installers and repairers ...	A	VL	VL	VL	A	VH	L	VL	E
Industrial machinery mechanics	H	H	L	H	H	H	A	VL	E
Millwrights	L	A	A	A	A	H	H	VL	PS E HS
Aircraft engine specialists	VL	L	H	VL	L	VH	L	VL	PS E
Automotive body and related repairers	H	H	H	H	H	A	H	L	E HS
Automotive mechanics ·..	VH	VH	A	VH	VH	A	A	L	PS E HS
Bus and truck mechanics and diesel engine specialists	H	H	A	A	H	A	A	VL	E HS
Motorcycle, boat, and small engine mechanics ...	L	L	L	L	L	-	H	A	PS E HS
Heat, air-conditioning, and refrigeration mechanics and installers	H	H	A	A	A	A	A	L	PS E
Home appliance and power tool repairers	L	VL	L	L	L	-	L	L	PS E HS
Office machine and cash register servicers	L	A	A	VL	L	A	L	L	PS E
Machinists	H	H	L	H	H	H	A	VL	PS E HS
Tool and die makers	A	L	L	L	A	VH	L	VL	PS E HS
Compositors and typesetters, precision, and machine operators[3]	L	L	A	L	L	-	L	A	PS E HS
Stationary engineers and boiler operators, low pressure[3] ...	L	L	L	VL	L	VH	L	VL	PS E
Water and liquid waste treatment plant and system operators	A	A	H	VL	A	-	VL	VL	PS E
OPERATOR, FABRICATOR, AND LABORER OCCUPATIONS									
Welders and cutters, machine operators, setters, and hand workers[3]	H	A	L	H	H	A	VH	VL	PS E HS
Metal molding machine operators and tenders, setters and setup operators	L	VL	VL	VL	L	L	VH	VL	PS E
Printing press operators	H	H	A	A	H	A	A	L	E HS
Bus drivers	VH	VH	VH	VH	VH	A	A	VH	E
Crane and tower operators	L	L	L	L	L	H	H	VL	E
Operating engineers	A	H	H	A	A	H	VH	VL	E

[1] Each characteristic, and its data source, is discussed in the "Data sources" section of chapter I.

[2] Codes for source of formal training are: HS = high school vocational training program, E = formal employer training, PS = postsecondary school training, but less than a bachelor's degree, CD = 4-year college degree program.

[3] This title does not appear in the National Industry-Occupation Matrix, but was formed by combining several matrix occupations in order to achieve Current Population Survey comparability.

NOTE: Rankings are based on all detailed occupations in the National Industry-Occupation Matrix and those in the Current Population Survey with 40,000 or more employees. Codes for describing the variables are: VH = "Very high," H = "High," A = "Average," L = "Low," and VL = "Very low."   A dash indicates data are not available.

Table 5. Rankings of occupations for which high school vocational training is useful, by selected characteristics[1]

Occupation as defined by National Industry-Occupation Matrix	Employ-ment, 1990	Employment change, 1988-2000		Annual average job openings, 1990-2005		Median earnings of full-time workers	Unem-ploy-ment rate	Part-time workers	Significant sources of formal training [2]
		Number	Percent	Growth plus total replace-ment needs	Growth plus net replace-ment needs				
TECHNICIAN OCCUPATIONS									
Electrical and electronic technicians and technologists	H	VH	VH	H	H	H	L	VL	CD PS E HS
Drafters	H	H	A	H	H	H	A	L	CD PS E HS
ADMINISTRATIVE SUPPORT OCCUPATIONS									
Billing, cost, and rate clerks	H	A	L	H	H	L	A	A	HS
Bookkeeping, accounting, and auditing clerks	VH	VL	VL	VH	VH	L	A	H	PS HS
Payroll and timekeeping clerks	A	L	L	A	A	L	L	A	HS
Interviewing clerks, except personnel and social welfare	A	H	VH	H	H	L	H	H	HS
Receptionists and information clerks	VH	VH	VH	VH	VH	VL	H	VH	HS
File clerks	H	H	L	VH	H	VL	H	VH	HS
Order clerks and customer service representatives, utilities[3]	H	A	L	H	H	A	L	A	HS
Secretaries	VH	VH	A	VH	VH	L	A	H	PS HS
Typists and word processors	VH	VL	VL	VH	VH	L	H	H	HS
Data entry keyers, except composing	H	H	L	VH	H	L	H	H	PS HS
General office clerks	VH	VH	H	VH	VH	L	A	VH	HS
PRECISION PRODUCTION, CRAFT, AND REPAIR OCCUPATIONS									
Bricklayers and stone masons	A	H	A	H	A	H	VH	L	PS E HS
Carpenters	VH	VH	A	VH	VH	A	VH	L	HS
Electricians	VH	VH	H	H	VH	H	H	VL	PS E HS
Plumbers, pipefitters, and steamfitters	H	H	A	H	H	H	H	L	E HS
Millwrights	L	A	A	A	A	H	H	VL	PS E HS
Automotive body and related repairers	H	H	H	H	H	A	H	L	E HS
Automotive mechanics	VH	VH	A	VH	VH	A	A	L	PS E HS
Bus and truck mechanics and diesel engine specialists	H	H	A	A	H	A	A	VL	E HS
Motorcycle, boat, and small engine mechanics	L	L	L	L	L	-	H	A	PS E HS
Home appliance and power tool repairers	L	VL	L	L	L	-	L	L	PS E HS
Machinists	H	H	L	H	H	H	A	VL	PS E HS
Tool and die makers	A	L	L	L	A	VH	L	VL	PS E HS
Compositors and typesetters, precision, and machine operators[3]	L	L	A	L	L	-	L	A	PS E HS
Upholsterers	L	L	L	L	L	-	A	A	HS
OPERATOR, FABRICATOR, AND LABORER OCCUPATIONS									
Machine tool cutting operators and tenders, metal and plastic	A	VL	VL	L	L	A	H	L	HS
Welders and cutters, machine operators, setters, and hand workers[3]	H	A	L	H	H	A	VH	VL	PS E HS
Printing press operators	H	H	A	A	H	A	A	L	E HS

[1] Each characteristic, and its data source, is discussed in the "Data sources" section of chapter I.

[2] Codes for source of formal training are: HS = high school vocational training program, E = formal employer training, PS = postsecondary school training, but less than a bachelor's degree, CD = 4-year college degree program.

[3] This title does not appear in the National Industry-Occupation Matrix, but was formed by combining several matrix occupations in order to achieve Current Population Survey comparability.

NOTE: Rankings are based on all detailed occupations in the National Industry-Occupation Matrix and those in the Current Population Survey with 40,000 or more employees. Codes for describing the variables are: VH = "Very high," H = "High," A = "Average," L = "Low," and VL = "Very low." A dash indicates data are not available.

Table 8. Awards and degrees by field of study, 1989-90

Classification of Instructional Program (CIP) codes and titles	Awards, curriculums of under 1 year	1- to 4-year awards	Associate degrees	Bachelor's degrees requiring 4 or 5 years	Master's degrees	Doctoral degrees	First professional degrees
Total, all programs	531,443	375,452	473,645	1,066,511	328,260	39,451	72,703
01. Agribusiness and agricultural production	3,866	2,130	2,937	4,544	729	211	–
01.01 Agricultural business and management	1,443	757	775	3,242	566	153	–
01.0101 Agricultural business and management, general	154	377	400	340	49	5	–
01.0102 Agricultural business	13	12	140	1,136	23	–	–
01.0103 Agricultural economics	–	–	104	1,638	483	148	–
01.0104 Farm and ranch management	1,276	345	115	86	6	–	–
01.0199 Agricultural business and management, other	–	22	16	42	5	–	–
01.02 Agricultural mechanics	165	209	147	227	4	1	–
01.0201 Agricultural mechanics, general	125	61	76	185	4	–	–
01.0203 Agricultural mechanics, construction, and maintenance skills	–	–	1	4	–	–	–
01.0204 Agricultural power machinery	40	136	58	9	–	–	–
01.0205 Agricultural structures, equipment, and facilities	–	–	2	8	–	–	–
01.0206 Soil and water mechanical practices	–	–	4	3	–	1	–
01.0299 Agricultural mechanics, other	–	12	6	18	–	–	–
01.03 Agricultural production	319	157	474	91	58	17	–
01.0301 Agricultural production, general	255	61	320	29	15	–	–
01.0302 Animal production	63	–	112	34	3	–	–
01.0303 Aquaculture	–	–	–	10	30	15	–
01.0304 Crop production	1	–	25	–	9	2	–
01.0305 Game farm management	–	–	–	18	–	–	–
01.0399 Agricultural production, other	–	–	17	–	1	–	–
01.04 Agricultural products and processing	–	–	13	12	2	1	–
01.0401 Agricultural product and processing, general	–	–	4	–	2	1	–
01.0402 Food products	–	–	9	2	–	–	–
01.0499 Agricultural products and processing, other	–	–	–	10	–	–	–
01.05 Agricultural services and supplies	663	201	364	65	–	–	–
01.0501 Agricultural services and supplies, general	8	15	128	–	–	–	–
01.0502 Agricultural services	–	–	49	2	–	–	–
01.0503 Agricultural supplies marketing	–	–	22	–	–	–	–
01.0504 Pet grooming	161	–	17	–	–	–	–
01.0505 Animal training	3	–	7	20	–	–	–
01.0506 Horseshoeing	254	–	5	–	–	–	–
01.0507 Horse handling and care	225	28	129	43	–	–	–
01.0599 Agricultural services and supplies, other	12	–	7	–	–	–	–
01.06 Horticulture	1,161	774	1,068	403	36	26	–
01.0601 Horticulture, general	818	298	423	117	25	19	–
01.0602 Arboriculture	2	–	–	–	–	–	–
01.0603 Ornamental horticulture	146	148	294	243	11	4	–
01.0604 Greenhouse operation and management	10	–	21	–	–	–	–
01.0605 Landscaping	144	130	171	34	–	–	–
01.0606 Nursery operation and management	31	–	45	1	–	–	–
01.0607 Turf management	8	–	77	7	–	–	–
01.0699 Horticulture, other	2	106	37	1	–	3	–
01.07 International agriculture	–	–	–	14	12	–	–
01.99 Agribusiness and agricultural production, other	115	29	96	490	51	13	–
02. Agricultural sciences	637	3,220	974	5,849	1,668	825	–
02.01 Agricultural sciences, general	58	41	242	893	169	3	–
02.02 Animal sciences	477	3,158	558	2,823	487	213	–
02.0201 Animal sciences, general	381	5	162	2,306	368	162	–
02.0202 Animal breeding and genetics	32	–	11	9	18	1	–
02.0203 Animal health	21	–	157	28	11	2	–
02.0204 Animal nutrition	–	–	–	–	3	10	–
02.0206 Dairy	–	–	16	143	31	15	–
02.0208 Livestock	–	–	102	2	–	–	–
02.0209 Poultry	43	–	26	122	22	11	–
02.0299 Animal sciences, other	–	–	84	213	34	12	–
02.03 Food sciences	–	–	–	528	301	122	–
02.04 Plant sciences	97	18	132	1,407	581	379	–
02.0401 Plant sciences, general	–	4	17	215	64	27	–
02.0402 Agronomy	94	–	17	495	298	229	–
02.0403 Horticulture science	–	–	58	527	144	92	–
02.0408 Plant protection (pest management)	3	–	2	23	15	–	–
02.0409 Range management	–	–	1	98	47	22	–
02.0499 Plant sciences, other	–	–	37	49	13	9	–
02.05 Soil sciences	–	–	5	100	90	80	–
02.99 Agricultural sciences, other	5	–	37	98	40	28	–
03. Renewable natural resources	140	1,082	1,037	2,775	994	236	–
03.01 Renewable natural resources, general	–	–	166	707	263	42	–
03.02 Conservation and regulation	22	870	119	208	28	1	–
03.0201 Conservation and regulation, general	–	–	85	108	3	–	–

Table 8. Awards and degrees by field of study, 1989-90 — Continued

Classification of Instructional Program (CIP) codes and titles	Awards, curriculums of under 1 year	1- to 4-year awards	Associate degrees	Bachelor's degrees requiring 4 or 5 years	Master's degrees	Doctoral degrees	First professional degrees
03.0202 Conservation	–	–	30	97	25	1	–
03.0203 Resources protection and regulation	22	–	–	–	–	–	–
03.0299 Conservation and regulation, other	–	–	4	3	–	–	–
03.03 Fishing and fisheries	–	–	36	104	94	18	–
03.04 Forestry production and processing	85	–	287	211	28	23	–
03.0401 Forestry production and processing, general	19	–	162	115	19	23	–
03.0403 Forest production utilization	1	–	41	2	–	–	–
03.0404 Forest products processing technology	22	–	37	46	–	–	–
03.0405 Logging	29	–	2	–	–	–	–
03.0499 Forestry production and processing, other	14	–	45	48	9	–	–
03.05 Forestry and related sciences	12	–	152	795	411	112	–
03.0501 Forestry and related sciences, general	–	–	84	427	311	88	–
03.0502 Forestry science	–	–	18	67	51	8	–
03.0504 Forest engineering	–	–	1	35	6	1	–
03.0506 Forest management	–	–	28	138	16	5	–
03.0509 Wood science	–	–	10	51	12	3	–
03.0599 Forestry and related sciences, other	12	–	11	77	15	7	–
03.06 Wildlife management	21	43	242	590	109	19	–
03.99 Renewable natural resources, other	–	16	35	160	61	21	–
04. Architecture and environmental design	258	2,492	2,067	9,348	3,505	97	–
04.01 Architecture and environmental design, general	48	3	13	549	102	4	–
04.02 Architecture	–	16	75	4,575	1,771	22	–
04.03 City, community, and regional planning	–	–	1	378	992	60	–
04.04 Environmental design	–	–	35	686	74	5	–
04.05 Interior design	209	584	1,924	1,811	39	3	–
04.06 Landscape architecture	1	–	3	918	318	1	–
04.07 Urban design	–	–	–	–	96	–	–
04.99 Architecture and environmental design, other	–	–	16	431	113	2	–
05. Area and ethnic studies	94	338	71	4,401	1,205	128	–
05.01 Area studies	88	–	6	3,755	1,007	100	–
05.0101 African studies	3	–	–	43	14	1	–
05.0102 American studies	1	–	6	1,413	210	65	–
05.0103 Asian studies	18	–	–	416	90	1	–
05.0104 East Asian studies	–	–	–	420	143	10	–
05.0105 Eastern European studies	–	–	–	98	18	–	–
05.0106 European studies	18	–	–	224	3	1	–
05.0107 Latin American studies	7	–	–	285	194	4	–
05.0108 Middle Eastern studies	7	–	–	61	69	11	–
05.0109 Pacific area studies	–	–	–	2	4	–	–
05.0110 Russian and Slavic studies	9	–	–	268	108	1	–
05.0111 Scandinavian studies	–	–	–	14	4	1	–
05.0112 South Asian studies	–	–	–	14	10	4	–
05.0113 Southeast Asian studies	–	–	–	10	1	–	–
05.0114 Western European studies	25	–	–	35	52	–	–
05.0115 Canadian studies	–	–	–	26	–	–	–
05.0199 Area studies, other	–	–	–	426	87	1	–
05.02 Ethnic studies, total	6	71	65	541	93	18	–
05.0201 Afro-American (black) studies	6	–	10	235	37	1	–
05.0202 American Indian studies	–	–	6	19	10	1	–
05.0203 Hispanic-American studies	–	–	3	83	13	–	–
05.0204 Islamic studies	–	–	–	–	3	3	–
05.0205 Jewish studies	–	69	46	166	19	3	–
05.0299 Ethnic studies, other	–	–	–	38	11	10	–
05.99 Area and ethnic studies, other	–	–	–	105	105	10	–
06. Business and management	81,647	26,849	54,493	244,297	77,367	1,142	–
06.01 Business and management, general	3,103	1,862	12,304	42,868	13,937	184	–
06.02 Accounting	1,452	1,978	5,828	45,038	3,290	60	–
06.03 Banking and finance	9	69	463	26,111	5,336	48	–
06.04 Business administration and management	2,760	2,480	26,937	70,259	39,685	563	–
06.0401 Business administration and management, general	2,704	1,934	25,290	67,216	37,274	545	–
06.0402 Contract management and procurement/purchasing	2	69	146	748	472	–	–
06.0403 Product management	34	–	13	384	93	5	–
06.0499 Business administration and management, other	20	467	1,488	1,911	1,846	13	–
06.05 Business economics	239	–	2	3,691	172	33	–
06.06 Human resources development	88	–	22	2,227	1,043	11	–
06.07 Institutional management	878	753	3,303	5,804	443	2	–
06.0701 Hotel/motel management	727	420	1,980	3,518	150	1	–
06.0702 Recreational enterprises management	–	–	51	237	38	–	–
06.0703 Resort management	–	–	51	13	–	–	–
06.0704 Restaurant management	12	212	416	126	2	–	–
06.0705 Transportation management	122	–	98	761	62	1	–
06.0799 Institutional management, other	17	96	707	1,149	191	–	–

Table 8. Awards and degrees by field of study, 1989-90 — Continued

Classification of Instructional Program (CIP) codes and titles	Awards, curriculums of under 1 year	1- to 4-year awards	Associate degrees	Bachelor's degrees requiring 4 or 5 years	Master's degrees	Doctoral degrees	First professional degrees
06.08 Insurance and risk management	1,608	–	7	533	47	3	–
06.09 International business management	52	–	37	1,565	1,860	14	–
06.10 Investments and securities	145	–	30	373	252	–	–
06.11 Labor/industrial relations	16	–	136	1,069	717	17	–
06.12 Management information systems	17	345	406	3,143	1,105	9	–
06.13 Management science, total	11	–	309	2,610	1,188	60	–
06.1302 Operations research (quantitative methods)	–	–	–	935	515	49	–
06.1303 Management science, general	–	–	210	505	241	–	–
06.1399 Management science, other	11	–	99	1,170	432	11	–
06.14 Marketing management and research	1,043	343	1,704	30,635	2,383	51	–
06.1401 Marketing management	1,036	292	1,631	29,158	2,179	46	–
06.1402 Marketing research	–	–	–	178	18	1	–
06.1499 Marketing management and research, other	7	10	73	1,299	186	4	–
06.15 Organizational behavior	–	–	3	561	166	30	–
06.16 Personnel management	17	–	28	1,605	230	9	–
06.17 Real estate	67,221	13,527	622	824	290	–	–
06.18 Small business management and ownership	254	233	474	135	8	–	–
06.19 Taxation	316	64	1	–	960	–	–
06.20 Trade and industrial supervision and management	145	116	662	825	76	–	–
06.99 Business and management, other	2,273	4,029	1,215	4,421	4,179	48	–
07. Business and office	58,921	55,033	45,010	3,436	34	–	–
07.01 Accounting, bookkeeping, and related programs	7,775	7,933	10,621	345	18	–	–
07.0101 Accounting, bookkeeping, and related programs, general	1,992	4,359	7,778	142	18	–	–
07.0102 Accounting and computing	4,103	2,689	2,594	192	–	–	–
07.0103 Bookkeeping	816	377	154	–	–	–	–
07.0104 Machine billing, bookkeeping, and computing	65	55	–	–	–	–	–
07.0199 Accounting, bookkeeping, and related programs, other	799	453	95	11	–	–	–
07.02 Banking and related financial programs	643	925	626	22	–	–	–
07.0201 Banking and related financial programs, general	64	527	561	19	–	–	–
07.0203 Insurance clerk	4	–	10	–	–	–	–
07.0205 Teller	554	–	–	–	–	–	–
07.0299 Banking and related financial programs, other	21	270	55	3	–	–	–
07.03 Business data processing and related programs	13,147	6,941	8,904	477	8	–	–
07.0301 Business data processing and related programs, general	5,488	2,681	4,186	355	8	–	–
07.0302 Business computer and console operation	2,853	1,444	275	–	–	–	–
07.0303 Business data entry equipment operation	3,521	1,018	244	–	–	–	–
07.0304 Business data peripheral equipment operation	26	–	17	–	–	–	–
07.0305 Business data programming	664	716	3,260	29	–	–	–
07.0306 Business systems analysis	9	–	245	61	–	–	–
07.0399 Business data processing and related programs, other	586	1,017	677	32	–	–	–
07.04 Office supervision and management	538	781	1,763	1,121	7	–	–
07.05 Personnel and training programs	88	–	102	–	–	–	–
07.0501 Personnel and training programs, general	4	–	35	–	–	–	–
07.0502 Training assisting	9	–	45	–	–	–	–
07.0503 Personnel assisting	75	–	22	–	–	–	–
07.06 Secretarial and related programs	18,426	20,427	16,529	1,340	–	–	–
07.0601 Secretarial and related programs, general	6,939	5,688	6,048	506	–	–	–
07.0602 Court reporting	184	1,402	617	26	–	–	–
07.0603 Executive secretarial	692	2,944	3,178	146	–	–	–
07.0604 Legal secretarial	3,379	2,374	1,590	14	–	–	–
07.0605 Medical secretarial	1,138	2,360	1,257	–	–	–	–
07.0606 Secretarial	2,797	3,679	3,199	633	–	–	–
07.0607 Stenographic	319	308	96	–	–	–	–
07.0699 Secretarial and related programs, other	2,978	1,672	544	15	–	–	–
07.07 Typing, general office, and related programs	8,708	9,080	918	43	1	–	–
07.0701 Typing, general office, and related programs, general	1,817	1,886	615	43	1	–	–
07.0702 Clerk-typist	1,763	4,040	83	–	–	–	–
07.0705 General office clerk	2,512	791	170	–	–	–	–
07.0707 Receptionist and communication systems operation	302	794	7	–	–	–	–
07.0708 Shipping, receiving, and stock clerk	55	–	–	–	–	–	–
07.0709 Traffic, rate and transportation clerk	–	–	2	–	–	–	–
07.0799 Typing, general office, and related programs, other	2,259	1,527	41	–	–	–	–
07.08 Word processing	6,961	4,993	2,034	47	–	–	–
07.99 Business (office administrative support), other	2,635	3,936	3,513	41	–	–	–
08. Marketing and distribution	39,746	13,117	14,429	5,553	161	2	–
08.01 Apparel and accessories marketing	13,382	3,430	4,360	1,649	–	2	–
08.0101 Apparel and accessories marketing, general	298	119	176	255	–	–	–
08.0102 Fashion merchandising	385	1,027	4,154	1,391	–	2	–
08.0103 Fashion modeling	12,654	2,208	24	–	–	–	–
08.0105 Jewelry marketing	–	–	3	–	–	–	–
08.0199 Apparel an accessories marketing, other	45	–	3	3	–	–	–
08.02 Business and personal services marketing	57	44	377	766	1	–	–
08.0201 Business and personal services marketing, general	–	15	98	531	–	–	–

Table 8. Awards and degrees by field of study, 1989-90 — Continued

Classification of Instructional Program (CIP) codes and titles	Awards, curriculums of under 1 year	1- to 4-year awards	Associate degrees	Bachelor's degrees requiring 4 or 5 years	Master's degrees	Doctoral degrees	First professional degrees
08.0202 Display	–	20	265	–	–	–	–
08.0203 Marketing of business or personal services	–	–	14	235	1	–	–
08.0299 Business and personal services marketing, other	57	–	–	–	–	–	–
08.03 Entrepreneurship	–	–	140	60	38	–	–
08.04 Financial services marketing	125	10	54	2	–	–	–
08.05 Floristry, farm and garden supplies marketing	380	–	18	–	–	–	–
08.0501 Floristry, farm and garden supplies marketing, general	143	–	7	–	–	–	–
08.0503 Floristry	142	–	11	–	–	–	–
08.0599 Floristry, farm and garden supplies marketing, other	95	–	–	–	–	–	–
08.06 Food marketing	104	60	69	2	–	–	–
08.0601 Food marketing, general	104	–	40	2	–	–	–
08.0604 Supermarket marketing	–	19	22	–	–	–	–
08.0699 Food marketing, other	–	–	7	–	–	–	–
08.07 General marketing	4,947	1,669	3,440	2,388	93	–	–
08.0701 Auctioneering	171	–	–	–	–	–	–
08.0702 Industrial sales	6	–	34	251	–	–	–
08.0703 Internal marketing	–	–	11	64	72	–	–
08.0704 Purchasing	82	39	50	130	2	–	–
08.0705 Retailing	538	505	1,119	286	–	–	–
08.0706 Sales	2,374	–	394	178	–	–	–
08.0708 Marketing, general	171	356	559	650	19	–	–
08.0799 General marketing, other	1,605	–	1,273	829	–	–	–
08.08 Home and office products marketing	34	17	60	17	–	–	–
08.0801 Home and office products marketing, general	–	–	33	–	–	–	–
08.0802 Appliance marketing	34	–	–	–	–	–	–
08.0803 Building materials marketing	–	–	6	–	–	–	–
08.0805 Furniture marketing	–	–	21	–	–	–	–
08.0806 Hardware marketing	–	8	–	–	–	–	–
08.0808 Speciality home furnishing marketing	–	–	–	17	–	–	–
08.09 Hospitality and recreation marketing	928	935	175	148	–	–	–
08.0901 Hospitality and recreation marketing, general	18	–	162	23	–	–	–
08.0902 Marketing of hotel/motel services	14	–	–	–	–	–	–
08.0903 Marketing of recreational services	–	–	6	73	–	–	–
08.0904 Recreational products marketing	489	–	–	–	–	–	–
08.0905 Waiter/waitress and related services	299	–	–	–	–	–	–
08.0999 Hospitality and recreation marketing, other	108	–	7	52	–	–	–
08.10 Insurance marketing	1,602	–	25	–	–	–	–
08.11 Transportation and travel marketing	16,522	6,120	2,405	293	29	–	–
08.1101 Transportation and travel marketing, general	2,370	2,357	356	45	–	–	–
08.1102 Transportation marketing	331	–	38	5	–	–	–
08.1104 Tourism	2,107	1,006	1,124	231	29	–	–
08.1105 Travel services marketing	10,788	2,120	843	2	–	–	–
08.1106 Warehouse services marketing	403	–	12	–	–	–	–
08.1199 Transportation and travel marketing, other	523	–	32	10	–	–	–
08.12 Vehicles and petroleum marketing	14	158	81	10	–	–	–
08.1201 Vehicles and petroleum marketing, general	6	–	2	6	–	–	–
08.1203 Automotive vehicles and accessories marketing	8	124	79	4	–	–	–
08.99 Marketing and distribution, other	1,651	315	3,225	218	–	–	–
09. Communications	6,733	1,229	1,724	50,440	4,080	263	–
09.01 Communications, general	46	74	632	24,042	1,490	177	–
09.02 Advertising	55	171	273	2,917	227	1	–
09.03 Communications, research	–	–	2	112	26	12	–
09.04 Journalism (mass communications)	7	59	333	11,662	1,309	40	–
09.05 Public relations	–	–	9	1,804	109	–	–
09.06 Radio/television news broadcasting	421	–	146	1,033	27	–	–
09.07 Radio/television, general	21	–	193	5,601	267	12	–
09.08 Telecommunications	6,005	98	83	727	146	–	–
09.99 Communications, other	178	–	53	2,542	479	21	–
10. Communication technologies	968	835	2,166	1,220	299	6	–
10.01 Communications technology	968	835	2,166	1,220	299	6	–
10.0101 Educational media technology	–	–	84	–	9	1	–
10.0102 Motion picture technology	–	–	4	37	–	–	–
10.0103 Photographic technology	528	114	268	39	–	–	–
10.0104 Radio and television production and broadcasting technology	83	218	659	1,052	264	5	–
10.0105 Sound recording technology	243	–	52	16	–	–	–
10.0106 Video technology	100	–	16	10	–	–	–
10.0199 Communications technologies, other	14	453	1,083	66	26	–	–
11. Computer and information sciences	27,102	12,640	8,842	27,700	9,644	623	–
11.01 Computer and information sciences, general	5,915	927	2,902	21,396	7,867	596	–
11.02 Computer programming	8,528	6,714	2,250	584	124	–	–
11.03 Data processing	4,527	1,811	1,548	531	73	–	–

Table 8. Awards and degrees by field of study, 1989-90 — Continued

Classification of Instructional Program (CIP) codes and titles	Awards, curriculums of under 1 year	1- to 4-year awards	Associate degrees	Bachelor's degrees requiring 4 or 5 years	Master's degrees	Doctoral degrees	First professional degrees
11.04 Information science and systems	436	343	1,169	3,735	1,167	17	–
11.05 Systems analysis	–		26	265	67	2	–
11.06 Microcomputer applications	4,180	1,750	542	5	–	–	–
11.99 Computer and information sciences, other	3,516	397	405	1,184	346	8	–
12. Consumer, personal, and miscellaneous services	55,893	51,924	886	80	–	–	–
12.01 Drycleaning and laundering services	452	–	2	–	–	–	–
12.02 Entertainment services, other	5,975	–	25	–	–	–	–
12.0202 Bartending	3,089	–	25	–	–	–	–
12.0203 Card dealing	598	–	–	–	–	–	–
12.0204 Umpiring	2,288	–	–	–	–	–	–
12.03 Funeral services	36	751	594	79	–	–	–
12.04 Personal services	49,241	50,346	261	–	–	–	–
12.0401 Personal services, general	1,038	–	55	–	–	–	–
12.0402 Barbering	2,624	3,102	4	–	–	–	–
12.0403 Cosmetology	37,101	44,587	202	–	–	–	–
12.0404 Electrolysis	150	–	–	–	–	–	–
12.0405 Massage	4,172	522	–	–	–	–	–
12.0406 Make-up artistry	897	–	–	–	–	–	–
12.0499 Personal services, other	3,259	1,072	–	–	–	–	–
12.99 Consumer, personal, and miscellaneous services, other	189	–	4	1	–	–	–
13. Education	6,488	3,845	8,166	107,297	86,357	6,952	–
13.01 Education, general	38	867	3,706	2,218	9,126	1,207	–
13.02 Bilingual/crosscultural education	54	1,134	3	132	195	34	–
13.0201 Bilingual/crosscultural education	54	1,130	3	125	187	34	–
13.0299 Bilingual/crosscultural education, other	–	–	–	7	8	–	–
13.03 Curriculum and instruction	2,619	–	–	529	5,206	730	–
13.04 Education administration, total	–	–	26	27	10,091	2,019	–
13.0401 Education administration, general	–	–	–	9	6,532	1,403	–
13.0402 Administration of special education	–	–	–	13	9	13	–
13.0403 Adult and continuing education administration	–	–	–	–	166	52	–
13.0404 Educational supervision	–	–	–	–	826	38	–
13.0405 Elementary and secondary education administration	–	–	26	–	1,638	57	–
13.0406 Higher education administration	–	–	–	5	262	345	–
13.0407 Community college education administration	–	–	–	–	102	4	–
13.0499 Educational administration, other	–	–	–	–	556	107	–
13.05 Educational media	–	–	–	42	808	29	–
13.06 Evaluation and research, total	–	–	–	5	181	129	–
13.0601 Evaluation and research, general	–	–	–	3	74	49	–
13.0603 Educational statistics and research	–	–	–	2	26	30	–
13.0604 Educational testing, evaluation, and measurement	–	–	–	–	74	22	–
13.0606 Higher education research	–	–	–	–	7	20	–
13.0699 Evaluation and research, other	–	–	–	–	–	8	–
13.07 International comparative education	–	–	1	–	29	3	–
13.08 School psychology	–	–	1	158	1,454	492	–
13.09 Social foundations	–	–	–	–	198	139	–
13.10 Special education, total	183	88	164	6,966	9,053	213	–
13.1001 Special education, general	1	40	102	4,552	6,797	170	–
13.1002 Education of culturally disadvantaged	–	–	–	–	8	–	–
13.1003 Education of the deaf and hearing impaired	–	–	31	219	154	1	–
13.1004 Education of the gifted and talented	–	–	–	4	168	7	–
13.1005 Education of the emotionally handicapped	–	–	–	221	205	2	–
13.1006 Education of the mentally handicapped	–	–	5	612	203	5	–
13.1007 Education of the multiple handicapped	–	–	–	93	81	–	–
13.1008 Education of the physically handicapped	–	–	3	30	29	3	–
13.1009 Education of the visually handicapped	–	–	–	17	25	–	–
13.1010 Remedial education	160	–	–	1	39	2	–
13.1011 Specific learning disabilities	–	–	–	374	736	13	–
13.1012 Speech correction	–	–	–	547	256	–	–
13.1099 Special education, other	22	17	23	296	352	10	–
13.11 Student counseling and personnel services	–	–	–	48	10,546	418	–
13.12 Teacher education, general programs, total	467	473	2,455	60,242	19,861	402	–
13.1201 Adult and continuing education	32	–	38	83	703	158	–
13.1202 Elementary education	6	82	1,195	49,697	12,026	88	–
13.1203 Junior high/middle school education	–	–	–	869	551	–	–
13.1204 Pre-elementary education	79	241	736	4,880	1,616	17	–
13.1205 Secondary education	205	9	285	4,237	3,660	80	–
13.1299 Teacher education, general programs, other	145	40	201	476	1,305	59	–
13.13 Teacher education, specific subject areas	356	445	829	35,957	15,893	843	–
13.1301 Agricultural education	–	–	9	522	265	35	–
13.1302 Art education	–	–	39	1,175	533	38	–
13.1303 Business education	–	–	42	1,964	554	15	–
13.1304 Driver and safety education	–	–	–	54	61	–	–
13.1305 English education	136	62	15	2,010	456	23	–

Table 8. Awards and degrees by field of study, 1989-90 — Continued

Classification of Instructional Program (CIP) codes and titles	Awards, curriculums of under 1 year	1- to 4-year awards	Associate degrees	Bachelor's degrees requiring 4 or 5 years	Master's degrees	Doctoral degrees	First profes-sional degrees
13.1306 Foreign languages education	–	–	1	462	159	19	–
13.1307 Health education	1	–	36	1,675	808	109	–
13.1308 Home economics education	–	–	16	491	199	7	–
13.1309 Industrial arts education	–	–	32	1,937	602	35	–
13.1310 Marketing and distributive education	–	–	–	270	18	1	–
13.1311 Mathematics education	51	–	18	1,770	780	40	–
13.1312 Music education	–	–	31	2,916	899	72	–
13.1313 Nutritional education	3	–	4	–	17	–	–
13.1314 Physical education	–	–	497	13,052	3,484	200	–
13.1315 Reading education	–	–	–	222	3,538	75	–
13.1316 Science education	–	–	5	1,695	790	48	–
13.1317 Social science education	–	–	13	822	168	2	–
13.1318 Social studies education	7	–	12	1,743	212	5	–
13.1319 Technical education	–	–	34	274	231	23	–
13.1320 Trade and industrial education	60	–	3	1,348	524	56	–
13.1321 Computer education	–	–	14	15	579	–	–
13.1399 Teacher education, other	98	42	8	1,540	1,016	40	–
13.14 Teaching English as a second language/foreign language	813	559	–	72	868	2	–
13.15 Teaching assisting	151	–	225	3	–	–	–
13.99 Teacher education, specific areas, other	1,807	121	756	898	2,848	292	–
14. Engineering	612	575	2,968	64,798	24,022	4,953	–
14.01 Engineering, general	202	39	1,561	2,569	1,116	242	–
14.02 Aerospace, aeronautical, and astronautical engineering	1	–	12	3,051	1,029	178	–
14.03 Agricultural engineering	9	–	1	467	186	78	–
14.04 Architectural engineering	–	–	49	530	34	–	–
14.05 Bioengineering and biomedical engineering	–	–	11	701	364	112	–
14.06 Ceramic engineering	–	–	25	349	90	42	–
14.07 Chemical engineering	–	–	35	3,527	1,040	564	–
14.08 Civil engineering	–	30	57	7,353	2,829	513	–
14.09 Computer engineering	253	–	16	1,954	787	86	–
14.10 Electrical, electronics, and communications	39	358	477	21,150	7,246	1,169	–
14.1001 Electrical, electronics, and communications engineering	1	355	477	21,150	7,246	1,169	–
14.1002 Microelectronic engineering	38	–	–	–	–	–	–
14.11 Engineering mechanics	–	–	–	146	184	91	–
14.12 Engineering physics	–	–	–	328	73	33	–
14.13 Engineering science	–	5	70	223	305	73	–
14.14 Environmental health engineering	–	–	16	111	351	37	–
14.15 Geological engineering	–	–	–	65	40	6	–
14.16 Geophysical engineering	–	–	–	18	11	3	–
14.17 Industrial engineering	–	–	21	4,041	1,834	191	–
14.18 Materials engineering	–	–	–	446	492	261	–
14.19 Mechanical engineering	–	–	98	14,548	3,446	754	–
14.20 Metallurgical engineering	–	–	2	369	210	104	–
14.21 Mining and mineral engineering	–	–	–	88	57	30	–
14.22 Naval architecture and marine engineering	–	–	–	316	45	6	–
14.23 Nuclear engineering	–	–	–	258	243	111	–
14.24 Ocean engineering	–	–	–	82	94	17	–
14.25 Petroleum engineering	–	–	–	307	165	54	–
14.26 Surveying and mapping sciences	–	–	8	107	26	2	–
14.2601 Surveying and mapping sciences	–	–	8	81	22	2	–
14.2602 Cartography	–	–	–	26	4	–	–
14.27 Systems engineering	–	–	–	327	314	25	–
14.28 Textile engineering	–	89	394	39	22	1	–
14.99 Engineering, other	108	–	115	1,328	1,389	170	–
15. Engineering and engineering-related technologies	16,299	19,055	45,051	17,930	895	12	–
15.01 Architectural technologies	33	213	1,672	811	11	–	–
15.0101 Architectural design and construction technology	33	197	1,509	692	–	–	–
15.0102 Architectural interior design technology	–	–	53	–	–	–	–
15.0199 Architectural technologies, other	–	–	110	119	11	–	–
15.02 Civil technologies	741	1,293	3,868	771	1	–	–
15.0201 Civil technology	31	164	999	368	–	–	–
15.0202 Drafting and design technology	688	1,049	2,431	256	–	–	–
15.0203 Surveying and mapping technology	22	79	194	33	–	–	–
15.0299 Civil technologies, other	–	–	244	114	1	–	–
15.03 Electrical and electronic technologies	4,823	9,862	23,598	4,698	46	–	–
15.0301 Computer technology	638	643	1,750	291	7	–	–
15.0302 Electrical technology	846	1,353	1,274	868	–	–	–
15.0303 Electronic technology	2,891	6,753	16,588	3,212	–	–	–
15.0304 Laser electro-optic technology	1	37	252	27	7	–	–
14.0399 Electrical and electronic technologies	447	1,076	3,734	300	32	–	–
15.04 Electromechanical instrumentation and maintenance technologies	1,311	1,166	3,434	416	11	1	–
15.0401 Biomedical equipment technology	–	87	481	3	–	–	–

APPENDIX D: Projections for Self-Employed Workers[1]

Self-employment is an alternative to traditional employment for a growing number of people. This appendix provides information on the projected growth in employment in the major occupations where self-employed people work. By reviewing this information, you can learn where most of the self-employed work and the growth projections for these occupations.

Self-employed workers made up 8.3 percent (10.2 million workers) of the nearly 123 million job total in 1990. The number of self-employed workers is projected to grow by 1.5 million, a total of 15 percent, between 1990 and 2005. This rate of growth is somewhat slower than the projected total increase of 21 percent for wage and salary employees. There is, however, a great deal of variation in the projected growth of self-employed workers among the various occupations.

More than half of all the self-employed are in the services and retail trade industries. Virtually all of the recent job growth among self-employed workers has been in services. The fastest growing services for the self-employed include the construction, finance, insurance, and real estate industries. Employment declines among the self-employed have been recorded in agriculture, forestry, fishing and in retail trade.

About one-third of the increase (508,000 of 1.5 million) in self-employed workers is projected to occur among the executive, administrative, and managerial occupations. The recent trend of faster job growth among self-employed managers than among their wage and salary counterparts is expected to continue through 2005, as many individuals continue to start up their own businesses.

The next largest increase in self-employment (442,000 jobs) will occur in service occupations. Many other opportunities (210,000) are expected for self-employed child care workers, as more and more families seek child care outside the home. Other occupations with projected increases in self-employed workers include janitors and cleaners, including maids and housekeeping cleaners (111,000), and hairdressers, hairstylists, and cosmetologists (76,000).

Other opportunities for self-employment will exist in the professional specialty occupations (281,000 jobs) and precision production, craft and repair (246,000 jobs). Both of these groups include many different occupations with a relatively high proportion of self-employed workers.

Although the marketing and sales fields had the most self-employed workers in 1990, they are projected to grow by only 72,000 workers (4 percent), from 1990 to 2005. Higher numbers of salaried employees in medium-size and large establishments employing marketing and sales workers will out pace the increases among self-employed workers. However, in many sales occupations, the self-employed will still account for a sizable portion of total employment in 2005.

Within the major group "agriculture, forestry, fishing, and related occupations," the number of self-employed farmers is projected to continue its decline and to shrink by about 224,000, due to the dwindling number of smaller farms. The one occupation in this major group that is expected to experience growth in the number of self-employed workers is gardeners and groundskeepers (up 84,000).

1 The narrative and chart in this appendix are based on "Occupational Employment Projections," in "Outlook 1990-2005," Bulletin 2402, published by the U.S. Department of Labor.

Table 6. **Self-employed workers in occupations with 50,000 workers or more, actual 1990 and projected to 2005**

[Numbers in thousands]

Occupation	1990			2005			Change in self-employed, 1990–2005	
	Total employment	Self-employed workers	Percent of total employment	Total employment	Self-employed workers	Percent of total employment	Number	Percent
Total, all occupations	122,573	10,161	8.3	147,191	11,663	7.9	1,502	14.8
Executive, administrative, and managerial occupations......	12,451	1,598	12.8	15,866	2,106	13.3	508	31.8
Managerial and administrative occupations..................	8,838	1,328	15.0	11,174	1,778	15.9	450	33.9
Food service and lodging managers	595	247	41.5	793	280	35.3	33	13.4
Property and real estate managers	225	89	39.5	302	110	36.5	21	23.6
Management support occupations..................	3,613	270	7.5	4,691	328	7.0	58	21.5
Accountants and auditors	985	102	10.4	1,325	110	8.3	8	7.8
Management analysts	151	68	44.9	230	100	43.4	32	47.1
Professional specialty occupations	15,800	1,446	9.2	20,907	1,727	8.3	281	19.4
Social scientists	224	65	29.0	320	106	33.1	41	63.1
Psychologists	125	51	40.9	204	90	44.1	39	76.5
Lawyers and judicial workers	633	198	31.3	850	205	24.1	7	3.5
Lawyers	587	198	33.8	793	205	25.9	7	3.5
Teachers, librarians, and counselors...................	5,687	134	2.4	7,280	165	2.3	31	23.1
Other teachers and instructors ..	757	108	14.3	963	135	14.0	27	25.0
Adult and vocational education teachers	517	108	20.9	669	135	20.2	27	25.0
Instructors, adult (nonvocational) education ...	219	108	49.3	289	135	46.7	27	25.0
Health diagnosing occupations ...	855	271	31.7	1,101	310	28.1	39	14.4
Dentists	174	92	52.7	196	103	52.6	11	12.0
Physicians	580	139	24.0	776	160	20.6	21	15.1
Health assessment and treating occupations..................	2,305	69	3.0	3,304	89	2.7	20	29.0
Writers, artists, and entertainers ..	1,542	517	33.5	1,915	603	31.5	86	16.6
Artists and commercial artists ...	230	143	62.2	303	190	62.8	47	32.9
Designers	339	114	33.6	428	123	28.7	9	7.9
Designers, except interior designers.................	270	86	31.9	335	90	26.9	4	4.7
Musicians	252	75	29.7	276	85	30.8	10	13.3
Writers and editors, including technical writers.............	232	78	33.6	292	89	30.5	11	14.1
Technicians and related support occupations	4,204	107	2.5	5,754	132	2.3	25	22.9
Marketing and sales occupations	14,088	1,831	13.0	17,489	1,903	10.9	72	4.0
Insurance sales workers	439	139	31.7	527	150	28.5	11	7.9
Real estate agents, brokers, and appraisers	413	255	61.8	492	281	57.2	26	10.4
Sales agents, real estate	300	199	66.3	355	220	62.0	21	10.6
Salespersons, retail.............	3,619	187	5.2	4,506	200	4.4	13	7.0
Administrative support occupations, including clerical	21,951	338	1.5	24,835	382	1.5	44	13.0
Financial records processing occupations..................	2,860	147	5.1	2,750	164	6.0	17	11.6
Bookkeeping, accounting, and auditing clerks	2,276	143	6.3	2,143	160	7.5	17	11.9
Secretaries, stenographers, and typists..................	4,680	88	1.9	5,110	110	2.2	22	25.0

Outlook: 1990–2005: Occupational Employment

Table 6. **Continued—Self-employed workers in occupations with 50,000 workers or more, actual 1990 and projected to 2005**

[Numbers in thousands]

Occupation	1990			2005			Change in self-employed, 1990–2005	
	Total employment	Self-employed workers	Percent of total employment	Total employment	Self-employed workers	Percent of total employment	Number	Percent
Service occupations	19,204	1,220	6.4	24,805	1,662	6.7	442	36.2
Cleaning and building service occupations, except private household	3,435	238	6.9	4,068	352	8.7	114	47.9
Janitors and cleaners, including maids and housekeeping cleaners	3,007	221	7.4	3,562	332	9.3	111	50.2
Food preparation and service occupations	7,706	79	1.0	10,031	80	.8	1	1.3
Chefs, cooks, and other kitchen workers	3,069	50	1.6	4,104	55	1.3	5	10.0
Personal service occupations	2,192	824	37.6	3,164	1,112	35.1	288	34.9
Barbers	77	59	76.8	76	59	77.8	0	0.0
Child care workers	725	466	64.3	1,078	676	62.7	210	45.0
Cosmetologists and related workers	636	296	46.5	793	374	47.1	78	26.4
Hairdressers, hairstylists, and cosmetologists	597	287	48.1	742	363	48.9	76	26.5
Agriculture, forestry, fishing, and related occupations	3,506	1,380	39.4	3,665	1,250	34.1	−131	−9.5
Farm operators and managers	1,223	1,074	87.8	1,023	850	83.1	−224	−20.9
Farmers	1,074	1,074	100.0	850	850	100.0	−224	−20.9
Gardeners and groundskeepers, except farm	874	166	19.0	1,222	250	20.5	84	50.6
Precision production, craft, and repair occupations	14,124	1,686	11.9	15,909	1,932	12.1	246	14.6
Blue-collar worker supervisors	1,792	130	7.3	1,912	143	7.5	13	10.0
Construction trades	3,763	936	24.9	4,557	1,158	25.4	222	23.7
Carpenters	1,057	373	35.3	1,209	450	37.2	77	20.6
Electricians	548	58	10.6	706	75	10.6	17	29.3
Painters and paperhangers, construction and maintenance .	453	214	47.2	564	289	51.2	75	35.0
Plumbers, pipefitters, and steamfitters	379	65	17.2	459	75	16.4	10	15.4
Mechanics, installers, and repairers	4,900	407	8.3	5,669	411	7.3	4	1.0
Machinery and related mechanics, installers, and repairers	1,675	56	3.3	1,980	65	3.3	9	16.1
Vehicle and mobile equipment mechanics and repairers	1,568	240	15.3	1,892	225	11.9	−15	−6.3
Automotive mechanics	757	152	20.1	923	145	15.7	−7	−4.6
Other mechanics, installers, and repairers	1,002	73	7.3	1,180	77	6.5	4	5.5
Production occupations, precision .	3,134	205	6.5	3,208	212	6.6	7	3.4
Textile, apparel, and furnishings workers, precision	272	90	33.0	302	96	31.8	6	6.7
Custom tailors and sewers	116	61	52.7	137	70	51.0	9	14.8
Operators, fabricators, and laborers	17,245	555	3.2	17,961	570	3.2	15	2.7
Machine setters, set-up operators, operators, and tenders	4,905	93	1.9	4,579	97	2.1	4	4.3
Hand workers, including assemblers and fabricators	2,675	103	3.9	2,307	119	5.2	16	15.5
Transportation and material moving machine and vehicle operators . .	4,730	285	6.0	5,743	278	4.8	−7	−2.5
Motor vehicle operators	3,417	248	7.3	4,301	242	5.6	−6	−2.4
Truckdrivers	2,701	196	7.3	3,360	174	5.2	−22	−11.2
Truckdrivers, light and heavy . .	2,362	182	7.7	2,979	160	5.4	−22	−12.1
Helpers, laborers, and material movers, hand	4,935	74	1.5	5,332	76	1.4	2	2.7

More Good Books by JIST Works, Inc.

America's Top 300 Jobs
A Complete Career Handbook
Edited and Compiled by
J. Michael Farr—$17.95 T300

Based on information provided by the U.S. Department of Labor. This book provides detailed descriptions of more than 250 of the most popular jobs in the country and includes summary information on many more. Complete job descriptions feature Nature of Work, Training and Advancement, Earnings, Related Occupations, Future Outlook, and more.

America's Top Technical and Trade Jobs
Good Jobs That Don't Require Four Years of College
Edited and Compiled by
J. Michael Farr—$9.95 ATT

Like the other books in this series, this book provides job descriptions for more than 50 of the top technical and trade jobs in the U.S. economy. As many as 80 percent of the new jobs created do not require a college degree but do require technical skills! Determine which skills to upgrade to remain competitive in the work force and move up in your career.

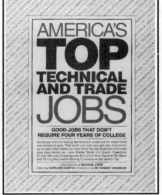

America's Top Medical Jobs
Good Jobs in Health Related Occupations
Edited and Compiled by
J. Michael Farr—$9.95 ATM

This book highlights one of the fastest growing areas in our economy—the medical field. It describes all the major medical occupations, the salaries, growth potential, education required, and other details. The medical industry offers good opportunities for people at all educational levels and this book provides the needed information to explore the possibilities of a career in this lucrative industry.

America's Federal Jobs
A Complete Directory of Federal Career Opportunities Developed by the U.S. Office of Personnel Management
$14.95 AFJ

This book provides the most helpful and up-to-date information on applying for a job with the nation's largest employer—the federal government. Major sections describe more than 150 agencies and departments, application procedures, student training opportunities, affirmative employment programs, pay scales and benefits, and much more. In addition, the index cross-references agencies by college major and types of experience.

America's Top Office, Management, and Sales Jobs
Good Jobs That Offer Advancement and Excellent Pay
Edited and Compiled by
J. Michael Farr—$9.95 ATO

This book was created in response to the need for good career information by people trying to increase their incomes by upgrading their skills or changing jobs. The service economy has seen tremendous growth in the last decade and the job descriptions in this book reflect that growth. Besides the office, managerial, and sales jobs, added sections include labor market trends and career planning.

Career Guide to America's Top Industries
Essential Information on Opportunities and Trends in All Major Industries
Compiled by the U.S. Department of Labor—*New!* $11.95 CGTI

This is the newest book in the America's series. It contains business forecasts for 350 industries and detailed information on more than 40 major industries, comprising about 75 percent of all jobs in our economy. The guide provides an overview of economic and industrial trends emphasizing how these factors can affect career decisions. Anyone interested in the labor market and making career decisions should consult this book.

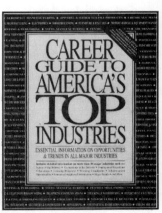

Call your
favorite dealer or local bookstore
to place orders now!

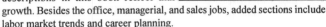